TEACHER CERTIFICATION TESTS

Elna M. Dimock

Prentice Hall
New York • London • Toronto • Sydney • Tokyo • Singapore

Prentice Hall General Reference
15 Columbus Circle
New York, NY 10023

An Arco Book

Arco, Prentice Hall, and colophons are
registered trademarks of Simon & Schuster, Inc.

Library of Congress Cataloging-in-Publication Data

Dimock, Elna M.
    Teacher certification tests / Elna M. Dimock.—3rd ed.
    p. cm.
    "An Arco book."
    1. Examinations—United States—Study guides.
2. Examinations—United States—Questions. 3. Teachers—
Certification—United States. I. Title. II. Title: Arco Teacher
certification tests.
LB1762.D55   1993   87-11393
370'.7'76—dc20   CIP
ISBN 0-671-86526-9

Manufactured in the United States of America

1   2   3   4   5   6   7   8   9   10

CONTENTS

HOW TO GET THE MOST
OUT OF THIS BOOK

Teaching is considered a portable skill, which is very convenient in our increasingly mobile society. It used to be relatively easy to get a teaching position when moving from one state to another. Enter the testing requirement for a teaching credential, and all is confusion. More and more states are adding a requirement that candidates for a teaching credential must pass the state-designated test. The problem is that nearly all of them are different. The plethora of tests increases the difficulty of a teacher in one state getting a credential to teach in another state. Here is help!

This book gives you information about each state: the testing requirements, addresses, and telephone numbers of the credential or certification office. Directions are given about which parts of the review section you will need to study for each state, and which parts of the tests to practice. Finally, there are seven sample tests, each a different type.

HOW TO PROCEED

If you want a credential in a specific state, take the following steps:

1. Look up the state on page 7.

2. Find the test requirements for that state.

3. Call or write the state to:
   a) double-check the requirements;
   b) find out when the tests are given;
   c) learn when you must sign up for the test;
   d) ask for the forms and requirements to be sent.

4. Sign up for the tests you need.

5. Study test-taking techniques and the appropriate review sections.

6. Take the practice tests, remembering to practice the test-taking techniques. Do your thinking with your pencil on the practice tests, just as you will on the test itself. Some tests do not allow scratch paper, so practicing in this book will pay big dividends. After you have corrected each test, study the explanations, turning to the review sections as necessary.

If you want to know which states use certain tests, the National Teacher Examinations (NTE), the Pre-Professional Skills Test (PPST), or none at all, turn to page 7.

STATE TEST REQUIREMENTS

The information in this book is as up-to-date as publishing deadlines allow. Do call the credentials department of the state that you are interested in teaching in to make sure that requirements have not changed. The testing requirement has not passed in several states in which it was considered, but it may be brought up in the next session of the legislature.

This book deals only with testing requirements. In addition to degrees, some states have requirements such as taking a class or passing a test in state school law, history, or constitution.

DEPARTMENT OF EDUCATION

ALABAMA
50 N. Ripley St., Montgomery 36130-3901
(Phone: 205-242-9977)

ALASKA
801 W. 10th St., Suite 200, Juneau 99801-1894
(Phone: 907-465-2831)

ARIZONA
1535 W. Jefferson St., Phoenix 85007
(Phone: 602-542-5468)

ARKANSAS
4 State Capitol Mall, Little Rock 72201-1011
(Phone: 501-682-4475)

CALIFORNIA
721 Capitol Mall, Sacramento 95814
(Phone: 916-445-7256)

COLORADO
201 E. Colfax Ave., Denver 80203
(Phone: 303-866-6628)

CONNECTICUT
165 Capitol Ave., Hartford 06106
(Phone: 203-566-5497)

DELAWARE
State Department of Public Instruction, Office of Certification, P.O. Box 1402, Dover 19903
(Phone: 1-800-433-5292)

FLORIDA
325 W. Gaines St., Florida Education Center, Suite 203, Tallahassee 32399-0400
(Phone: 904-488-2317)

GEORGIA
1866 Twin Towers East, Atlanta 30334-5040
(Phone: 404-656-2406)

HAWAII	1390 Miller St., Honolulu 96813 (Phone: 808-586-3310)
IDAHO	650 W. State St., Boise 83720 (Phone: 208-334-3301)
ILLINOIS	100 N. First St., Springfield 62777 (Phone: 217-782-2221)
INDIANA	Indiana Professional Standards Board, State House, Room 229, Indianapolis 46204 (Phone: 317-232-9010)
IOWA	State Department of Education, Grimes State Office Building, Des Moines 50319-0146 (Phone: 515-281-5294)
KANSAS	120 S.E. Tenth St., Topeka 66612-1103 (Phone: 913-296-3201)
KENTUCKY	500 Mero St., Frankfort 40601 (Phone: 502-564-4606)
LOUISIANA	P. O. Box 94064, Baton Rouge 70804 (Phone: 504-342-3490)
MAINE	State Department of Education, State House Station No. 23, Augusta 04333 (Phone: 207-287-5944 or 5945)
MARYLAND	200 W. Baltimore St., Baltimore 21201-2595 (Phone: 301-333-2142)
MASSACHUSETTS	1385 Hancock St., Quincy 02169 (Phone: 617-770-7517)
MICHIGAN	P.O. Box 30008, Lansing 48909 (Phone: 517-373-3310)
MINNESOTA	712 Capitol Square Building, 550 Cedar St., St. Paul 55101 (Phone: 612-296-2046)
MISSISSIPPI	P.O. Box 771, Jackson 39205-0771 (Phone: 601-359-3513)
MISSOURI	State Department of Elementary and Secondary Education, P.O. Box 480, Jefferson City 65102 (Phone: 314-751-3503)

MONTANA Office of Public Instruction, Capitol Building,
  Helena 59620 (Phone: 406-444-3150)

NEBRASKA P.O. Box 94987, 301 Centennial Mall, South,
  Lincoln 68509-4987 (Phone: 402-471-2497)

NEVADA 400 W. King St., Carson City 89710
  (Phone: 702-687-3115)

NEW HAMPSHIRE State Office Park South, 101 Pleasant St.,
  Concord 03301 (Phone: 603-271-3494)

NEW JERSEY C.N. 503, Trenton 08625-0503
  (Phone: 609-292-2070)

NEW MEXICO State Capitol, Santa Fe 87503
  (Phone: 505-827-6587)

NEW YORK Cultural Education Building, Rm 5A11, Albany
  12230 (Phone: 518-474-5704)

NORTH CAROLINA State Department of Public Instruction,
  Education Building, 116 West Edenton St.,
  Raleigh 27603-1712
  (Phone: 919-733-4125)

NORTH DAKOTA State Department of Public Instruction, State
  Capitol Building, 600 Boulevard Ave. East,
  Bismarck 58505 (Phone: 701-224-2264)

OHIO Ohio Departments Building, 65 South Front St.,
  Rm 1012, Columbus 43266-0308
  (Phone: 614-466-3593)

OKLAHOMA Oliver Hodge Memorial Education Building, 2500
  N. Lincoln Blvd., Oklahoma City 73105-4599
  (Phone: 405-521-3337)

OREGON Salem 97310 (Phone: 503-378-3586)

PENNSYLVANIA 333 Market St., Harrisburg 17126-0333
  (Phone: 717-787-2967)

RHODE ISLAND 22 Hayes St., Providence 02908
  (Phone: 401-277-2675)

SOUTH CAROLINA 1015 Rutledge Building, 1429 Senate St.,
  Columbia 29201 (Phone: 803-734-8466)

SOUTH DAKOTA Kneip Building, Pierre 57501
                 (Phone: 605-773-3553)

TENNESSEE   North Wing, 6th floor, Nashville 37243-0377
                 (Phone: 615-741-1644)

TEXAS   Texas Education Agency, 1701 North Congress,
                 Austin 78701 (Phone: 512-463-8976)

UTAH   State Office of Education, 250 East 500, South,
                 Salt Lake City 84111
                 (Phone: 801-538-7740)

VERMONT   120 State St., Montpelier 05620-2501
                 (Phone: 802-828-2445)

VIRGINIA   P.O. Box 6-Q, Richmond 23317
                 (Phone: 804-225-2022)

WASHINGTON   State Department of Public Instruction,
                 7510 Armstrong St., S.W.,
                 Tumwater 98504
                 (Phone: 206-753-6773)

WEST VIRGINIA 1900 Kanawha Blvd. East, Bldg. 6, Rm 337,
                 Charleston 25305-0330
                 (Phone: 304-558-2703)

WISCONSIN   State Department of Public Instruction,
                 125 S. Webster St., Box 7841,
                 Madison 53707-7841
                 (Phone: 608-266-1027)

WYOMING   Hathaway Building, Cheyenne 82002
                 (Phone: 307-777-6261)

SUMMARY OF TEST REQUIREMENTS

1. No test.
2. Test required.
3. Test requirement under consideration.
4. NTE (National Teacher Examinations) core battery required.
5. NTE specialty examinations required.
6. State-developed or adopted basic skills test required.
7. State-developed or adopted professional knowledge test required.
8. State-developed or adopted teaching specialty test required.
9. Test required for entrance to education programs at state colleges and universities.
10. Special requirements; see state section that follows.

State	1	2	3	4	5	6	7	8	9	10
AL		✔					✔	✔	✔	✔
AK	✔									
AZ		✔				✔				✔
AR		✔		✔	✔					✔
CA		✔				✔				✔
CO		✔								✔
CT		✔				✔				✔
DE		✔				✔				✔
FL		✔				✔	✔	✔		✔
GA		✔					✔	✔		✔
HI		✔		✔	✔					✔
ID		✔		✔						✔
IL		✔				✔		✔		✔
IN		✔		✔	✔					✔
IA	✔									
KS		✔		✔		✔	✔			✔
KY		✔		✔	✔	✔			✔	✔
LA		✔		✔	✔					✔
ME		✔		✔						✔
MD		✔		✔	✔					✔

State	1	2	3	4	5	6	7	8	9	10
MA	✔									
MI		✔				✔		✔		✔
MN		✔				✔				✔
MS		✔		✔	✔					✔
MO		✔			✔					✔
MT		✔		✔						✔
NE		✔				✔				✔
NV		✔		✔		✔	✔			✔
NH	✔									✔
NJ		✔		✔						✔
NM		✔		✔						✔
NY		✔		✔						✔
NC		✔		✔	✔					✔
ND	✔									
OH		✔		✔						✔
OK		✔						✔		✔
OR		✔		✔		✔				✔
PA		✔		✔	✔					✔
RI		✔		✔						✔
SC		✔		✔					✔	✔
SD	✔									
TN		✔		✔						✔
TX		✔					✔	✔		✔
UT	✔									
VT	✔									
VA		✔		✔	✔					✔
WA		✔								✔
WV		✔						✔		✔
WI		✔				✔				✔
WY		✔								✔

INFORMATION ABOUT STATES THAT REQUIRE TESTS

ALABAMA   Prospective teachers who began their collegiate study in the Fall 1989 semester or quarter or thereafter must earn a passing score on a comprehensive examination and complete a class B (Bachelor's degree level) teacher education program approved by the Alabama State Board of Education. The comprehensive exam is designed by the college or university to cover the content of the teaching field(s) and professional education. Successful completion of an admissions test designated by the state superintendent of education or a passing score on the Alabama English Language Proficiency Test is required for admission to professional studies.

ARIZONA   The Arizona Teacher Proficiency Exam is given monthly in Phoenix, Tucson, and Flagstaff. The deadline for signing up is two weeks before the test date, but register early to get your first-choice date and place. The cost is $10.00. The basic skills test (reading, mathematics, and grammar) takes 130 minutes and has 150 questions. Each section contains 50 questions. You will get your scores in about two weeks. The test is valid for only seven years from the test date; after that, it must be retaken. Special arrangements may be made for the handicapped to take the Arizona Teacher Proficiency Exam.

ARKANSAS   The core battery, professional knowledge, and area specialty examinations of the NTE are required for initial certification. Each teaching area requires different scores on the tests. Current teachers and holders of teaching credentials must pass a test of functional academic skills. There are provisions for instruction and retesting for those who do not pass.

CALIFORNIA   The California Basic Educational Skills Test is required to get a first-time credential, to renew a provisional credential, or to get a different credential. It is given six times a year, in February, April, June, August, October, and December. Sign up at least five weeks before the test. Cost is $35.00. The reading, mathematics, and writing portions of the test each take about one hour. The required total score is 123, with no single score being less than 37.

COLORADO   The California Achievement Test (level 19, form C or D) is used for initial certification. It tests reading, mathematics, spelling, and grammar. You must demonstrate your ability to express yourself in oral English before a panel of judges or document that you have passed a college course in public speaking with a grade of B or higher. The test is administered at colleges in Colorado and costs $30.00. Contact the college where you will be taking the test for more information. The test is scheduled to change in 1994. It has not yet been decided whether a national test will be adopted.

CONNECTICUT   A candidate for a teaching credential must take the Connecticut Competency Examination for Prospective Teachers (CONNCEPT), score 70 percent correct on the mathematics portion, and get a scaled score of 71 on the reading and 6 on the writing. The test is given three times a year, in November, March, and July.

DELAWARE The following scores on the PPST are required for initial certification: reading—175, writing—172, mathematics—175. The test takes three hours and costs $65.00. It is given at three colleges six times a year. The test is always given in October and January; the four other dates vary. Register one month before through the Educational Testing Service in Oakland, CA.

FLORIDA The Florida Teacher Certification Examination is required to get a credential. The test is given four times a year in January, April, August, and October. The registration deadline is 50 days before the examination date. Late registration is 30 days; late charges are $15.00. The examination is two days long: basic skills and professional knowledge are tested on the first day, and subject area specialty tests on the second. (The days are not consecutive, and must be scheduled separately.) The basic skills test includes writing, reading, and mathematics, and it is free of charge. There is a fee of $25.00 for the professional knowledge test, and the specialty tests are $25.00 per subject area.

GEORGIA The Georgia Teacher Certification Testing Program is required for initial certification in any one of thirty subject area fields. You are tested on your knowledge of the subject matter in your particular area of specialization, and on the professional knowledge required of educators. All of the teacher certification tests consist of multiple-choice questions and are scored by computer. Your performance on a test is evaluated against an established criterion. Sign up at least six weeks before the test date. There is a $35.00 registration fee, and a $10.00 late fee for any registration form postmarked after the registration deadline. You will receive your test score report in about six weeks.

HAWAII The core battery and area specialty exams of the NTE are required. Passing scores for the core battery are: communication skills —651, general knowledge—647, professional knowledge—648.

IDAHO The core battery of the NTE is required with the following scores: communication skills—652, general knowledge—646, professional knowledge—648.

ILLINOIS All persons applying for credentials as teachers, social workers, counselors, and administrators are required to pass two tests. The basic skills test covers reading, writing, grammar, and mathematics. The other test assesses each specialty area. For information about test dates, cost, registration procedures, deadlines, and passing scores, contact the certification office.

INDIANA The core battery and specialty areas of the NTE are required, with these scores: general knowledge—647, professional knowledge—646, and communication skills—653. Required scores for area specialty tests vary.

KANSAS The PPST and the professional knowledge test of the NTE are required for initial certification. Passing scores for the PPST are: reading—168, mathematics—168, writing—170. The passing score on the NTE is 642. The NTE is administered nationally. Check with any college or state department of education for information. Check with the Kansas State Department of Education for sites and dates for the PPST.

KENTUCKY The California Test of Basic Skills (CTBS) is required for entry to educational programs. Teachers obtaining an initial credential or teachers from out-of-state with fewer than two years of experience must take the NTE and will intern for one year. During that year they will be assisted and evaluated by a three-member team. Upon successful completion of the year they will receive a regular credential. Passing scores for the NTE are: communication skills—646, general knowledge—643, professional knowledge—644. Passing scores on the area specialty tests vary

LOUISIANA NTE core battery is required with the following scores: communication skills—645, general knowledge—644, professional knowledge—645. The scores needed for the specialty areas vary.

MAINE The core battery of the National Teachers Examination is required for initial certification. Passing scores are: communication skills—656, general knowledge—649, professional knowledge—648.

MARYLAND The core battery and specialty area exams of the NTE are required with these scores: communication skills—648, general knowledge—645, professional knowledge—648. Passing scores on the area specialty tests vary.

MICHIGAN The Michigan Teacher Certification Testing Program is required for certification. Developed by the National Evaluation System, it consists of basic skills (reading, writing, math) and subject area tests. Both the basic skills test and the subject area tests are 4 1/2 hours long. The test is administered four times a year; specific testing months vary. Call the Michigan Department of Education for lists of passing scores.

MINNESOTA The PPST is required for certification with scores as follows: reading—173, writing—172, math—169. Out-of-state applicants may get a one-year license without test completion; then a renewal is required. Minnesota also requires a Human Relations Program for teacher certification. Out-of-state applicants need not have this for their first license, but it will be needed for renewal.

MISSISSIPPI The NTE core battery is required with the following scores: communication skills—651, general knowledge—646, professional knowledge—649. The passing score on the area specialty tests varies. The passing level will increase every two years.

MISSOURI The specialty areas of the NTE are required for certification. If there is no specialty exam for your particular area, then the NTE core battery test of professional knowledge is required. A list of qualifying scores for all specialty areas is available; contact the Missouri Board of Education for information.

MONTANA The core battery test of the NTE is required for initial certification or reinstatement of a lapsed credential. Scores required to pass are: communication skills—648, general knowledge—644, professional knowledge—648.

NEBRASKA Candidates must pass the PPST for certification.

NEVADA The PPST or the NTE is required for certification. Required scores for the PPST are: reading—173, mathematics—170, writing—172. The required score for the NTE is professional knowledge—651.

NEW HAMPSHIRE   Candidates need either a Masters degree in Education or a statement from their college proving proficiency in reading, writing, and math for certification.

NEW JERSEY   The NTE core battery test of general knowledge is required for certification.

NEW MEXICO   The core battery of the NTE is required for certification. Passing scores are: communication skills—644, general knowledge—645, professional knowledge—630.

NEW YORK   The core battery of the NTE is required for certification. Required scores are: general knowledge—649, professional knowledge—646, communication skills—650.

NORTH CAROLINA   The core battery of the NTE is required for certification. The required score is professional knowledge—646. The passing score on the area specialty test varies.

OHIO   Candidates who entered a teacher preparation program after 1987 are required to take the core battery of the NTE. The required scores are: general knowledge—642, professional knowledge—642.

OKLAHOMA   The Oklahoma Teacher Competency Proficiency Test, a state-developed test, is required for certification. It tests specialty areas. It is administered in February, May, August, and November at various locations in the state.

OREGON   The California Basic Educational Skills Test (CBEST) or the NTE is required for certification. The required scores for the NTE are: communication skills—659, general knowledge—654.

PENNSYLVANIA   The core battery of the NTE is required for certification. The required scores are: communication skills—646, general knowledge—644, professional knowledge—643. The passing score on the area specialty tests varies.

RHODE ISLAND   The core battery of the NTE is required for certification. The required scores are: communication skills—657, general knowledge—649, professional knowledge—648.

SOUTH CAROLINA   The Education Entrance Exam (EEE), a basic skills test, is required for entrance to the teacher education program. It is administered by the individual colleges. The NTE core battery test is required for certification. The required score is professional knowledge—642.

TENNESSEE   The core battery of the NTE is required for certification, with the following scores: communication skills—651, general knowledge—647, professional knowledge—643.

TEXAS   Candidates must pass the Examination for the Certification of Educators in Texas (ExCET). It is composed of a professional development test and content specialization tests.

VIRGINIA The NTE core battery and area specialty exams are required for initial certification. Passing scores on the three core battery tests are as follows: communication skills—649, professional knowledge—639, general knowledge—639. Passing scores for the area specialty exams vary from one examination to another.

WASHINGTON Candidates must pass a state-developed knowledge requirement test, which covers school, society, school law, and human growth and development, for certification.

WEST VIRGINIA Candidates must pass the Content Specialization Test, a state-developed test, for certification. A Multi-Subject Test is required for elementary teaching fields.

WISCONSIN Candidates must pass the PPST for certification.

WYOMING You must take a course about the United States and Wyoming constitutions or pass a test on each in order to obtain a teaching credential. Out-of-state teachers may send for a booklet containing the information covered in the Wyoming constitution test, study the information, and take the test. Any district or county superintendent may administer the test.

WHICH SECTIONS TO STUDY FOR YOUR TEST

ALABAMA

Test-Taking Techniques
Review—Professional Knowledge
Sample Test 5 (ExCET)—Professional Knowledge
Sample Test 6—Professional Knowledge

ARIZONA

Test-Taking Techniques
Review—Reading, Mathematics, Grammar, Professional Knowledge
Sample Test 4 (CONNCEPT)—Reading, Mathematics

CALIFORNIA

Test-Taking Techniques
Review—Reading, Mathematics, Writing
Sample Test 1 (CBEST)—Reading, Mathematics, Writing
Sample Test 2 (CBEST)—Reading, Mathematics, Writing
Sample Test 3 (PPST)—Reading, Mathematics, Writing
Sample Test 4 (CONNCEPT)—Mathematics, Writing
Sample Test 6—Mathematics, Writing

COLORADO

Test-Taking Techniques
Review—Mathematics, Grammar
Sample Test 1 (CBEST)—Mathematics
Sample Test 2 (CBEST)—Mathematics
Sample Test 3 (PPST)—Mathematics
Sample Test 4 (CONNCEPT)—Mathematics
Sample Test 6—Mathematics

CONNECTICUT	Test-Taking Techniques Review—Reading, Mathematics, Writing Sample Test 1 (CBEST)—Reading, Mathematics, Writing Sample Test 2 (CBEST)—Reading, Mathematics, Writing Sample Test 3 (PPST)—Reading, Mathematics, Writing Sample Test 4 (CONNCEPT)—Reading, Mathematics, Writing Sample Test 6—Reading, Mathematics, Writing
DELAWARE	Test-Taking Techniques Review—Reading, Mathematics, Writing Sample Test 1 (CBEST)—Reading, Mathematics, Writing Sample Test 2 (CBEST)—Reading, Mathematics, Writing Sample Test 3 (PPST)—Reading, Mathematics, Writing Sample Test 4 (CONNCEPT)—Mathematics, Writing Sample Test 6—Writing, Mathematics
FLORIDA	Test-Taking Techniques Review—Reading, Mathematics, Writing, Professional Knowledge Sample Test 1 (CBEST)—Mathematics, Writing Sample Test 2 (CBEST)—Mathematics, Writing Sample Test 3 (PPST)—Mathematics, Writing Sample Test 4 (CONNCEPT)—Reading, Writing, Mathematics Sample Test 5 (ExCET)—Professional Knowledge Sample Test 6—Writing, Reading, Mathematics, Professional Knowledge
GEORGIA	Test-Taking Techniques Review—Professional Knowledge Sample Test 5 (ExCET)—Professional Knowledge Sample Test 6—Professional Knowledge

ILLINOIS

Test-Taking Techniques
Review—Reading, Writing, Grammar, Mathematics
Sample Test 1 (CBEST)—Reading, Mathematics, Writing
Sample Test 2 (CBEST)—Reading, Mathematics, Writing
Sample Test 3 (PPST)—Reading, Writing, Mathematics
Sample Test 4 (CONNCEPT)—Mathematics, Reading, Writing
Sample Test 6—Writing, Mathematics, Reading

KANSAS

Test-Taking Techniques
Review—Reading, Mathematics, Writing
Sample Test 1 (CBEST)—Reading, Mathematics, Writing
Sample Test 2 (CBEST)—Reading, Mathematics, Writing
Sample Test 3 (PPST)—Reading, Mathematics, Writing
Sample Test 4 (CONNCEPT)—Mathematics, Writing
Sample Test 6—Mathematics, Writing

KENTUCKY
(*entry test*)

Test-Taking Techniques
Review—Reading, Mathematics, Grammar

MICHIGAN

Test-Taking Techniques
Review—Reading, Mathematics, Writing
Sample Test 1 (CBEST)—Reading, Mathematics, Writing
Sample Test 2 (CBEST)—Reading, Mathematics, Writing
Sample Test 3 (PPST)—Reading, Mathematics, Writing
Sample Test 4 (CONNCEPT)—Mathematics, Writing
Sample Test 6—Mathematics, Writing

MINNESOTA	Test-Taking Techniques
	Review—Reading, Mathematics, Writing
	Sample Test 1 (CBEST)—Reading, Mathematics, Writing
	Sample Test 2 (CBEST)—Reading, Mathematics, Writing
	Sample Test 3 (PPST)—Reading, Mathematics, Writing
	Sample Test 4 (CONNCEPT)—Mathematics, Writing
	Sample Test 6—Mathematics, Writing
NEBRASKA	Test-Taking Techniques
	Review—Reading, Mathematics, Writing
	Sample Test 1 (CBEST)—Reading, Mathematics, Writing
	Sample Test 2 (CBEST)—Reading, Mathematics, Writing
	Sample Test 3 (PPST)—Reading, Mathematics, Writing
	Sample Test 4 (CONNCEPT)—Mathematics, Writing
	Sample Test 6—Mathematics, Writing
NEVADA	Test-Taking Techniques
	Review—Reading, Mathematics, Writing
	Sample Test 1 (CBEST)—Reading, Mathematics, Writing
	Sample Test 2 (CBEST)—Reading, Mathematics, Writing
	Sample Test 3 (PPST)—Reading, Mathematics, Writing
	Sample Test 4 (CONNCEPT)—Mathematics, Writing
	Sample Test 6—Mathematics, Writing
OREGON	Test-Taking Techniques
	Review—Reading, Mathematics, Writing
	Sample Test 1 (CBEST)—Reading, Mathematics, Writing
	Sample Test 2 (CBEST)—Reading, Mathematics, Writing
	Sample Test 3 (PPST)—Reading, Mathematics, Writing
	Sample Test 4 (CONNCEPT)—Mathematics, Writing
	Sample Test 6—Mathematics, Writing

SOUTH CAROLINA
(entry test)

Test-Taking Techniques
Review—Reading, Mathematics, Writing, Grammar
Sample Test 1 (CBEST)—Reading, Mathematics, Writing
Sample Test 2 (CBEST)—Reading, Mathematics, Writing
Sample Test 3 (PPST)—Reading, Mathematics, Writing
Sample Test 4 (CONNCEPT)—Reading, Mathematics, Writing
Sample Test 6—Writing, Reading, Mathematics

TEXAS

Test-Taking Techniques
Review—Professional Knowledge
Sample Test 5 (ExCET)—Professional Knowledge
Sample Test 6—Professional Knowledge

WISCONSIN

Test-Taking Techniques
Review—Reading, Mathematics, Writing
Sample Test 1 (CBEST)—Reading, Mathematics, Writing
Sample Test 2 (CBEST)—Reading, Mathematics, Writing
Sample Test 3 (PPST)—Reading, Mathematics, Writing
Sample Test 4 (CONNCEPT)—Mathematics, Writing
Sample Test 6—Writing, Mathematics

TEST-TAKING TECHNIQUES

GENERAL

Your score on a test depends on how much you know, your level of test anxiety, and your test-taking skills. This section will help you master your anxiety and improve your skills. The knowledge requirement is handled in the review chapter.

TEST ANXIETY

There are a few people who don't experience test anxiety. Lucky for them! For the rest of us, test anxiety manifests itself in many forms—from sweaty palms, inability to eat, digestion problems, and lumps in the throat to memory loss and paralysis. It is no laughing matter. You may not be able to get rid of test anxiety entirely, but it can be tamed. A bit of it can keep you alert. Here is what you can do.

Prepare for the test psychologically. Imagine the scene: You arrive at the test site. You're in plenty of time. You have all your supplies with you. You meet people who are there to take the test, too. What will they say? "I'm so nervous. Aren't you?" "I heard this was the worst test. No one passes." You cannot control others completely, but you can control your reactions and responses. Sometimes people who are negative are trying to make you as nervous as they are. You don't need to play their ain't-it-awful game. You can say, "No, I'm not nervous." You can ignore them, walk away, or say, "I'd rather not talk right now. I'll talk to you later." Your job now is to protect yourself and keep positive images. What others do is unimportant. How you react inwardly is all-important.

Now you walk into the room, get checked off the master list, go to your assigned place, and sit down. There is no rush, because you have plenty of time.

Be an island of calm. Don't let the nervous atmosphere penetrate your invisible shield. You're here to do your very best. This test can get you a credential that will be professionally and financially rewarding. Relax; look around you. You have energy and confidence. Other peoples' problems are not yours right now. Disturbances are all outside your shield and don't enter your calm world.

TEST-TAKING SKILLS

RELAXATION TECHNIQUES

Practice the following techniques to avoid tension and gain serenity. It's important to practice these before the test so that you will use them automatically during the test.

Escape. Close your eyes and take a mini-vacation. Picture the calmest environment possible—the beach, the mountains, a garden. Picture yourself there. Enjoy the tranquility. After fifteen to thirty seconds you will open your eyes, feeling relaxed and refreshed.

Breathe slowly, breathing out all tension.

Unkink your muscles. Stretch your legs and relax. Rotate your ankles. Stretch your arms forward and relax them. Clench your fists and relax them. Rotate your shoulders to release the tension in the muscles between your shoulder blades. Close your eyes and roll your head on your neck, four times to the right and four times to the left. These techniques are useful any time, not just during the test.

BEFORE THE TEST

Several days before the test, check the test site out. How long does it take to get there? Where do you park? Where is the testing room? Where are the rest rooms?

Get happy. Avoid arguments and depressing situations if possible. Get rid of any anger you may have, or at least put it on the shelf for the time being. If you have a friend who always has problems and always "shares" them, stay away from that friend the week before the test. Worry only about what is real and what you can do something about. Anything else is unproductive. Anger and worry drain a great deal of energy. You need that energy for the test.

The night before the test, follow your regular routine. Don't do any special studying. Most of all, you need a clear head for thought and analysis. Have ready what you need for the test: #2 pencils, eraser, pen, admission ticket, identification, watch, and perhaps a sweater. If the test is very long, take a snack or lunch.

The morning of the test, eat lightly or as usual. Don't take any artificial stimulants or relaxants.

Wear comfortable, layered clothing that can be put on or taken off as necessary for comfort. Do not dress sloppily or too casually or you won't do your best.

Arrive thirty minutes early to give yourself plenty of time to park, get to the room, and get checked in without rushing.

If you have a choice of seats, sit where you can concentrate—not by a door, aisle, pencil sharpener, or distracting people. If you're left-handed, request a left-handed desk. You may not get it, but it doesn't hurt to ask.

DURING THE TEST

Be enthusiastic. This test is your means to the credential you want.

Use the relaxation techniques while the test administrator reads the directions. They are very helpful. Expect the preliminaries to take half an hour. During the test, breathe slowly. Relax and unkink your muscles every half hour, using the techniques you have practiced. Escape on your mini-vacation every hour or whenever you feel your eyes crossing or the words blurring.

Don't let others bother you. If someone near you sighs as though he's dying or another writes and erases furiously, just block them out. Don't let their problems become yours. Think only of doing your best. You know a lot more than you think you do. You know what to expect.

Keep on going; don't get bored. This is a game of sorts—a game you will win. It's worth the effort.

MECHANICS OF TEST-TAKING

Be sure your name and all supplementary information are correct. Even though you are familiar with the directions, read them carefully.

Mark machine-scored answer sheets carefully and completely. Outline O , then fill in ◕ ●. Erasures should be complete.

PACING YOURSELF

When the proctor says you may start, write the time on the answer sheet at question one. Add half the time allotted for the section, or a little less, and write that time at the middle question. Write the ending time at the last question. When you get to the half-way point as you work on the test, you can check the time to see whether you are ahead of or behind schedule. This system allows some review time at the end. You will not need to look at your watch all the time either. Erase the times on your answer sheet before you hand your test in.

INSURANCE

Before you start the test, mark the last ten answers in the section with the same letter (all Bs or Cs, for instance). Thus, if you haven't finished when the time is up, you have at least one chance in four or five of getting the last ten correct. If you don't mark them, you have no chance of getting them right. As you work through the test and come to the last questions, you can readily change the answers. Remember, there is no penalty for guessing.

TACKLING A QUESTION

You have paid for the test. Unless you are given scratch paper, write, mark, and solve problems on the test.

Read the questions carefully. Don't jump to conclusions. Does it say *must* or *may*, *and* or *or, always* or *sometimes*? Break complicated questions into parts. Check your answer against each part. Underline key words.

Example:
12.   The fraction $^{12}/_{11}$ is between the numbers given in each of the following pairs except

Underline *between* and *except*.

You may sometimes find it useful to cross out the answers that you can easily see are unlikely or impossible.

Example:
5. $\sqrt{31}$ is between

(A) 100 and 1,000
(B) 3 and 4
(C) 5 and 6
(D) 15 and 16
(E) 60 and 64

The square root of 31 must be less than 31. Eliminate A and E. Answer D is half of 31, which is unlikely.

If you cannot decide between two answers, choose one, circle it and put a mark by the number of the question.

Example:

5. $\sqrt{31}$ is between

    (A) 100 and 1,000
    (B) 3 and 4
    (C) 5 and 6
    (D) 15 and 16
    (E) 60 and 64

Indicate your choice on the answer sheet, and put a mark by the number.

         A B C D E
      – 5 ○ ○ ● ○ ○

(Be sure to erase all extra marks on the answer sheet before you hand it in.) Don't leave an answer unmarked. You will lose your place more easily if you do, as well as missing a chance to get the right answer.

A question must earn your time and attention. If you haven't decided on an answer after one minute, mark it as above and go on. If you have no idea what the answer is, choose B or C or D, but not the same letter as the answer just above or just below. Don't leave an answer blank. The mark by the number shows that you should go back to it after you have finished the section, if you have enough time. If the question is a super-puzzler, put two marks by it. There are only a few two-mark questions. As you review each questionable answer, look only at the choices not crossed out. Make your decision, and *erase* the mark by the number of the question on the answer sheet. Do the super-puzzlers (two marks) last. Since all the questions count equally, spend your time on those that are easiest for you. It's not a good idea to spend five minutes on a single question when in the same time you could be answering five questions.

When you guess, avoid such answers as "none of the above" and "it cannot be determined." They are usually put in when the test-maker cannot think of another choice. Of course, they must be correct once in a while, just to keep you guessing, but the averages are against it.

If you have a choice of combinations of numbered answers, and you're not sure of the answer, choose the one with the number that is used most often in the answers.

Example:
(A)   I
(B)   II
(C)   III
(D)   II and III
(E)   I and II

I is used two times. II is used three times. III appears twice. The best guess is B.

Work quickly, but not hastily. Mark your answers carefully. Go over the test after you have finished, making sure that all your answers are in the right spaces. Return to those questions you·checked for further thought. Reread the directions, questions and answers. Check your calculations. Don't be afraid to change an answer. *Erase all extra marks on the answer sheet.* Check identical answers on successive questions carefully, especially if there are three or more in a row.

STRATEGIES FOR SPECIFIC QUESTIONS

READING

You will read a short passage, from one sentence to several paragraphs. There will be from one to five questions after each passage. First, quickly read the stems of the questions that pertain to the passage.

Example:

13. The most appropriate title is

    (A) Clarity
    (B) The Placement of Modifiers
    (C) The Purpose of Writing
    (D) The First Rule
    (E) Ideals

"The most appropriate title is" constitutes the stem of the question.

Decide whether the question involves interpretation or facts. Put I for interpretation or F for facts by the question.

Then read the passage carefully, keeping the questions in mind. Underline key words as you go, especially those that present facts. Answer as many of the questions as you can. Then reread the passage and answer the remaining questions. If absolutely necessary, read the paragraph a third time. Take your best shot at the remaining questions. Remember the marking technique.

Check the answer. Re-read the sentence that supports the answer to be sure it is correct. Be certain the answer covers all parts of the question.

Don't add facts you happen to know. The questions test your ability to read and understand *only* a given passage. Forget your own conclusions.

Don't expect to find the answer to an inferential question stated word for word in a passage.

Don't pick a specific answer when a general one is asked for.

If you are still unsure about a question even after three readings of the passage, don't return to it unless you have extra time at the end. It takes too long to reread the passage.

SENTENCE COMPLETION

As you read the sentence, look for clues in its structure or rhythm that tell you what kinds of words will be best suited for filling in the blanks. Watch for key words in the sentence. Guess at the answer even before consulting the choices. One choice will likely match or approximate your guess.

Look for clue words that indicate the blanks have contrasting meanings. For example, *not . . . but, rather than,* and *whereas.* Be alert to clues of similarity, such as *not only . . . but also* and *as well as.*

The part of the sentence without the blank will often define or suggest what the missing word should be. Start with that part of the sentence and work backward.

When there are two blanks and you don't find an answer choice that fits the first one, try to find choices that fit the second one. Then go back to the first blank.

MATHEMATICS

Some tests give formulas at the beginning of the test, others don't. Look for them, and if they are given, be sure to use them. Don't depend on their being there, however.

Read each question carefully, so that you solve for what is asked. Estimate the answer first, then work it out. Do all of your work on the test, unless scratch paper is provided. Cross out answers that are not possible. This narrows your choices and may leave you with only one answer.

Study graphs carefully. Are they to scale?

Round off amounts when you're asked for an approximate answer.

Draw a diagram or sketch and label it.

Check your calculations. Copy correctly. Make your work columns and figures neat to avoid errors. Work quickly, but don't get sloppy.

Watch for mixed units of measure in the questions and answers. Eliminate answers with wrong units and, when in doubt, those with the highest and lowest figures.

When a question asks you to find an exception, look for some element common to all the choices except one. The choice without that element is your answer.

You can try each answer out to see whether it works in the question. Usually there is a very simple or short-cut solution. Be alert for it.

Most of your mistakes will be due to carelessness in reading, not to your inability to do the math. Reread the question. Triple check the problem if there is time.

What to do if you don't have any idea what the answer is:

> If all the answer choices form a series, such as 4, 6, 8, 10, 12, avoid the extremes: 4 and 12. If you are to find the largest number that will work, pick the largest or next-to-largest number. Remember, there is no penalty for guessing.

WRITING

The topics are drawn from your personal observations and experiences. The topics are analytical or expressive. They are usually changed each time the tests are given. Everyone taking the test on the same day ordinarily writes on the same topic(s).

Spend ten minutes on each topic, organizing your thoughts.

Do not stray from the topic title, or your essay will not count. If you don't like the topic and think you could write a better essay on another topic, resist the impulse.

Support your generalizations with specific examples. Be as specific and concrete as possible.

Write with care and precision. Scoring is based on organization, flow, cohesiveness, focus on the subject matter, level of vocabulary, strength of supporting arguments, mechanics, and style.

> **One essay**—You will have forty-five minutes to write on one of two topics. Write on the topic with which you are most comfortable.
>
> **Two essays**—You will be asked to write about two topics in sixty minutes. Spend thirty minutes on each or twenty minutes on one and forty minutes on the other. Write on the topic that you feel most comfortable about first.

GRAMMAR

Generally, choose the answer that "sounds" best to you. Remember that the grammar being tested is written, not spoken usage; therefore, the language will be somewhat formal. Beware, however, of sentences that sound too formal.

PROFESSIONAL KNOWLEDGE

Some questions are factual, and you'll choose the answer you've learned or the one that seems most logical.

When questions deal with opinion, keep in mind current attitudes of educators and administrators. When in doubt, ask yourself: Which answer will benefit the child most? Which answer asks everyone's opinion? Which answer gets the most people involved?

REVIEW OF SKILLS
AND KNOWLEDGE

READING REVIEW

The questions in the reading section are designed to test your ability to interpret, analyze and evaluate a reading passage. You do not need to draw on outside knowledge. Work only with what is stated or implied in the passage.

Familiarize yourself with the main categories of reading questions:

- Interpreting a passage
- Drawing inferences
- Drawing conclusions
- Knowing the meanings of specific words
- Paraphrasing a portion of the text
- Determining what the next sentence might be
- Applying the information in the passage to another situation
- Determining the main idea
- Completing a sentence
- Analyzing a graph

The length of the passages varies from one sentence to several paragraphs. There are from one to five questions after each passage. If you are short of time toward the end of the test, it is better to read two short passages and answer one question about each than it is to tackle a long passage and not have time to answer any of the accompanying questions.

TYPES OF QUESTIONS

1. **Fill in a word (or words) to complete the sentence.**
   Example:
   38. Blue is a calming color. Men may fish, not
        so much for the _____ but for the
        _____ of the stream and sky.

        (A) sport . . . excitement
        (B) thrill . . . movement
        (C) fish . . . action
        (D) excitement . . . tumbling
        (E) catch . . . serenity

   Strategy: Before looking at your answer choices:

        • Read the sentence through, filling in your own words. Choose simple words.

- Then look at the answer choices and decide whether any of them are synonyms for your words.
- Try each set of words out in the sentence. Remember, the sentence must flow. If the sentence is written in an erudite style, the missing words will be complex. If the sentence is colloquial, the words will be simple.
- If there is more than one word to be filled in, look at the first word of the choices and eliminate those that don't fit. In the above example, they all fit.
- Go on to the second word. Which words don't fit? *Excitement, movement, action* and *tumbling* don't fit with *calming* in the sentence. We are now left with E. Note that this passage has a *not . . . but* construction.
- Read the sentence again, incorporating the words from E to see whether it makes sense.
- If at any point during this process you hit on the right answer, mark it and go on.

2. **Choose the most logical interpretation.** Notice the word *most*. There may be several interpretations that fit, but you need to find the most obvious one, or the one you think the testmakers had in mind. This is no time for innovative thinking.

   Example:

   7. The expressionist painters at the turn of the century tried to depict a state of mind rather than to make a realistic copy of some object. In other words,

   (A) expressionist paintings resemble camera snapshots.
   (B) most expressionist paintings are of people.
   (C) expressionist paintings are all done in oils.
   (D) expressionist paintings give the feeling rather than the appearance of things.
   (E) expressionist paintings are all done in pastels.

   Strategy: When you have read the sentence, underline the key points:

   state of mind and realistic copy

   You might even write *not* above *rather than*. The idea is "state of mind not copy." As you read each possible answer, draw a line through the ones that don't fit your conclusion. Then (A) is eliminated. Choices (B), (C), and (E) may be true, but no mention is made of these things in the passage. Choice (D) is best. *Feeling* takes the place of *state of mind* and *appearance* takes the place of *copy*.

3. **Determine the main idea.** This question can appear in several forms, such as: "Choose a title." "What is the central thought?" "What would a good topic sentence be?" "The author's purpose is . . . ." "The theme is . . . " "This passage illustrates . . . " The key to this type of question is that the answer you choose must be comprehensive. Choose the answer that is supported by the whole pas-

sage. You can think of the main idea or topic of a paragraph as a covering for the paragraph. It must fit snugly, but include everything in the paragraph; it must be general enough to include everything, but not too broad.

To illustrate the concept of finding a cover that fits, let's look at this question: What do Maserati, Porsche, Jaguar and Aston-Martin have in common?

Answer 1. They are all cars. (This statement is too general; the cover is too loose.)

Answer 2. They are all expensive cars. (A slightly better fit, but still too general.)

Answer 3. They are all expensive European cars. (This cover fits snugly. It narrows the field without becoming too specific.)

Answer 4. They are all expensive British cars. (Now the cover is too tight. Only Jaguar and Aston-Martin are British.)

The sample questions that follow further illustrate this strategy for answering main idea questions.

Example:

During the Second World War, the United States of America threw the full force of its raw materials, resourcefulness and energy into producing the goods necessary for the war. What would happen when the war ended? Historically, the end of war has meant the beginning of a depression. Factories shut down, causing unemployment, not to mention the soldiers whose expertise was suddenly no longer required, increasing the number of unemployed.

Instead, America turned all its factories, energy and know-how to producing the consumer goods for which people were clamoring. All production had gone into the war effort and few consumer goods were available—especially metal items such as appliances. People had saved their money, as there was nothing to spend it on during the war years. Now they were not only eager for the goods, but they could afford them. To satisfy the demand, the factories needed as many employees as previously.

23.   What is the main idea of this passage?

(A) America gears up for the war.
(B) The aftermath of the Second World War.
(C) Unemployment after the Second World War.
(D) Industry after the Second World War.
(E) American industry's post-Second World War transition.

Strategy: Look at each answer choice to determine how well it fits:

(A) too specific
(B) too general
(C) not in the passage

     (D) too general

     (E) the main idea

Use this system to eliminate items as you look for the main idea in any passage.

Example:

```
1   The physical language of time and space—movement, rhythm
2   and pacing—is a language that communicates a world of
3   significance, especially, perhaps, to preschool children, who
4   are still more fluent in body language than in verbal language.
5   One way people stand or move may mutely signal
6   importance, intimacy or consent; another may indicate that
7   the relationship is distant or that consent is to be withheld or
8   that the goings-on are unimportant, peripheral to the main
9   event. Children must learn the spatial codes for their own and
10  other cultures. Playacting—their own and dramatizations they
11  watch—is essential to this learning.
```

24. The information in the passage suggests that preschool teachers should be particularly aware of messages they communicate by their

     (A) tone of voice

     (B) movements and gestures

     (C) choice of words

     (D) choice of group discussion topics

     (E) scheduling of activities for the day

Throughout the passage nonverbal or body language is discussed. Choice E is completely out. Choices A, C and D are all verbal. Choice B, a synonym for body language, is correct.

Strategy:

- Read the stem of the question.
- Read the passage through as fast as you can to get an overall feel for it. What is your general impression?
- Read the answer choices. Eliminate any that don't fit.
- Read the passage again for refinement.
- Underline key points with your pencil or just note them with your eyes as you read the passage.
- Does one of the answers fit? Good. If not, eliminate answers that deal with only part of the passage.
- Does your final choice deal with the whole topic?

4. **Infer.** Inferential questions ask you to deduce something from the passage. You must understand the passage clearly to make inferences. Read the passage at the top of this page and use it to answer the following questions.

Example:

25. It can be inferred from the passage above that which of the following is true of spatial codes?

     (A) They are less easily understood by preschool children than by older children.

(B) They are most effectively learned in the classroom.

(C) They differ from culture to culture.

(D) They function in written as well as nonverbal communication.

(E) They are more frequently used to signal important rather than unimportant relationships.

Strategy:

Use elimination to find the answer:

(A) no—line 3

(B) no—lines 3 and 4

(C) maybe—lines 9 and 10

(D) no—lines 1, 2 and 4

(E) no—lines 5 through 7. They are used for both important and unimportant relationships.

The answer is C, since none of the other choices qualifies.

5. **Determine the meaning of words** as used in the text. Remember that you need to give the meaning as it is used in this particular passage. Even though you may know one meaning of a word, it may not be the one used in this passage.

Example:

9. The shell *evoked* sounds of the sea.
   Evoked in this sentence means

(A) recreated

(B) made

(C) brought to mind

(D) muffled

(E) simulated

Strategy:
• Read the stem and underline *evoked*.
• Read the passage and underline *evoked*. *Evoke* means "to bring forth from memory." Choice D doesn't fit at all. Choice C is closest.

6. **Find specific details**—facts. In this type of question you should be able to underline the answer. It will be there almost word for word.

Strategy:
• Read the stem first.
• Read the passage, underlining words that pertain to the question. You need only a general idea of what you are looking for.
• Read the question and the answer choices, eliminating the obviously wrong choices.
• Refer to the passage to find the answer.

Example:

1 They came from almost every place and for almost every
2 reason. They came not because of gold, but golden tans. They
3 came because they would look better. Didn't the people in the
4 commercials all look terrific? They came because they wanted
5 "the good life"—sun, sand and youth. They came because
6 you could do your own thing, whatever that was. They came
7 because it was the pot of gold at the end of the rainbow. They
8 came because it was California.

18. People came to California for all of the following reasons except

(A) to do what they wished
(B) the beach life
(C) hope of dreams fulfilled
(D) to stay young
(E) gold

Strategy:

Read the stem of the question and underline *except*. When a question has *except*, you must be able to find the other four answer choices in the passage. You will have to check all of the choices. Sometimes exactly the same words are given in the question as in the passage; at other times synonyms are used.

In this case, read the answer choices first. As you read the passage, underline the words that might fit. Read the answer choices again. Locate the terms in the passage and start eliminating. This is an elimination-process question, unless you are certain that one of the answer choices is not in the passage.

(A) to do what they wished—"do your own thing," line 6
(B) beach life—"sun, sand," line 5
(C) hope of dreams fulfilled—"pot of gold at the end of the rainbow," lines 7 and 8.
(D) to stay young—"youth," line 5
(E) gold—"*not* because of gold," line 2. This is it! (Don't be misled by "pot of gold," line 7. That is a proverbial expression, not intended literally.)

7. **Analyze logic and order.** This type of question gives you a lot of data to sort out. Don't let it throw you. Organize and conquer. Take the time to draw a chart of the information on the question booklet, using your own shorthand. This type of question takes time. If there is only one such question *and* if you're short of time, guess and come back to it later. The chart gives you a particular advantage if there are several questions dealing with the same information, because your work is all done. All you need to do is read the information from the chart.

Example:

39. The seventh grade is going on a two-day field trip. Each student's gear must include a sleeping bag, pup tent, backpack or rucksack and a poncho or a jacket with a rain hat. A sleeping bag with a rain cover may be used instead of a sleeping bag and pup tent.

Which of the following combinations of equipment is correct?

   I. sleeping bag with rain cover, jacket, rain hat
  II. sleeping bag, rucksack, jacket, rain hat
 III. sleeping bag, pup tent, backpack, poncho

(A) I only
(B) II only
(C) III only
(D) both II and III
(E) both I and III

Read the question. Make a chart

	SB/RC	PT	BP/RS	P/J&RH	*Eliminate*
I.	✔			✔	no; A, E
II.	✔		✔	✔	no; B, D
III.	✔	✔	✔	✔	yes

Choice C is your answer.

8. **Fill in words omitted in a reading passage.** Some tests have a series of reading passages with about ten words omitted in each. You are to fill in each space with one of four choices of words. The passages are usually on educational topics.

Example:

It has been said that we can't have another 1. _____ because wealth, especially stocks, is no longer 2. _____ in a few hands, but spread among many. In times of 3. _____, when people could save money, they didn't, because prices were going up and credit was 4. _____ available. More and more people borrowed heavily, expecting to repay with cheaper money and sell at even more 5. _____ prices. People seem to expect everything to continue to go up and are always 6. _____ when prices fall. The old adage "What goes up, must come down" is still 7. _____. Had business, government and people saved money 8. _____ borrowing, they and the economy would be better off. It is strange that our 9. _____, which claims to encourage saving, taxes savings and allows deductions for interest payments, in essence 10. _____ borrowing.

1. (A) war
    (B) famine
    (C) depression
    (D) inflation

2. (A) dispersed
    (B) concentrated
    (C) only
    (D) spread

3. (A) peace
    (B) wealth
    (C) war
    (D) inflation

4. (A) readily
    (B) not
    (C) somewhat
    (D) everywhere

5. (A) inflated
    (B) gross
    (C) deflated
    (D) difficult

6. (A) comforted
    (B) surprised
    (C) encouraged
    (D) depressed

7. (A) questionable
    (B) valid
    (C) trite
    (D) gospel

8. (A) in addition to
    (B) to increase
    (C) instead of
    (D) while

9. (A) government
    (B) population
    (C) president
    (D) bank

10. (A) decrying
    (B) taxing
    (C) defeating
    (D) subsidizing

Strategy:

- Fill your own word in first. Then, of the four choices, choose the word closest to your own word. Write the word in the space. Follow this procedure for the rest of the passage.
- Read the passage with the filled-in words to see whether it makes sense.
- Circle the words you used. Transfer your circled choices to the answer sheet.

Answers: 1. **C**   2. **B**   3. **D**   4. **A**   5. **A**   6. **B**   7. **B**   8. **C**   9. **A**   10. **D**

GRAMMAR REVIEW

Remember the basic rule: Choose the answer that "sounds right" to you. Keep a secretarial handbook by your side (at home, of course, not at the test). It answers many grammar and usage questions concisely.

1. **Be sure you know and use the proper case form for pronouns.**

Case	Forms				
Subjective	I	we	he, she	they	who
Objective	me	us	him, her	them	whom
Possessive	my (mine)	our (ours)	his, her (hers)	their (theirs)	whose

Examples:

(He, Him) and (I, me) agreed to meet for lunch.

The pronouns needed are subjects of the verb *agreed*; therefore, the correct choices are the subjective pronouns *He* and *I*.

The test was hard for Bill and (I, me).
The pronoun needed is the object of the preposition *for*; therefore, you should choose the objective pronoun *me*.

(Who's, Whose) gloves are these?
This sentence needs a possessive pronoun. The possessive form of "who" is *whose*. *Who's* is a contraction meaning "who is."

In formal writing, reflexive pronouns (myself, himself, etc.) are used only after the antecedent. *Myself* is used after *I* or *me*; *himself* after *he* or *him*.

CORRECT: I myself will go.
　　NOT: No one will go except myself.
　　BUT: No one will go except me.

2. **A verb must be in the right tense.**

English Verb Time Lines

Simple Tenses:	Past	Present	Future
	I walked	I walk	I will walk
	I walked three miles yesterday	I walk three miles each day.	I will walk three miles tomorrow.
	(past activity at a specific time)	(habitual activity)	(activity to take place at some later time)

Perfect Tenses:	Past Perfect	Present Perfect	Future Perfect
	I had walked	I have walked	I will have walked
	I had walked three miles by the time you caught up with me.	I have walked three miles to get here.	I will have walked three miles by the time you catch up with me.
	(activity begun and completed in the past before some other past action)	(activity begun in the past, completed in the present)	(activity begun at any time and completed in the future)

Don't shift tenses needlessly within a sentence.
Example:
He ran for the bus and (jumps, jumped) on.
The first verb (ran) is in the past tense, so the second verb should also be in the past tense (jumped).

3. **Subjects and verbs must agree in number. Pronouns must agree with their antecedents.**

    Singular subjects require singular verbs; plural subjects require plural verbs.
    Example:
    The *suggestion* of the employees *seems* appropriate. (*singular*)
    The *suggestions* of the employees *seem* appropriate. (*plural*)

    Singular subjects joined by *and* are usually plural.
    Example: Tracy and Kim share an apartment.

    When singular and plural subjects are joined by *either . . . or* or *neither . . . nor*, the verb agrees with the noun closest to it.
    Example:
    Neither the teachers nor the *principal was* in the cafeteria.
    Neither the principal nor the *teachers were* in the cafeteria.

    Each, every, everyone take singular verbs and singular pronouns.
    Example:
    Everyone takes *her* (not their) turn at leading the discussion.
    Each student must take (his, their) books.

    Each student is singular; therefore, the singular pronoun *his* is correct.

4. **The subjunctive mood of a verb expresses a condition contrary to fact, such as a wish.**
    Example:
    If I were president, (however I am not) I would live in the White House.
    If I were you, (but I'm not) I would sell the car.

5. **Adjectives modify nouns or pronouns.**
    Examples:
    the *handsome* dog
    the *proud* mother
    the *eager* student

    Adjectives also follow forms of the verb *to be* or its equivalents—*feel, smell, taste, seem, appear, sound.*
    Examples:
    He feels *bad* (not badly).
    The flower smells *sweet* (not sweetly).

6. **Adverbs modify verbs adjectives and other adverbs.** They often end in "-ly."
    Examples:
    He runs *quickly*.
       (verb) (adverb)
    He was *deeply* tanned.
          (adverb) (adjective)
    He runs *really quickly*.
       (verb) (adverb)(adverb)

7. **Use the appropriate forms for comparisons:** the comparative for two things; the superlative for three or more.
   To form the comparative, add *-er* or use *more* (or *less*) with the word. To form the superlative, add *-est* or use *most* (or *least*) with the word.

Positive	**Comparative**	**Superlative**
tall	taller	tallest
eager	more eager	most eager
quickly	less quickly	least quickly

   Example: He is the *taller* of the two brothers.
   (Use the comparative to compare two.)

   She is the *tallest* member of the volleyball team.
   (Use the superlative for three or more.)

   NOT: He is taller than any boy in the class.
   (Then he would be taller than himself.)
   BUT: He is taller than any *other* boy in the class.

8. **A participial phrase used as an adjective must be immediately followed by the noun or pronoun it modifies.**

   INCORRECT: After having walked all day, the lake came into view.
   (This sounds as though the lake had walked all day.)

   CORRECT: After having walked all day, *she* saw the lake.
   or
   After she had walked all day, the lake came into view.

9. **Avoid sentence fragments.** A fragment is an incomplete sentence.
   Example:
   Our school is famous for its academics. *Especially our foreign language classes.*
   "Especially our foreign language classes" has neither subject nor verb; therefore, it cannot be a sentence. To correct this example, connect the fragment to the complete sentence with a comma:
   Our school is famous for its academics, especially our foreign language classes.

10. **Avoid run-on sentences and comma splices.**
    A run-on sentence is two complete sentences that are run together without appropriate punctuation.
    Example:
    He completed the assignment it was well done.

    A comma splice is two complete sentences linked only by a comma.
    Example:
    He completed the assignment, it was well done.

    To correct a run-on or comma splice:
    1) Make two sentences:
       He completed the assignment. It was well done.

2) Connect the sentences with a semicolon:
   He completed the assignment; it was well done.

3) Add transitional words to make one clause subordinate to the other:
   When he completed the assignment, he realized it was well done.
       (subordinate clause)   (main clause)

11. **Use parallel structure for sentence elements that are parallel in thought.**

    INCORRECT: He liked to go to the mountains to enjoy fishing, hunting and to relax.

    CORRECT: He liked to go to the mountains to enjoy fishing, hunting and re-laxing.

or

    He liked to go to the mountains to fish, to hunt and to relax.

12. **Paired words are "buddies."** If you use one, you must use the other also: either . . . or, neither . . . nor, not only . . . but also.

13. **Correct spelling is a matter of looking words up, memorizing them and practicing using them.** Use your dictionary to look up the spelling of words you are unsure of. Each time you look up a word, write it correctly ten times. (Remember fourth grade?) Repetition will help to fix the spelling in your memory.

The rules that follow should help you to avoid the most common spelling errors.

    RULE 1: *i* before *e*
                 Except after *c*
                 Or when sounded like *ay*
                 As in *neighbor* or *weigh*.
    Exceptions:
    Neither, leisure, foreigner, seized, weird, heights.

    RULE 2: If a word ends in *y* preceded by a vowel, keep the *y* when adding a suffix.
    Examples:
    day, days; attorney, attorneys

    RULE 3: If a word ends in *y* preceded by a consonant, change the *y* to *i* before adding a suffix.
    Examples:
    try, tries, tried; lady, ladies
    Exceptions:
    To avoid double *i*, retain the *y* before *-ing* and *-ish*.
    Examples:
    fly, flying; baby, babyish

    RULE 4: Silent *e* at the end of a word is usually dropped before a suffix beginning with a vowel.
    Examples:
    dine + ing = dining

locate + ion = location
use + able = usable
offense + ive = offensive
Exception:
Words ending in *ce* and *ge* retain *e* before *-able* and *-ous* in order to retain the
soft sounds of *c* and *g*.
Examples:
peace + able = peaceable
courage + ous = courageous

RULE 5:   Silent *e* is usually kept before a suffix beginning with a consonant.
Examples:
care + less = careless
late + ly = lately
one + ness = oneness
game + ster = gamester
Exceptions to Rules 4 and 5:
truly, duly, awful, argument, wholly, ninth, mileage, dyeing, acreage, canoe-
ing.

RULE 6:   A word of one syllable that ends in a *single* consonant preceded by
a *single* vowel doubles the final consonant before a suffix begin-
ning with a vowel or *y*.
Examples:
hit, hitting; drop, dropped; big, biggest; mud, muddy
But:
Help, helping because *help* ends in *two* consonants
Need, needing because the final consonant is preceeded by *two* vowels.

RULE 7:   A word of more than one syllable that accents the *last* syllable and
that ends in a *single* consonant preceded by a *single* vowel doubles
the final consonant when adding a suffix beginning with a vowel.
Examples:
begin, beginner; admit, admitted
But:
enter, entered because the accent is *not* on the last syllable.

RULE 8:   A word ending in *er* or *ur* doubles the *r* in the past tense if the word
is accented on the last syllable.
Examples:
occur, occurred; prefer, preferred; transfer, transferred

RULE 9:   A word ending in *er* does *not* double the *r* in the past tense if the
accent falls on other than the last syllable.
Examples:
answer, answered; offer, offered; differ, differed

RULE 10:   When *-full* is added to the end of a noun to form an adjective, the
final *l* is dropped.
Examples:
cheerful, cupful, hopeful

RULE 11:   All words beginning with *over* are one word.
Examples:
overcast, overcharge, overhear

RULE 12:   All words with the prefix *self* are hyphenated.
Examples:
self-control, self-defense, self-evident

14. **Know when to capitalize.**
    Capitalize names of specific persons, places and things; names of organizations and institutions; historical periods and events; members of national, political, racial and religious groups:
    Examples:
    Thomas Jefferson, San Francisco, Statue of Liberty, Internal Revenue Service, Yale University, Middle Ages, Civil War, Republican, Methodist, Japanese.

    Capitalize derivatives of proper names:
    Example:
    American history, Spanish-speaking countries, French bread

    Capitalize the first and last words and all other words except articles, conjunctions and short prepositions (four or fewer letters) in the title of books, plays, etc:
    Example:
    The Fall of Rome, *A Day in the Life of Ivan Denisovich*

    Capitalize personal titles when they precede a proper name, but *not* usually when they follow the name:
    Example:
    Professor Joseph Malone but Joseph Malone, a professor of history

    Capitalize specific course titles but not general courses of study:
    Example:
    I am taking History 102, English Composition 5 and Advanced Physics.
    but
    I am studying American history, English composition and physics.

    Capitalize the first word of every sentence, including a quotation within a sentence:
    Example:
    She asked, "Where are the children?"

15. **Use words correctly.**
    Some people are confused about the correct use and spelling of the following words. Check the dictionary for further information.
    Accidentally. Note the second *a*.

    Affect is most often used as a verb meaning "influence." *Effect* is sometimes used as a noun (as in "to have an *effect* on something") and sometimes as a verb meaning "to bring about."

    All right, not *alright.*

    Already means "previously." *All ready* means "all prepared."

Between two people or things, but *among* three or more people or things.

Use *number of* when something can be counted (cars) and *amount of* when it can't (flour).

Fewer is used with objects that can be counted, *less* with an amount that cannot ("fewer cars"; "less flour").

Anxious means "worried," while *eager* means "looking forward" to something.

"*Bring* the book" means that the book will be moved toward the speaker. "*Take* the book" means that the book will be moved away from the speaker.

Use *farther* when discussing actual distance and *further* when meaning metaphorical distance.
He ran *farther* than I.
I have gone *further* in my profession than anyone else in my class.

A speaker *implies* (suggests), while a listener *infers* (interprets).

Use *regardless*, not *irregardless*.

Latest means "most recent" while *last* means "after all others."
We had the *latest* news.
Harry came in *last* in the race.

To *raise* is to lift something else. To *rise* is to lift oneself.
The man who raises the profits will rise in the company as surely as the sun rises in the sky.

Scarcely and *hardly* do not take *not*.

To *set* is to place something. To *sit* is to seat oneself.

Perfect and *unique* do not need any strengthening adjectives. They represent the ultimate; words like *very* and *totally* are redundant with them.

Use *kind of*, not *kind of a*.
NOT: He led a wonderful kind of a life.
BUT: He led a wonderful kind of life.

Differentiate between between *angry* and *mad*.
You make me mad (insane).
You make me angry (irritated).

Aggravate means to make worse: *irritate* means to annoy.
WRONG: The slow traffic aggravates me.
RIGHT: The slow traffic irritates me.
RIGHT: The slow traffic aggravates (worsens) my headache.

Use *try to* or *be sure to*, not *try and* or *be sure and*.
NOT: Try and come to school on time.
BUT: Try to come to school on time.

NOT: Be sure and fill in the forms correctly.
BUT: Be sure to fill in the forms correctly.

The *reason is because* is redundant. Use *reason is that* or *because.*
WRONG: *The reason I am late is because my car had a flat tire.*
RIGHT: The *reason* I am late *is that* my car had a flat tire.
or
I am late *because* my car had a flat tire.

Then is an adverb meaning "at that time" or "next in time." *Than* is a conjunction used in comparisons.
First you walk; *then* you run.
This book is longer *than* that one.

Use *could have* or *should have,* not *could of* or *should of.*
I *should have* (not should of) gone with you.
He *could have* (not could of) won the race.

16.   **Synonyms** are words that have the same meaning.
Example:
The new program caused *controversy.* A synonym for *controversy* is
(A) *debate*
(B) anger
(C) comparison
(D) agreement

17.   **Antonyms** are words that have opposite meanings.
Example:
The antonym of *praise* is
(A) laud
(B) *chide*
(C) detest
(D) emulate

18.   **Be able to recognize similes**
Examples:
She looked *like* a rose
He was as helpless *as* a child
and **metaphors:** She *is* a rose

19.   **You should be able to discern whether a sentence makes a comparison, provides details, or gives a reason or an explanation.**

20.   **Finding the main idea is discussed in the reading review.**

WRITING REVIEW

The writing portion of the teacher's competency test is designed to measure your mastery of English and your ability to express your ideas clearly in written form. Neither your knowledge about a topic nor your viewpoint is a factor in the scoring. The topic is only a means of determining your ability to express yourself in standard English.

There are usually two types of topic in each test. One type asks you to express your thoughts about a remembered experience. The other type asks you to take a position on a subject and defend it. In both instances you will need to marshal your thoughts so that you have 1) a thesis, 2) subpoints that support or expand on your theme and 3) a conclusion.

When the instructions for the topic ask you to include specific considerations or supporting arguments, be sure that you include them all. Support your generalizations with specifics. Stay within the guidelines of the topic, and don't write more than the space allows. You may write less. Length is not the criterion, but you should fill at least half the space given.

You may want to pattern your essays on the basic five-paragraph style. The first paragraph states the thesis and makes brief mention of the supporting statements; the next three paragraphs expand on the three main supporting statements; the last paragraph restates the thesis in other words and wraps it all up.

The best way to prepare for the writing portion of the test is to practice. Writing improves tremendously with practice. Write one or two essays a day for several weeks. You will become more comfortable about writing on a variety of topics and more fluent in your writing.

If you have difficulty writing on a personal topic or expressing an opinion, make up your response. *You don't* have to tell the absolute truth. Test graders are only interested in how well you write, not true confessions.

When writing your essay, it is especially important that you develop an outline and stick to it. Don't add extra thoughts after the conclusion. Don't agonize over the outline. Adopt the shopping list method of outlining to leave yourself enough time to write the essay itself. Pay attention to the topic and write only about that.

Write legibly. This is a test of communication. If the reader can't read your essay, you haven't communicated and your essay score will reflect this fact. Concentrate on your handwriting as you practice.

If you have trouble finishing the essay on time, give yourself five minutes less time for the practice essays than the time allowed on your actual test. Then you'll have an easier time during the test.

Some people say, "I've always been a bad speller." That doesn't cure the problem. You *can* improve your spelling by concentrating on the spelling rules included in the Grammar Review, pages 38 to 40.

Go over the rest of the Grammar Review section for tips on writing correctly and effectively.

Ask a knowledgeable teacher or friend to correct your practice essays. Rewrite any essays in which you have more than ten errors. You will see what your essay can look like and become accustomed to correct writing.

For each topic, spend a third of your time jotting down your ideas, putting them in order and making an outline. Take half of the time to write the essay. This will leave you a few minutes to reread the essay(s) carefully, correcting mechanical errors. When you have to write on two topics, write on the one that is easiest for you first. If you have enough time, improve phrasing and vocabulary. The mechanics of written English are a major consideration in scoring: grammar, punctuation, sentence structure, vocabulary, paragraphing.

As you write and edit, keep in mind consistency of viewpoint, supporting arguments, organization, logic, appropriateness to audience, unity and cohesiveness. Scoring is done on a holistic basis, taking into consideration all of these points.

PRACTICE TOPICS

Here are topics you can use for practice.

What event in your life affected you most profoundly? Relate how it changed you and explain why the change was for the better or worse.

"A teacher has not taught until the student has learned." In which situations would you agree with this statement and under what circumstances would you disagree?

Which class in college has been of most benefit to you? Why?

Compare the practice of student teaching two periods a day for a year with student teaching all day for nine weeks. Which do you think is better? Support your opinions.

At some time in our lives we must face a situation about which we can do nothing. Relate such an incident, including how you dealt with it, your feelings at the time and its aftereffects on you.

Education is not an accumulation of facts, but the confidence of knowing that one can locate the facts when they are needed. Give reasons why you agree or disagree with this statement.

There are people who have greatly influenced our lives without knowing it. They could be famous people or people we have met only casually or even people we have never met. Describe the influence one such person has had on your life.

Do you think graded report cards in elementary school are beneficial or harmful to the students?

Which college class was most disappointing to you? If you were to teach that class, what changes would you make in it to improve it for the students?

It has been suggested that education professors and school district administrators teach an elementary or secondary school class every seventh year. Do you think this is a beneficial and workable idea or not?

What do you consider the most important character trait of a good teacher?

"Good teachers do not necessarily make good administrators." What is your opinion of this statement? Illustrate with examples from your experience, if possible.

MATHEMATICS REVIEW

The following are the types of math problems that you are most likely to face on the test. The distribution of problems on a particular test will vary. Check the sample test for the topics you need to cover. Not everything in the review is used on each test.

Problem Type	Approximate Distribution
Word problems	20%
Equations	10–15%
Fractions	10%
Graphs	10%
Ratio and proportion	5–10%
Percentages	5%
Substitution in formulas	5%
Comparing and ordering numbers	5%
Estimation	5%
Measurement	5%
Logical reasoning	5–10%

TERMS

Perimeter—the distance around the edge of something.

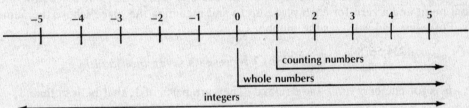

The perimeter is 3 + 4 + 3 + 4 = 14

Area—the size of the enclosed space. The area of the above rectangle is 3 × 4 = 12 square units.

Prime number—a number that can be divided evenly only by itself and by 1, such as 2, 3, 5, 7.

Ratio—the comparison of two quantities, such as 10:13 or $^{10}/_{13}$.

Proportion—two ratios equal to each other, such as $^{10}/_{13} = {}^{20}/_{26}$.

Counting numbers—1, 2, 3, 4 . . . .

Whole numbers—0, 1, 2, 3, 4 . . . .

Integers—. . . −4 −3, −2, −1, 0, 1, 2, 3, 4 . . .

Factor—a number that divides evenly into another number.

$$3 \times 4 = 12$$
3 and 4 are factors of 12

Square—the product of a number multiplied by itself.

The square of 5 is 25
$$5 \times 5 = 25$$
Written: $5^2 = 25$

Square root—a number that, when multiplied by itself, equals a given number.

The square root of 25 is 5
$$5 \times 5 = 25$$
Written: $\sqrt{25} = 5$

Cylinder—the shape of a tin can.

Cube—a block whose length, width and height are all the same.

NUMBER PLACEMENT

1	2	3	4	.	5	6	7	8
THOUSANDS	HUNDREDS	TENS	ONES	.	TENTHS	HUNDREDTHS	THOUSANDTHS	TENTHOUSANDTHS
1,000	200	30	4		$\frac{5}{10}$	$\frac{6}{100}$	$\frac{7}{1,000}$	$\frac{8}{10,000}$

To find what a number to the left of the decimal represents, put a 1 under the number and add zeros up to the decimal point.

$$1234.5678 \qquad \text{so, 2 represents two } hundreds.$$
$$100.$$

To find out what a number to the right of the decimal represents, put a 1 below the decimal point and a zero for each place up to and including the place where the number is. Put a line and a 1 over the number.

$$\frac{1234.5678}{1000} = \frac{1}{1,000} \qquad \text{so, 7 represents seven } thousandths.$$

Hint: *-th* is for numbers *after* the decimal. They are parts of 1, that is, less than 1.

ROUNDING OFF

To round off, write the number you are rounding off to under the number. Your answer will have the same number of zeros. If the number above the first zero on the left is less than 5, leave the number on the left alone, and put zeros in the places to the right of the 1.

Example: Round off to the nearest 1,000.

63,456.

1,000.
Write: 63,000

If the number above the first zero is 5 or more, add 1 to the number on the left and put zeros in the places to the right of the 1.

Example: Round off to the nearest 1,000.

63,654

1,000
64,000
Write: 64,000

ESTIMATING

When you are asked to add a column of numbers, estimate the answers first, then check the answer choices. You may not need to do more. Sometimes you have to find the sum of the last digits.

Example:

1,234	Answers (A)	12,027	Estimate	1,000
2,347	(B)	120,266		2,000
3,789	(C)	12,026		4,000
4,656	(D)	1,226		5,000
	(E)	12,025		12,000

Eliminate D (too small) and B (too large). A, C and E differ only in the last digit. Add up the last digits: the total is 26. The answer is C. Another clue is that three answers end in 6 and three answers are around 12,000. Only C has both.

NUMBER LINE

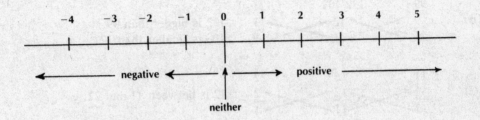

Example:

34. The fraction $^{12}/_{11}$ is between each of the following pairs of numbers except

(A) $^2/_3$ and $^4/_3$
(B) $^9/_{11}$ and $^{11}/_9$
(C) 1 and 2
(D) 0.9 and 1.1
(E) $^{11}/_{12}$ and $^{12}/_{12}$

Underline the word *except*.

Draw a number line.

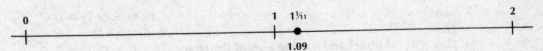

Change $^{12}/_{11}$ to $1\,^1/_{11}$ ($12 \div 11 = 1\,^1/_{11}$). Change $^{12}/_{11}$ to a decimal: $12 \div 11 = 1.09$.

Locate your results on the number line. Mark it with a dot. Write the fraction above the line and the decimal below the line. You're ready to compare $^{12}/_{11}$ (or $1\,^1/_{11}$ or 1.09) with either fractions or decimals, instead of converting each pair.

Locate each pair on the number line, putting fractions above the line and decimals below it. Connect each pair. Is the dot between each pair? The correct pair is the one that doesn't have the dot between them.

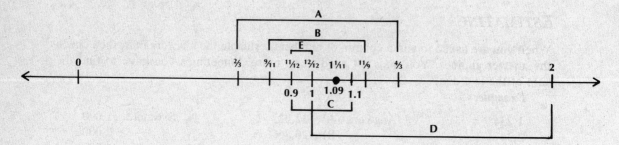

The correct answer is (E).

Another way to solve this problem is to compare fractions (see page 52). For this method, first change all decimals to fractions. Next cross-multiply as indicated by the arrows below.

(A) $\frac{2}{3}$ $\frac{12}{11}$ $\frac{4}{3}$ 36 is between 22 and 44.

(B) $\frac{9}{11}$ $\frac{12}{11}$ $\frac{11}{9}$ 132 is bigger than 99.
108 is smaller than 121.

(C) $\frac{1}{1}$ $\frac{12}{11}$ $\frac{2}{1}$ 12 is between 11 and 22.

(D) $\frac{9}{10}$ $\frac{12}{11}$ $\frac{11}{10}$ 120 is between 99 and 121.

(E) $\frac{11}{12}$ $\frac{12}{11}$ $\frac{12}{12}$ 144 is *not* between 121 and 132.

OPERATIONS WITH SIGNED NUMBERS

Addition.

+ plus + = +
− plus − = −
+ plus − = subtract and use the sign of the larger

$(+4) + (+2) = 6$
$(-4) + (-2) = -6$
$4 + (-2) = 2$
$(-4) + (+2) = -2$

Two positive numbers added result in a positive.
   Example:
   $(+3) + (+5) = +8$

Two negative numbers added result in a negative.
   Example:
   $(-3) + (-5) = -8$ or $-3 -5 = -8$

To add a positive and a negative number find the difference between the numbers and use the sign of the larger number.

> *Example:*
> $(+3) + (-5) = -2$ or $+3 -5 = -2$
>   BUT
> $(-3) + (+5) = 2$

Subtraction.

Two positive numbers subtracted result in the sign of the larger number.

> *Example:*
> $5 - 3 = 2$
> $3 - 5 = -2$

This is the same as addition of numbers with unlike signs.

To subtract two negative numbers, take the difference and use the sign of the larger number (two minus signs next to each other equal a plus sign).

> *Example:*
> $(-3) - (-5) =$
> $(-3) + 5 = 2$
>
> $(-5) - (-3) =$
> $-5 + 3 = -2$

To subtract a positive and a negative number, add them and take the sign of the larger number.

> $(-5) - (+3) =$
> $-5 - 3 = -8$
> $(+5) - (-3) =$
> $5 + 3 = 8$

Multiplication.

$$+ \times + = + \qquad 4 \times 2 = \quad 8$$
$$+ \times - = - \qquad 4 \times (-2) = -8$$
$$- \times - = + \qquad (-4)(-2) = \quad 8$$

Positive times positive equals positive.

> *Example:*
> $(+3)\,(+5) = 15$

Negative times negative equals positive.

> *Example:*
> $(-3)\,(-5) = 15$

Positive times negative equals negative.

> *Example:*
> $(+3)\,(-5) = -15$
> $(-3)\,(+5) = -15$

Division. A positive divided by a positive equals positive.
 Example:
 $$\frac{+8}{+4} = 2$$

A negative divided by a negative equals positive.
 Example:
 $$\frac{-8}{-4} = 2$$

A positive divided by a negative equals a negative.
A negative divided by a positive equals a negative.
 Example:
 $$\frac{+8}{-4} = -2 \qquad \frac{-8}{+4} = -2$$

Signs in division are the same as in multiplication.

$$+ \div + = + \qquad \frac{8}{4} = 2$$

$$+ \div - = - \qquad \frac{8}{-4} = -2 \ or \ -\frac{8}{4} = -2 \ or \ \frac{-8}{4} = -2$$

$$- \div - = + \qquad \frac{-8}{-4} = 2$$

Brackets

Remove brackets in pairs from the innermost brackets or parentheses to the outer-most. Remember that a minus in front of parentheses changes all the signs inside the parentheses when you remove the parentheses. This is as if you are multiplying by -1.
 Example:
 $7 - [4 - (5 - 3) + 3] =$
 $7 - [4 - (2) + 3] =$
 $7 - [4 - 2 + 3] =$
 $7 - [5] =$
 $7 - 5 = 2$

Try this:
 $16 - 3[7 - 2(6 - 3) - 5(-8 - 1)] =$
 $16 - 3[7 - 2(3) - 5(-9)] =$
 $16 - 3[7 - 6 + 45] =$
 $16 - 3[46] =$
 $16 - 138 = -122$

This will also work with unknowns such as these:
 $16 - 3[a - 2(b - 3) - 5(c - 1)] =$
 $16 - 3[a - 2b + 6 - 5c + 5] =$
 $16 - 3[11 + a - 2b - 5c] =$
 $16 - 33 - 3a + 6b + 15c =$
 $-17 - 3a + 6b + 15c$

Order of operations is:

(1) parentheses, powers and square roots.

(2) Multiplication and division are from left to right.

(3) Addition and subtraction are from left to right.

Examples:

( )	$10 - \sqrt{36} + 3 \times 4 - (7 - 3)^2 + 12 \div 6 =$
powers and square roots	$10 - \sqrt{36} + 3 \times 4 - 4^2 + 12 \div 6 =$
$\times, \div$	$10 - 6 + 3 \times 4 - 16 + 12 \div 6 =$
$+, -$	$10 - 6 + 12 - 16 + 2 = 2$

DIVISION

To check your answer, multiply the answer by the number you divided by. The result should be the number you started with.

$$12 \div 3 = 4$$
$$\text{Check: } 4 \times 3 = 12$$

To find out whether a number is divisible (can be divided evenly) by a certain number, remember:

A number is divisible by 2 if it ends in an even number: 2, 4, 6, 8.

A number is divisible by 3 if the digits add up to a number divisible by 3.

Is 1,542 divisible by 3?
Add the digits: $1 + 5 + 4 + 2 = 12$.
Is 12 divisible by 3? $12 \div 3 = 4$
Yes, 1,542 is divisible by 3.

A number is divisible by 5 if it ends in 0 or 5.

A number is divisible by 9 if the digits add up to a number divisible by 9.

A number is divisible by 10 if it ends in 0.

FRACTIONS

$$\frac{3}{5} = \frac{\text{numerator}}{\text{denominator}}$$

Adding fractions. To add fractions with the same denominator, simply add the numerators and repeat the denominator in the answer. Do *not* add the denominators.

$$\frac{1}{4} + \frac{2}{4} = \frac{3}{4}$$

To add fractions of unequal denominators, you must find the *common denominator* (CD for short) of these fractions. The CD is the number that all the denominators in the problem will divide into evenly.

$$\frac{1}{9} + \frac{2}{3}$$

Here, the CD is 9, since both 9 and 3 divide evenly into 9. One easy way to find the CD is to multiply the denominators by each other.

$$\frac{1}{2} + \frac{1}{3} \quad \text{The CD is } 2 \times 3 = 6$$

To add these two fractions, multiply both terms (numerator and denominator) of the first fraction by the denominator of the second fraction. Then multiply both terms of the second fraction by the denominator of the first fraction.

$$\frac{1 \times 3}{2 \times 3} + \frac{1 \times 2}{3 \times 2} = \frac{3}{6} + \frac{2}{6} = \frac{5}{6}$$

Sometimes this system results in large numbers that are unwieldy.

$$\frac{1}{8} + \frac{1}{12} - \frac{1}{15} \qquad \text{The CD is } 8 \times 12 \times 15 = 1,440.$$

Here we use the *lowest common denominator* (LCD), which is the smallest number that each denominator will divide into evenly.

Here's how. Divide the denominators by their factors. Start dividing by the smallest number that you can see will go evenly into at least one of the denominators. In this example, your first factor is 2. Continue with the same factor until you need to try a larger one. Factor until each denominator is down to 1.

Factor		Denominators		
	8	12	15	$8 \div 2 = 4,\ 12 \div 2 = 6$
2	4	6	15	Since 2 won't go
2	2	3	15	evenly into 15, just
2	1	3	15	bring 15 down.
3	1	1	5	
5	1	1	1	

Multiply the factors together to get the LCD: $2 \times 2 \times 2 \times 3 \times 5 = 120$.

Now divide each denominator into the LCD. This is the number that you will multiply both the numerator and denominator of each fraction by.

$$120 \div 8 = 15$$
$$120 \div 12 = 10$$
$$120 \div 15 = 8$$

$$\frac{1 \times 15}{8 \times 15} + \frac{1 \times 10}{12 \times 10} - \frac{1 \times 8}{15 \times 8} =$$

$$\frac{15}{120} + \frac{10}{120} - \frac{8}{120}$$

$$\frac{15 + 10 - 8}{120} = \frac{17}{120}$$

Comparing fractions
   Example:
   16. Which is bigger, $\frac{4}{5}$ or $\frac{11}{13}$?

$$\text{Cross-multiply} \quad \overset{52}{\frac{4}{5}} \times \overset{55}{\frac{11}{13}}$$

$$4 \times 13 = 52; \ 11 \times 5 = 55$$

55 is bigger than 52, therefore $\frac{11}{13}$ is bigger than $\frac{4}{5}$.

You can repeat this process for a question like the following.

Example:

23. Which fraction is smallest?
    (A) ⅔
    (B) ¾
    (C) ⁷/₁₁
    (D) ⁶/₁₀
    (E) ⁵/₉

Underline *smallest*.

Compare $\quad \dfrac{2}{3} \overset{8}{\diagdown}\hspace{-0.4em}\overset{9}{\diagup} \dfrac{3}{4}$ $\quad$ ⅔ is smaller; cross out B (¾)

Compare $\quad \dfrac{2}{3} \overset{22}{\diagdown}\hspace{-0.4em}\overset{21}{\diagup} \dfrac{7}{11}$ $\quad$ ⁷/₁₁ is smaller; cross out A (⅔)

Compare $\quad \dfrac{7}{11} \overset{70}{\diagdown}\hspace{-0.4em}\overset{66}{\diagup} \dfrac{6}{10}$ $\quad$ ⁶/₁₀ is smaller; cross out C (⁷/₁₁)

Compare $\quad \dfrac{6}{10} \overset{54}{\diagdown}\hspace{-0.4em}\overset{50}{\diagup} \dfrac{5}{9}$ $\quad$ ⁵/₉ is smaller; cross out D (⁶/₁₀)

E (⁵/₉) is the answer.

Reducing fractions to their lowest terms. Divide the numerator and denominator by the same number until one number can't be divided any more. Start with the smallest or easiest numbers first, for example, 2, 3 or 10.

$$\frac{42 \div 2}{48 \div 2} = \frac{21}{24} \qquad \frac{21 \div 3}{24 \div 3} = \frac{7}{8}$$

or

$$\frac{\cancel{\cancel{42}}^{\,21^{\,7}}}{\cancel{\cancel{48}}_{\,24_{\,8}}} = \frac{7}{8}$$

Mixed fractions. Change a mixed fraction to an improper fraction. Multiply the denominator by the whole number and add the fraction. Put the result over the denominator.

Example:

$$2¼ = \frac{2 \times 4 + 1}{4} = \frac{9}{4}$$

Change an improper fraction into a mixed number.

Example:

$$\frac{13}{4} = \begin{array}{r} 3\text{ R}1 \\ 4\overline{)\ 13} \\ -12 \\ \hline 1 \end{array}$$
Divide the denominator into the numerator.

$$\frac{13}{4} = 3¼$$
The remainder stays as a fraction.

Adding mixed numbers with like denominators

Example:

$$2\frac{1}{3} \qquad 2\frac{2}{3}$$
$$+3\frac{1}{3} \qquad +2\frac{2}{3}$$
$$\overline{5\frac{2}{3}} \qquad \overline{4\frac{4}{3}} =$$
$$4 + \frac{3}{3} + \frac{1}{3} =$$
$$4 + 1 + \frac{1}{3} = 5\frac{1}{3}$$

Adding mixed numbers with unlike denominators.

Example:

$$2\frac{1}{3} = 2\frac{4}{12} \qquad \text{The common denominator is 12.}$$
$$+3\frac{1}{4} = 3\frac{3}{12}$$
$$\overline{5\frac{7}{12}}$$

Subtracting mixed fractions with like denominators.

Example:

$$\text{Borrow } 1 = \frac{3}{3}$$

$$3\frac{2}{3} \qquad 3\frac{1}{3} = 2 + 1 + \frac{1}{3} \;=\; 2 + \frac{3}{3} + \frac{1}{3} \;=\; 2\frac{4}{3}$$
$$-2\frac{1}{3} \qquad -2\frac{2}{3} = 2\frac{2}{3} \qquad\qquad = 2\frac{2}{3} \qquad = 2\frac{2}{3}$$
$$\overline{1\frac{1}{3}} \qquad\qquad\qquad\qquad\qquad\qquad\qquad\qquad\qquad \overline{\frac{2}{3}}$$

Subtracting mixed fractions with unlike denominators.

Example:

$$3\frac{1}{4} = 3\frac{3}{12} \quad \text{Borrow } 1 = \frac{12}{12} \qquad 2\frac{15}{12} \quad \text{The common denominator is 12.}$$
$$-2\frac{1}{3} = -2\frac{4}{12} \qquad\qquad\qquad\qquad -2\frac{4}{12}$$
$$\qquad\qquad\qquad\qquad\qquad\qquad\qquad\qquad \overline{\frac{11}{12}}$$

Multiplying mixed fractions (no common denominator necessary).

$$2\frac{1}{3} \times 3\frac{1}{4} = \frac{7}{3} \times \frac{13}{4} = \frac{91}{12} = 7\frac{7}{12}$$

$$4\frac{1}{5} \times 1\frac{2}{3} = \frac{\overset{7}{\cancel{21}}}{\underset{1}{\cancel{5}}} \times \frac{\overset{1}{\cancel{5}}}{\underset{1}{\cancel{3}}} = \frac{7}{1} = 7 \qquad \text{Cancel if possible.}$$

Dividing mixed fractions (no common denominator necessary).

$$4\frac{1}{4} \div 2\frac{1}{3} = \frac{17}{4} \div \frac{7}{3} = \frac{17}{4} \times \frac{3}{7} = \frac{51}{28} = 1\frac{23}{28}$$

DECIMALS

To compare decimals, add zeros so that each decimal number has the same number of digits to the right of the decimal. Extra zeros at the end of a decimal do not change the number.

Example:

$$.5 = .50 = .500$$

Example:
Which decimal number is greatest?

(A) 0.0150
(B) 0.095
(C) 0.1050
(D) 0.1105
(E) 0.115

Add zeros so that each decimal has four places. Then line up the decimals as if you're going to add them and you will see that E is greatest.

(A) 0.0150
(B) 0.0950
(C) 0.1050
(D) 0.1105
(E) 0.1150

Adding decimals. Arrange the numbers vertically with the decimal points lined up. Fill in the empty spaces to the right of the decimal point if necessary. This will prevent most errors.
Example:
Add 1.7 + 25.34 + .007 + 26 + 1.0556

```
   1.7      Arrange the numbers vertically.
  25.34     The number with the most places after the decimal is 1.0556.
    .007    Fill in the other decimal places so that each decimal number
  26        has four digits after the decimal point.
   1.0556
```

```
   1.7000   Now add.
  25.3400
    .0070
  26.0000
   1.0556
  54.1026
```

Subtracting decimals. Use the same system for subtraction of decimals.
Example:
46.32 − 27.5671 =

```
  46.3200
 −27.5671
  18.7529
```

Multiplying decimals. Multiply the numbers and add the decimal places.
Example:
2.4 × 1.7

```
   2.4        One decimal place
   1.7        One decimal place
  168         (Estimate 2 × 2 = 4.)
  24
  4.08        There are two decimal places.
```

Try this: 4.8 × 1.3106

Estimate 5 × 1 = 5

```
 1.3106
    4.8
 104848
 52424
6.29088
```

There are five decimal places.

Dividing decimals.

Example:

$3\overline{)45.9}$ Put the decimal in the answer directly above the decimal in the dividend.

$\begin{array}{r} 15.3 \\ 3\overline{)45.9} \end{array}$ Now divide.

$3.1\overline{)41.23}$

$3.1.\overline{)41.2.3}$

$\begin{array}{r} 13.3 \\ 31\overline{)412.3} \end{array}$

You need to get rid of the decimal in the divisor. Move it one place to the right. Move the decimal in the dividend the same number of places to the right. Now divide as usual.

Add 0s to the dividend if necessary to move the decimal the required number of spaces.

$.31\overline{)2976}$ Move the decimals two places to the right.

$.31.\overline{)2976.00.}$ Now divide.

$\begin{array}{r} 9{,}600 \\ 31\overline{)297{,}600.} \end{array}$ Approximate $3000 \div \frac{1}{3} = 3000 \times \frac{3}{1} = 9000$

Fraction, Decimal and Percent Equivalents

Memorize:

$\frac{1}{2}$	= 0.5	= 50%	$\frac{5}{6}$	= 0.83	= 83%
$\frac{1}{3}$	= 0.33	= 33%	$\frac{1}{7}$	= 0.14	= 14%
$\frac{2}{3}$	= 0.67	= 67%	$\frac{1}{8}$	= 0.125	= 12½%
$\frac{1}{4}$	= 0.25	= 25%	$\frac{3}{8}$	= 0.375	= 37½%
$\frac{3}{4}$	= 0.75	= 75%	$\frac{5}{8}$	= 0.625	= 62½%
$\frac{1}{5}$	= 0.2	= 20%	$\frac{7}{8}$	= 0.875	= 87½%
$\frac{2}{5}$	= 0.4	= 40%	$\frac{1}{9}$	= 0.11	= 11%
$\frac{3}{5}$	= 0.6	= 60%	$\frac{1}{10}$	= 0.1	= 10%
$\frac{4}{5}$	= 0.8	= 80%	$\frac{1}{11}$	= 0.09	= 9%
$\frac{1}{6}$	= 0.17	= 17%	$\frac{1}{12}$	= 0.08	= 8%

Memory aids:

$\frac{1}{7}$ = 0.14 (14 is double 7)

$\frac{1}{9}$ = 0.11 $\frac{1}{11}$ = 0.09

Fraction to decimal. To obtain the decimal equivalent of a fraction, divide the numerator by the denominator.

   Example:

$$\frac{3}{4} = 4\overline{)3.00} = 0.75$$

Decimal to fraction. Put 1 and as many zeros as there are numbers to the right of the decimal in the denominator. Drop the decimal point and write the given number as the numerator. You have converted the decimal to a fraction. Now reduce the fraction to its lowest terms.

   Example:

$$0.75 = \frac{75}{100} = \frac{3}{4}$$

Fraction to percent. Multiply the numerator by 100, divide by the denominator and add a percent sign.

   Example:

$$\frac{3}{4} = \frac{3 \times 100}{4} = 75\%$$

Remember, *percent* means *part of 100.*

   0.75 means 75 parts of 100, and is $\frac{75}{100}$

   75% means 75 parts of 100, and is $\frac{75}{100}$

Percent to fraction. Put the number before the percent sign in the numerator and 100 in the denominator; reduce.

   Example:

$$75\% = \frac{75}{100} = \frac{3}{4}$$

Decimal to percent. Move the decimal point two places to the right (in other words, multiply by 100). Add the percent sign.

   Example:

   .75 = .75 = 75.%
   delete point: 75%

Percent to decimal. Move the decimal point two places to the left (in other words, divide by 100). Drop the percent sign.

   Example:

   75% = .75. = .75

RATIO AND PROPORTION

Ratio is the comparison of two quantities. For instance, a quantity of 4 and a quantity of 20 compare on a ratio of 1 to 5 (1:5). The quantities 4 and 20 are written in fraction form as $^4/_{20}$ or in ratio form as 4:20 and, when reduced, become $^1/_5$ or 1:5 (in this instance, the result of dividing both the numerator and the denominator by 4). Therefore, 4 compares with 20 the same as 1 compares with 5. They compare on a *ratio* of 1 to 5 or 1:5.

Example:

6.   Which pair of numbers has a ratio of 4 to 9?

   (A) 49 and 94
   (B) 18 and 23
   (C) 63 and 28
   (D) 28 and 63
   (E) 94 and 49

In numbers having a ratio of 4 to 9, the first number is divisible by 4 and the second by 9. When you divide the first number by 4 and the second by 9, the answers should be the same. The order of numbers is important. Here the smaller number is first. 4 is less than 9. 4 to 9 is not the same as 9 to 4. Are 8 and 18 in a ratio of 4 to 9?

$$8 \div 4 = 2 \quad and \quad 18 \div 9 = 2$$

or $\quad \begin{aligned} 8 \div 4 &= 2 \\ 18 \div 9 &= 2 \end{aligned} \quad$ *or* $\quad \begin{aligned} 8 \div 2 &= 4 \\ 18 \div 2 &= 9 \end{aligned}$

Strategy:

Eliminate choices in which the numbers are in the wrong order, as in C and E, above. Now look at the remaining choices.

   (A) 49 cannot be divided evenly by 4
   (B) 18 cannot be divided evenly by 4
   (D) 28 can be divided evenly by 4: $28 \div 4 = 7$
        63 can be divided evenly by 9: $63 \div 9 = 7$

   (D) is the answer. Check: $\dfrac{28}{63} = \dfrac{4}{9}$

Example:

47.   On an assignment, a pupil did 15 problems correctly and 6 problems incorrectly. What is the ratio of correct to incorrect problems?

Strategy:

Underline *correct* and *incorrect*.

ratio is $\dfrac{correct}{incorrect} = \dfrac{15}{6} = \dfrac{5}{2}$ *or* 5 to 2 *or* 5:2

   (reduce if possible)

Example:

48.   The scale of a drawing is 1:36. This means that

   (A) 1 in. = 36 ft
   (B) 3 ft = 6 yd
   (C) 1 ft = 3 yd
   (D) 1 ft = 12 yd
   (E) 1 ft = 3 ft

To compare, you must use the same unit of measurement. Change each to the same measurement, and you will have

   (A) 1 in. = 432 in.
   (B) 3 ft = 18 ft

(C) 1 ft = 9 ft
(D) 1 ft = 36 ft
(E) 1 ft = 3 ft

The answer is clearly D.

A *proportion* is two ratios with an equal sign between them.

$$\frac{5}{6} = \frac{10}{12} \text{ or } 5:6 = 10:12 \text{ or } 5:6::10:12$$

Example:

33. At the rate of 5 items for 24¢, how many items can you get for 96¢?

$$\frac{24¢}{96¢} = \frac{5 \text{ items}}{\text{i items}} \qquad 24i = 5 \times 96 \qquad i = \frac{5 \times 96}{24} = 20$$

Example:

20. To get a C on her next test, Susan needs at least 70%, which is 91 questions correct. How many questions are there on the test?

$$\frac{\text{part}}{\text{whole}} = \frac{\text{part}}{\text{whole}} \qquad \frac{70\%}{100\%} = \frac{91 \text{ questions}}{\text{total questions}} \qquad \frac{70}{100} = \frac{91}{x}$$

Cross-multiply $70x = 91 \times 100$

Divide by 70 $\dfrac{70x}{70} = \dfrac{91 \times 100}{70}$

$x = 130$ questions.

Don't multiply too soon, because often you can cancel to get the correct answer.

$$\frac{\overset{13}{\cancel{91}} \times \overset{10}{\cancel{100}}}{\underset{\underset{1}{7}}{\cancel{70}}} = 130$$

When you are asked, "What part of something is something else?" just remember "is over of" $\left(\dfrac{\text{is}}{\text{of}}\right)$ and you won't get confused.

Example:

What part <u>of 6</u> <u>is</u> 4? $\qquad \dfrac{\text{is}}{\text{of}} \qquad \dfrac{4}{6} = \dfrac{2}{3}$

<u>4 is</u> what part <u>of 6</u>? $\qquad \dfrac{\text{is}}{\text{of}} \qquad \dfrac{4}{6} = \dfrac{2}{3}$

Example:

15 is what % of 20? To find percent (part of 100), just multiply by 100.

$$\frac{\text{is}}{\text{of}} \qquad \frac{15}{20} \times 100 = 75\%$$

Example:

28% of what number is 70? Estimate 28% is close to 25% or ¼. You want the total number (100%), so the answer will be about $4 \times 70 = 280$.

$$\frac{\text{is}}{\text{of}} \qquad \frac{\overset{10}{\cancel{70}} \times \overset{25}{\cancel{100}}}{\underset{\underset{1}{\cancel{4}}}{\cancel{28}}} = 250$$

FACTORS

Factors are numbers that, multiplied together, make up a given number.

$2 \times 3 \times 4 = 24$

factors

Another way of saying this is that a factor is a number that will divide evenly into a given number.

Factors of 12 are 2, 3, 4, 6

A *prime number* is a number that is divisible only by itself and 1. 0 and 1 are not primes. The primes are 2, 3, 5, 7, 11, 13, 17, 19, 23, 29. . . .

A *prime factor* is a factor that is prime. The prime factors of 12 are 2 and 3 ($4 = 2 \times 2$; $6 = 2 \times 3$). To find the prime factors of a number, divide by prime numbers until the number is completely factored. Start with easy numbers.

Example:

```
2 | 12
2 |  6
3 |  3
      1     2 × 2 × 3 = 12
```

Use the indicators of divisibility on page 51.

Example:

15.   What is the smallest prime factor of 1,683?

(A) 0
(B) 1
(C) 2
(D) 3
(E) 11

Strategy:
Underline *smallest prime*. 0 and 1 are not primes, so cross out answer choices A and B. The number is not even, so it can't be divided by 2; therefore cross out C. To find out whether 1,683 is divisible by 3, add the digits: $1 + 6 + 8 + 3 = 18$. Divide by 3. $18 \div 3 = 6$. D is the answer. You don't need even to try E since you have your answer in D. If you divide 1,683 by 11, you'll find it is a factor, but it isn't the *smallest prime* factor.

SQUARES AND SQUARE ROOTS

The *square* of a number is the number multiplied by itself.

the square of $9 = 9 \times 9 = 9^2 = 81$

The *square root* of a number is the opposite of the square; it is the number which multiplied by itself produces the square. The square root of 9 is 3.

Example:
$\sqrt{9} = \sqrt{3 \times 3} = \sqrt{3^2} = 3$

Memorize:

Squares	**Square Roots**
$1^2 = 1$	$\sqrt{1} = 1$
$2^2 = 4$	$\sqrt{4} = 2$
$3^2 = 9$	$\sqrt{9} = 3$
$4^2 = 16$	$\sqrt{16} = 4$
$5^2 = 25$	$\sqrt{25} = 5$
$6^2 = 36$	$\sqrt{36} = 6$
$7^2 = 49$	$\sqrt{49} = 7$
$8^2 = 64$	$\sqrt{64} = 8$
$9^2 = 81$	$\sqrt{81} = 9$
$10^2 = 100$	$\sqrt{100} = 10$
$11^2 = 121$	$\sqrt{121} = 11$
$12^2 = 144$	$\sqrt{144} = 12$

Estimating square roots. For every two digits under the square root sign there is one digit in the answer. To determine the number of digits in the answer, underline groups of two digits, moving left from the imaginary decimal. If there are an odd number of digits, count one place for the extra digit.

$$\sqrt{12\ \underline{34}} \qquad\qquad \sqrt{1\ \underline{23}\ \underline{45}}$$

Estimate: Two places in the answer

$\sqrt{12}$ is between $\sqrt{9} = 3$ and $\sqrt{16} = 4$
Answer is between 30 and 40.
$30^2 = 900$ and $40^2 = 1,600$
1200 is closer to 900 than 1,600,
so try 33.

$33 \times 33 = 1089$ too small
$35 \times 35 = 1225$ closest

Three places in the answer

$\sqrt{1} = 1$
Answer is between 100 and 200.
$100^2 = 10,000$ and $200^2 = 40,000$
Answer is closer to 100.

$110 \times 110 = 12,100$ too small
$115 \times 115 = 13,225$ too big
$113 \times 113 = 12,769$ too big
$111 \times 111 = 12,321$ closest

Simplification: Inspect the number to see if it can be factored into one or more numbers which are perfect squares.

$$\sqrt{400} = \sqrt{4} \times \sqrt{100} = 2 \times 10 = 20$$
$$\sqrt{75} = \sqrt{25 \times 3} = \sqrt{25} \times \sqrt{3} = 5\sqrt{3}$$
$$\sqrt{500} = \sqrt{100 \times 5} = \sqrt{100} \times \sqrt{5} = 10\sqrt{5}$$

Division:

$$\sqrt{\frac{400}{16}} = \frac{\sqrt{400}}{\sqrt{16}} = \frac{20}{4} = 5$$

or

$$\sqrt{25} = 5$$

Multiplication:

$$\sqrt{25} \times \sqrt{49} =$$
$$5 \times 7 = 35$$

Addition:

$$\sqrt{9 + 16} = \sqrt{25} = 5$$

not

$$\sqrt{9} + \sqrt{16} =$$

$$3 + 4 = 7$$ Addition or subtraction under square root sign is like brackets. These factors can't be separated.

$$\sqrt{25 - 16} = \sqrt{9} = 3$$

not

$$\sqrt{25} - \sqrt{16} = 5 - 4 = 1$$

The *cube* of a number is the number multiplied by itself twice.

$$1^3 = 1 \times 1 \times 1 = 1$$
$$2^3 = 2 \times 2 \times 2 = 8$$
$$3^3 = 3 \times 3 \times 3 = 27$$
$$4^3 = 4 \times 4 \times 4 = 64$$
$$5^3 = 5 \times 5 \times 5 = 125$$

AVERAGES, MEDIANS AND MODES

An *average* is the sum of a group of items divided by the number of items. Another word for average is *mean*.

The average of 7, 11, 13 and 19 is

$$\frac{7 + 11 + 13 + 19}{4} = \frac{40}{4} = 10$$

(4 numbers)

Example:

11. John tries to average 5 miles a day. He ran 4 miles on Monday and Wednesday, 3 on Tuesday, 5 on Thursday, 6 on Friday and 8 on Saturday. How many miles will he have to run on Sunday to make his goal?

To average 5 miles a day, he needs to run a total of $5 \times 7 = 35$ miles. The total for Monday through Saturday is $4 + 4 + 3 + 5 + 6 + 8 = 30$. He needs to run 5 miles on Sunday. $(35 - 30 = 5)$

Median is the middle number in a group of numbers listed in order from smallest to largest.

Range is the difference between the largest number and the smallest number in a group.

Examples:

The students in Mr. Jelmini's class had the following grades
44, 75, 61, 78, 70, 82, 68, 82, 50, 98, 75, 37, 82, and 78.

1. The median is
   (A) 61   (B) 70   (C) 75   (D) 78   (E) 82
2. The mode is
   (A) 61   (B) 70   (C) 75   (D) 78   (E) 82
3. The mean is
   (A) 61   (B) 70   (C) 75   (D) 78   (E) 82
4. The range is
   (A) 61   (B) 70   (C) 75   (D) 78   (E) 82

Strategy:

Arrange the numbers in a column from smallest to largest. This will automatically show you the median and the mode. Use this also to find the mean and the range. If a group of numbers is arranged in numerical order from smallest to largest, the median is the middle number.

1. Since there are fourteen numbers, the median is halfway between the seventh and eighth number; that is halfway between 75 and 75, or 75. If there were an odd number of numbers, then it would be the middle number. The answer to Example 1 is C.

37	1
44	2
50	3
61	4
68	5
70	6
75	7 Median
75	8
78	9
78	10
82	11
82	12 Mode
82	13
98	14

2. The *mode* is the number that appears most frequently. 82 appears three times, 78 and 75 twice and all the others once each. Therefore, 82 is the mode and the answer to Example 2 is E.

3. The *average* is the sum of the numbers divided by the number of items.

   $$\frac{980}{14} = 70 \qquad \text{The answer to Example 3 is B.}$$

4. The range is the largest number minus the smallest number, in this case $98 - 37 = 61$. The numbers range from 37 to 98, or have a range of 61. The answer to Example 4 is A.

BASIC UNITS OF MEASURE

	Imperial		**Metric**
When we use	pound (lb)	others use	kilogram (kg)
	ounce (oz)		gram (g)
	foot (ft) or yard (yd)		meter (m)
	inch (in.)		centimeter (cm)
	gallon (gal) quart (qt)		liter (l)
	mile (mi)		kilometer (km)

Approximate Equivalents
1 meter = 1 yd plus
2½ cm = 1 in.
1 kg   = 2 lb plus
30 g   = 1 oz
l liter = 1 qt
1 km   = ½ mi plus

Temperature

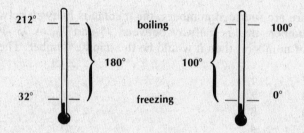

Conversion formula: $\frac{5}{9}(F - 32) = C$ $\frac{9}{5}C + 32 = F$

Approximation: $\dfrac{F - 30}{2} \approx C$ $2C + 30 \approx F$

WORD PROBLEMS

Do you shudder at the thought of word problems? The key is that they are translation problems. You need to translate from English to the international language of mathematics. Mathematics is a language like music, chemistry and physics; symbols replace words. Underline the key facts and what you want to know.

Example:

25. The cost of a cabin rental is $20 per night plus $5 for each person. How much will it cost Adele and her seven friends to stay three nights?

base cost @ night $20
number of people 8
cost per person $5
number of nights 3

(base cost + cost per person × no. of people) × (no. of nights) = total cost

$$(\$20 + 5 \times 8) \times (3) =$$
$$(\$20 + 40) \times (3) =$$
$$\$60 \times 3 = \$180$$

Example:

40. A total of 2,315 football fans will be travelling to a game in buses. Each bus can carry 50 passengers. How many buses will be needed?

Strategy:

$$\frac{\text{number of people}}{\text{number in each bus}} = \text{number of buses}$$

$$\frac{2315}{50} = 46\frac{15}{50} \text{ buses}$$

Can you hire $^{15}/_{50}$ of a bus? No. You need 1 more bus for a total of 47 buses.

Always check an answer to see that it makes sense. When there are large numbers, substitute small ones to get the formula. Try to make the answer you're looking for the unknown.

Discounts

Example:

37. What is the price of a $50.00 chair after it has been marked down by 10% and then 20%?

   (A) $45.00
   (B) $36.00
   (C) $35.00
   (D) $9.00
   (E) $4.00

Strategy:

Long way:
$50.00 × 0.10 = $5.00
$50.00−$5.00 = $45.00
$45.00 × 0.20 = $9.00
$45.00 − $9.00 = $36.00

Short way:
$50.00 × 0.90 = $45.00
$45.00 × 0.80 = $36.00

Note: It is not 30% off, because you take 20% off the $45.00, not off the $50.00.

Age

Example:

18. Louisa is four years older than Gilbert.
   Eight years ago she was twice as old as he.
   How old is Louisa?

   (A) 24
   (B) 16
   (C) 12
   (D) 8
   (E) 4

Strategy:
You want to find Louisa's age now.

Ages now are L, G
Ages 8 years ago are L − 8, G − 8
Your two equations are:
L = G + 4
L − 8 = 2(G − 8)

You want to find L, so try to get rid of G.

$$L = G + 4$$

Subtract 4. $\quad\quad\quad\quad\quad$ $\dfrac{-4 = \quad -4}{}$

Use this in place of G. $\quad$ L − 4 = G
Substitute. $\quad\quad\quad\quad$ L − 8 = 2 (L − 4 − 8)
Now solve for L. $\quad\quad$ L − 8 = 2 (L − 12) $\quad$ Tidy up.
$$L - 8 = 2L - 24$$
$$\dfrac{-L \quad\quad\quad -L}{-8 = L - 24}$$ $\quad$ Get L on one side only.
$$\dfrac{+24 = \quad + 24}{16 = L}$$ $\quad$ Get L all alone on one side.
$\quad\quad\quad\quad\quad\quad\quad$ 16 = G + 4 $\quad$ Substitute to find G:
$\quad\quad\quad\quad\quad\quad\quad$ 12 = G
Check $\quad\quad\quad\quad\quad$ 16 − 8 = 2(12 −8)
$\quad\quad\quad\quad\quad\quad\quad\quad$ 8 = 2 × 4

This looks long, and you may take some shortcuts, but you *can* solve it. You can also substitute the answers given, and see whether they work:

$\quad\quad$ (A) 24 $\quad$ (B) 16 $\quad$ (C) 12 $\quad$ (D) 8 $\quad$ (E) 4

Substitute choice A: L = 24, G = 20 $\quad$ 24 − 8 $\overset{?}{=}$ 2(20 − 8)
$\quad\quad\quad\quad\quad\quad\quad\quad\quad\quad\quad\quad\quad$ 16 $\overset{?}{=}$ 2 × 12 $\quad$ No.

Substitute choice B: L = 16, G = 12 $\quad$ 16 − 8 $\overset{?}{=}$ 2(12 −8)
$\quad\quad\quad\quad\quad\quad\quad\quad\quad\quad\quad\quad\quad$ 8 $\overset{?}{=}$ 2 × 4 $\quad$ Yes.

Try another problem, using the choices provided.
Example:

2. The difference between a two-digit number and the numbers reversed is 27. The sum of the digits is 7. What is the number?

   (A) 18
   (B) 43
   (C) 52
   (D) 61
   (E) 70

Strategy:
What are they looking for? Numbers like 61 and 16. The number must meet two criteria. Check the easiest part first: do the digits add up to 7? 8 + 1 = 9; eliminate A. The others are still in the game. Check to see whether the difference is 27. Subtract the reversed numbers.

(B)	43	(C)	52	(D)	61	(E)	70
	$\underline{-34}$		$\underline{-25}$		$\underline{-16}$		$\underline{-\ 7}$
	9		27 Bingo!		45		63

You can eliminate some without subtraction, because an estimate will show you that the difference isn't close to 27.

GRAPHS

Read the information carefully. Use your pencil as a ruler to read the chart. Use the answer sheet as a straight-edge to draw grid lines, if necessary.

FORMULAS

Interest = Principal × Rate × Time

I = PRT

Total amount to be repaid = P + I (Principal and Interest)

Distance = Rate × Time

D = RT

GEOMETRY

Perimeter is distance around, such as fencing or fringe on a tablecloth.

Draw a rough diagram.

P = 2L + 2w *or* 2(L + w)

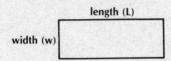

If you are unsure, substitute small numbers.

L = 3
w = 2

2 × 3 + 2 × 2 = 6 + 4 = 10

Area is the total space within a two-dimensional figure.
The area of a rectangle = length × width: A = L × W. In the diagram above, the area is 2 × 3 = 6.

Volume is the total space contained within a three-dimensional figure.

The volume of a rectangular solid
is length × width × height.

V = L × w × h
 = 6 × 4 × 5
 = 120 cubic inches

L = 6 in.
w = 4 in.
h = 5 in.

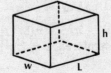

Area of triangles

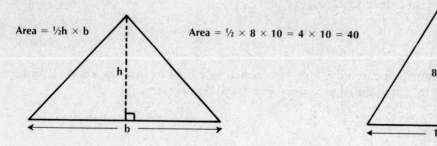

Area = ½h × b

Area = ½ × 8 × 10 = 4 × 10 = 40

Area of rectangles

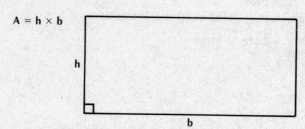

A = h × b

Area of parallelograms

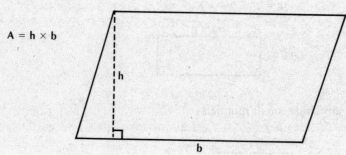

A = h × b

Circles

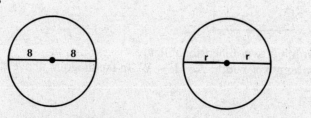

A circle has 360°.

Radius: from center of circle to edge = r (8)

Diameter: from one edge through the center to the other edge d = 2r (16)

$\pi = 3.14$ or $\frac{22}{7}$

Area = $\pi r^2 = \pi(8)^2 = 64\pi$

Circumference = $2 \pi r = 2 \pi (8) = 16 \pi$

Angles

A *right angle* contains 90°.

An angle less than a right angle is an *acute angle*.

If the two sides of an angle extend in opposite directions forming a straight line, the angle is a *straight angle* and contains 180°.

An angle greater than a right angle (90°) and less than a straight angle (180°) is an *obtuse angle*.

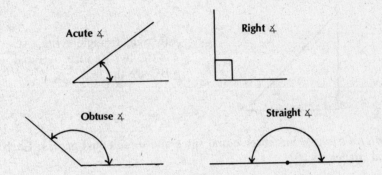

Vertical or opposite angles formed by intersecting straight lines are equal, so a = c, and b = d.

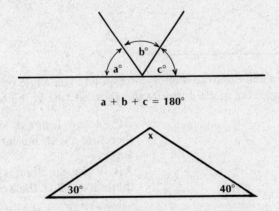

The sum of the angles on one side of a straight line equal 180°.

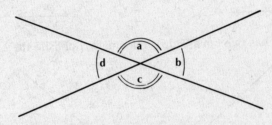

a + b + c = 180°

The sum of the interior (inside) angles of a triangle = 180°. So, to find x:

$$30 + 40 + x = 180°$$
$$70 + x = 180$$
$$x = 180 - 70 = 110°$$

Triangles

A triangle with a right angle is called a *right triangle*. In a right triangle, the side opposite the right angle is called the *hypotenuse* and is the longest side. The other two sides are called *legs*.

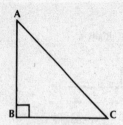

In right triangle ABC, AC is the hypotenuse. AB and BC are the legs.

An *equilateral triangle* has three equal sides and three equal angles. Each angle of an equilateral triangle is 60°.

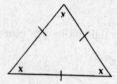
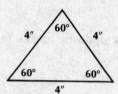

An *isosceles* triangle has two equal sides. The angles opposite the equal sides are also equal.

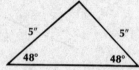

A *scalene* triangle has no equal sides and no equal angles.

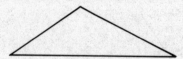

In a triangle the sides and opposite angles correspond. The angle opposite the longest side is the largest angle; the angle opposite the shortest side is the smallest angle.

BC is the longest side; therefore ∠1 is the largest angle.
AB is the smallest side; therefore ∠3 is the smallest ∠.

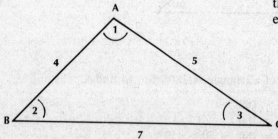

ALGEBRA

Don't be thrown by the word algebra. Instead of using horses, books and people, algebra uses a, b, c . . . x, y, z to stand for anything you want to use. It's shorthand. You can then plug in numbers or horses or books or people. Caution! Do not confuse the x that represents an item, such as one of the horses, with the $\times$ that indicates multiplication.

Addition

$$7a^2 + 3a + 2a^2 = ?$$

You *can* add $7a^2 + 2a^2$ to get $9a^2$. Think: 7 horses + 2 horses = 9 horses. Add the numbers in front of the a^2s (or horses). These numbers are called the *coefficients*. Do not add the *exponents* (powers).

$$7a^2 + 2a^2 = (7 + 2)a^2 = 9a^2$$

(*not* $9a^4$; that is multiplying.) You *cannot* add a^2 and a. They are different animals.

$$7a^2 + 3a + 2a^2 = 9a^2 + 3a$$

Example:

17.   Find the perimeter

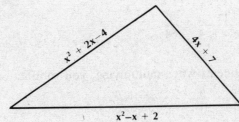

Perimeter is distance around. Add the sides by first lining up the figures. Put x^2 under x^2 and x under x.

$$
\begin{array}{r}
x^2 + 2x - 4 \\
4x + 7 \\
x^2 - x + 2 \\
\hline
2x^2 + 5x + 5
\end{array}
$$

Add each column

If there is no number in front of an x or x^2, it is 1.

Subtraction. Remember that if there is a minus sign in front of a bracket and the bracket is removed, the sign of every term inside the bracket is changed.

$$3b^2 - 4b + c - (3b^2 + b - c) =$$

this is positive

$$3b^2 - 4b + c - 3b^2 - b + c =$$

Now add up.

$$3b^2 - 3b^2 - 4b - b + c + c =$$

$$0 \qquad -5b \quad + \quad 2c \quad = 2c - 5b$$

Multiplication. A dot (•) is used to indicate multiplication, as well as $\times$ and nothing (as in 3a).

coefficient $\longrightarrow 3a^2 \longleftarrow$ exponent (power)

base

Add the exponents (powers) if the base is the same.

$$a \times a = a^1 \times a^1 = a^{1+1} = a^2$$

$$a^2 \times a^4 = a^{(2+4)} = a^6$$

$$a^2 \times b^3 = a^2b^3$$

Multiply the coefficients.

$$2a^2 \times 3a^3 = (2 \times 3)a^{(2+3)} = 6a^5$$
$$4a^2 \cdot 5b^3 = 20a^2b^3$$

Coefficients. 1 to any power is 1

$$1^2 = 1 \times 1 = 1; \ 1^3 = 1 \times 1 \times 1 = 1$$

Any number to the zero power is 1.

$$2^0 = 1 \qquad 463^0 = 1$$

Any negative power is 1 over a number to that power in the denominator.

$$4^{-3} = \frac{1}{4^3} = \frac{1}{4 \times 4 \times 4} = \frac{1}{64}$$

Just as you add exponents when multiplying, you subtract exponents when dividing.

$$\frac{4^7}{4^3} = 4^{7-3} = 4^4$$

$$\frac{a^7}{a^3} = a^{7-3} = a^4$$

$$\frac{a^4b^3}{a^3b^2} = a^{(4-3)}b^{(3-2)} = a^1b^1 = ab$$

$$\frac{6a^6 \times 4b^5}{8a^3 \times b^5} = \frac{24a^{(6-3)} \cdot b^{(5-5)}}{8} = 3a^3 \cdot b^0 = 3a^3$$

An expression containing a single term is called a *monomial*. An expression containing more than one term is called a *polynominal*. Special polynomials are *binomials* (two terms) and *trinomials* (three terms).

To multiply a polynomial by a monomial, multiply each term of the polynomial by the monomial.

$$7a^2(a^2 - 2a + 3) =$$
$$(7a^2 \cdot a^2) - (7a^2 \cdot 2a) + (7a^2 \cdot 3) =$$
$$7a^4 - 14a^3 + 21a^2$$

To multiply a polynomial by a polynomial, multiply each term of the first polynomial by each term of the second polynomial, then add any like terms in the answer.
   Example:
   Multiply $(x + 5)(x - 4)$

$$
\begin{array}{ll}
\textit{Method 1} & \textit{Method 2} \\
(x + 5)(x - 4) = \quad or & x \; + \; 5 \\
x(x - 4) + 5(x - 4) = & \underline{x \; - \; 4} \\
x^2 - 4x + 5x - 20 = & x^2 + 5x \\
x^2 + x - 20 & \underline{\quad - 4x - 20} \\
& x^2 + \; x - 20
\end{array}
$$

or

Method 3

$$
(x + 5)\,(x - 4) = \quad x^2 + x - 20
$$

First ⌢ Last

$(x + 5) \qquad (x - 4) \qquad = \qquad$ F O I L

Inside
Outside

Example:
Multiply $(a - 2)(a + 2)$

$$
\begin{array}{l}
a - 2 \\
\underline{a + 2} \\
a^2 - 2a \\
\underline{\quad + 2a - 4} \\
a^2 + 0 \; - 4 \qquad \text{Notice that the middle term drops out.}
\end{array}
$$

Answer: $a^2 - 4$. This binomial is the difference of two squares. It has as its factors two binomials, one the sum of the square roots $(a + 2)$ and one the difference of the square roots $(a - 2)$.

Now the reverse problems:

Factor $a^2 - 4$

You will get the square root of the first term (a) *minus* the square root of the second term (2) *and* the square root of the first term (a) *plus* the square root of the second term (2).

$$
a^2 - 4 = (a + 2)(a - 2) \qquad \sqrt{a^2} = a \qquad \sqrt{4} = 2
$$

Multiply $(3b - 5)(3b + 5) =$
$\qquad (3b - 5)(3b + 5) = 9b^2 - 25$
Factor $16c^2 - 49$
$\qquad 16c^2 - 49 = (4c - 7)(4c + 7)$

Use this information to solve the next problem.

$$
(x - 2)(x + 2) = 15 \times 19
$$

What is x?

Look for an easy solution.

x has to be between 15 and 19.

If x is 17, then x − 2 =

$$17 - 2 = 15$$

and

$$x + 2 = 17 + 2 = 19$$

Another way to solve it is:

$$(x - 2)(x + 2) = 15 \times 19$$
$$x^2 - 4 = 285$$
$$x^2 = 289$$
$$x = \sqrt{289}$$

The $\sqrt{289}$ is more than 10 ($10 \times 10 = 100$) and less than 20 ($20 \times 20 = 400$). Since it ends in 9, it could be 13 or 17.

$$13^2 = 169 \qquad 17^2 = 289 \qquad x = 17$$

There is almost always more than one approach to a question. Look for the quickest and easiest way.

Factoring algebraic terms:

$$a^2 + 2a + 1 =$$

Set up brackets. (a)(a)	a^2 is a × a. Put a in each bracket.
(a 1)(a 1)	1 is 1 × 1. Put 1 in each bracket.
(a + 1)(a + 1) = (a + 1)²	The sign of the middle term (2a) is +, therefore signs are both +.

You can always take each answer and multiply it out, if you have the time.

Factor
a² − 14a + 49
(a   )(a   )
(a   7)(a   7)

(a − 7)(a − 7)	The sign of 49 is positive; therefore the missing signs are alike.
(a − 7)²	The sign of 14a is negative; therefore the missing signs are negative.

Factor
a² − 6a − 7
(a   )(a   )

	7 is 1 × 7
(a 1)(a 7)	Last sign is negative therefore signs are unlike
(a + 1)(a − 7)	Sign of 6a is negative therefore negative biggest

Example:
Factor: $4a^2 + 12a + 9$

$$4 \text{ could be } 1 \times 4 \text{ or } 2 \times 2$$
$$9 \text{ could be } 1 \times 9 \text{ or } 3 \times 3$$
Both signs are positive

Try: $(a \ +3)(4a \ + 3)$ Try: $(2a + 3)(2a \ + 3)$ or $(2a \ + 3)^2$

$$\begin{array}{l} 12a \\ \underline{3a} \\ 15a \text{ too big} \end{array} \qquad \begin{array}{l} 6a \\ \underline{6a} \\ 12a \text{ fits} \end{array}$$

Example:
$6b^2 - 7b - 20$

$$6 \text{ could be } 1 \times 6 \text{ or } 2 \times 3$$
$$20 \text{ could be } 1 \times 20 \text{ or } 2 \times 10 \text{ or } 4 \times 5$$
These signs are unlike and the negative total is largest.

$(b \ + \ )(b \ - \ )$

Trial and Success

Try: $(2b + 2)(3b - 10)$ Try: $(2b + 4)(3b - 5)$ Try: $(2b + 5)(3b - 4)$

$$\begin{array}{l} +6b \\ \underline{-20b} \\ -14b \end{array} \qquad \begin{array}{l} +12b \\ \underline{-10b} \\ + 2b \end{array} \qquad \begin{array}{l} +15b \\ \underline{-8b} \\ +7b \text{ Success!} \end{array}$$

If you get the right numbers but the wrong sign, switch the signs.

$(2b - 5)(3b + 4)$

You can also factor out a common term — same number or letter divided into each term.

$$3x^3 + 6x^2 + 12x = 3x(x^2 + 2x + 4)$$
$3x$ is the common factor

Solving Equations

Problem: Solve for x. $7x - 4 = 38$
    Add 4. $\underline{+ 4 = + 4}$

    Divide by 7. $\dfrac{7x}{7} = \dfrac{42}{7}$

    Solution: $x = 6$

You can also plug in the answer choices for x and see which one fits.

Problem: Find c.

$$b = 3c$$
$$340 + 3b + c - 120 = 280$$

You want to find c, so substitute 3c for b, eliminating b.

	$340 + 3(3c) + c - 120 =$	280
Clean up.	$340 + 9c + c - 120 =$	280
Add like terms.	$340 - 120 + 10c =$	280
	$220 + 10c =$	280
Subtract 220.	-220	-220
Divide by 10.	$10c =$	60
Solution:	$c =$	6

When you multiply two or more numbers together and get a product of 0, at least one of those numbers must be 0. The product of any number and zero is always zero.

$$(12)(6)(7)(4)(3)(0) = 0$$

Problem: Solve for x. $x(x + 4) = 0$

Either $x = 0$ or $x + 4 = 0$

If $x + 4 = 0$

$$\underline{-4 = -4}$$

then x $= -4$

Solution: $x = 0$, $x = -4$ (one or the other or both)

To solve the following type of problem, set each factor equal to 0 and solve.

$(x + 3)(x - 5) = 0$

$x + 3 = 0$ $x - 5 = 0$

$x = -3$ $x = 5$

Coordinates

Y - distance up or down
X - distance right or left

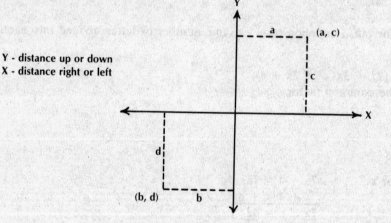

a is to the *right*, so it is positive (X)
b is to the *left*, so it is negative (X)
c is *up*, so it is *positive* (Y)
d is *down*, so it is *negative* (Y)

In general:

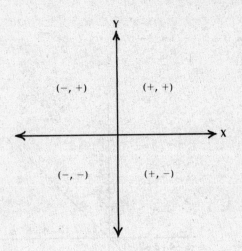

Points on a coordinate graph

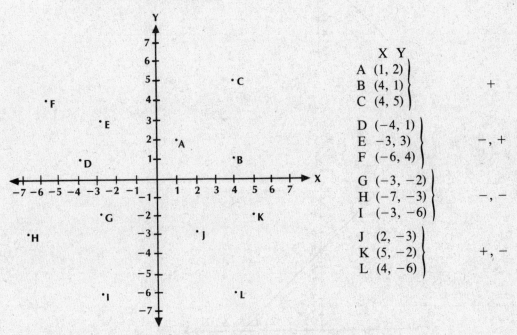

X	Y	
A	(1, 2)	
B	(4, 1)	+
C	(4, 5)	
D	(−4, 1)	
E	−3, 3)	−, +
F	(−6, 4)	
G	(−3, −2)	
H	(−7, −3)	−, −
I	(−3, −6)	
J	(2, −3)	
K	(5, −2)	+, −
L	(4, −6)	

To plot (draw or graph) these equations, plug numbers in.

$x = 2$
$y = -3$

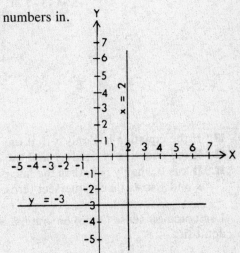

x = y
when x = 0, y = 0
when x = 1, y = 1
when x = 2, y = 2

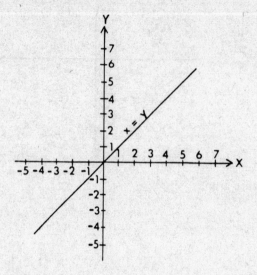

x + y = 5
when x = 0,   0 + y = 5   y = 5
when y = 0,   x + 0 = 5   x = 5

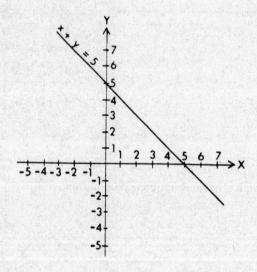

■ If the equation has only x in it (no y), then the graph is a vertical line.
■ If the equation has only y in it (no x), then the graph is a horizontal line.
■ If x is 0 when y is 0, then the line passes through the origin, the point at which the x and y axes (lines) intersect (cross).

Use common sense (logic) on graphs. Substitute numbers. Eliminate the answers that don't fit.

PROFESSIONAL-KNOWLEDGE REVIEW

Some tests ask factual questions: "Do you know this?" Other tests ask application questions: "Johnny has been absent five days. From other students you hear that he has been at the playground these days. What would you do?" All questions are designed to test your knowledge of teaching concepts, theory and educational law.

The tests are based on the following topics, which you should be familiar with:

CLASSROOM MANAGEMENT

Managing students effectively
Disciplining students appropriately
Promoting student motivation
Individualizing the pace of instruction
Using a lesson plan effectively
Understanding the principles of group process; involving students in decision-making
Using time management in planning
Communicating effectively
Making use of the cultural diversity of students

CURRICULUM AND INSTRUCTION

Knowing and using goals and objectives
Developing the curriculum
Planning lessons
Selecting appropriate resources
Mainstreaming

EVALUATION

Knowing testing terminology
Differentiating between evaluation and assessment
Developing tests
Choosing the appropriate test
Administering tests
Interpreting tests
Grading tests fairly
Reporting student performance to parents or administrators
Utilizing test results to improve student performance

GROWTH AND LEARNING THEORIES

Identifying abnormal behavior for referral
Knowing the basic theories of child development and learning
Recognizing the common characteristics of various levels of physical, mental, social and emotional development
Understanding theories of motivation

EDUCATIONAL FOUNDATIONS

Recognizing the major issues in American education
Identifying major educational theorists and their contributions
Appreciating the effect of culture on education; creating techniques for accommodating the variety of cultures
Maintaining professional skills with the appropriate resources
Understanding the major purposes of public education in America

ADMINISTRATION AND ORGANIZATION

Knowing the various responsibilities and roles in education at the federal, state and local levels
Following nondiscriminatory practices
Understanding state law as it applies to education
Undertaking the legal responsibilities of teachers
Implementing policies on the promotion of students
Recognizing revenue sources for education
Knowing the major legal rulings affecting education
Cooperating with coworkers and parents
Realizing teachers', parents' and students' rights and responsibilities
Holding effective parent-teacher conferences
Engaging in effective communication with the public

You may have to study the particular state educational law to prepare for the tests in some states.

ANSWER SHEET FOR SAMPLE TEST 1

READING

	A B C D E		A B C D E		A B C D E		A B C D E		A B C D E
1	○ ○ ○ ○ ○	11	○ ○ ○ ○ ○	21	○ ○ ○ ○ ○	31	○ ○ ○ ○ ○	41	○ ○ ○ ○ ○
2	○ ○ ○ ○ ○	12	○ ○ ○ ○ ○	22	○ ○ ○ ○ ○	32	○ ○ ○ ○ ○	42	○ ○ ○ ○ ○
3	○ ○ ○ ○ ○	13	○ ○ ○ ○ ○	23	○ ○ ○ ○ ○	33	○ ○ ○ ○ ○	43	○ ○ ○ ○ ○
4	○ ○ ○ ○ ○	14	○ ○ ○ ○ ○	24	○ ○ ○ ○ ○	34	○ ○ ○ ○ ○	44	○ ○ ○ ○ ○
5	○ ○ ○ ○ ○	15	○ ○ ○ ○ ○	25	○ ○ ○ ○ ○	35	○ ○ ○ ○ ○	45	○ ○ ○ ○ ○
6	○ ○ ○ ○ ○	16	○ ○ ○ ○ ○	26	○ ○ ○ ○ ○	36	○ ○ ○ ○ ○	46	○ ○ ○ ○ ○
7	○ ○ ○ ○ ○	17	○ ○ ○ ○ ○	27	○ ○ ○ ○ ○	37	○ ○ ○ ○ ○	47	○ ○ ○ ○ ○
8	○ ○ ○ ○ ○	18	○ ○ ○ ○ ○	28	○ ○ ○ ○ ○	38	○ ○ ○ ○ ○	48	○ ○ ○ ○ ○
9	○ ○ ○ ○ ○	19	○ ○ ○ ○ ○	29	○ ○ ○ ○ ○	39	○ ○ ○ ○ ○	49	○ ○ ○ ○ ○
10	○ ○ ○ ○ ○	20	○ ○ ○ ○ ○	30	○ ○ ○ ○ ○	40	○ ○ ○ ○ ○	50	○ ○ ○ ○ ○

MATHEMATICS

	A B C D E		A B C D E		A B C D E		A B C D E		A B C D E
1	○ ○ ○ ○ ○	11	○ ○ ○ ○ ○	21	○ ○ ○ ○ ○	31	○ ○ ○ ○ ○	41	○ ○ ○ ○ ○
2	○ ○ ○ ○ ○	12	○ ○ ○ ○ ○	22	○ ○ ○ ○ ○	32	○ ○ ○ ○ ○	42	○ ○ ○ ○ ○
3	○ ○ ○ ○ ○	13	○ ○ ○ ○ ○	23	○ ○ ○ ○ ○	33	○ ○ ○ ○ ○	43	○ ○ ○ ○ ○
4	○ ○ ○ ○ ○	14	○ ○ ○ ○ ○	24	○ ○ ○ ○ ○	34	○ ○ ○ ○ ○	44	○ ○ ○ ○ ○
5	○ ○ ○ ○ ○	15	○ ○ ○ ○ ○	25	○ ○ ○ ○ ○	35	○ ○ ○ ○ ○	45	○ ○ ○ ○ ○
6	○ ○ ○ ○ ○	16	○ ○ ○ ○ ○	26	○ ○ ○ ○ ○	36	○ ○ ○ ○ ○	46	○ ○ ○ ○ ○
7	○ ○ ○ ○ ○	17	○ ○ ○ ○ ○	27	○ ○ ○ ○ ○	37	○ ○ ○ ○ ○	47	○ ○ ○ ○ ○
8	○ ○ ○ ○ ○	18	○ ○ ○ ○ ○	28	○ ○ ○ ○ ○	38	○ ○ ○ ○ ○	48	○ ○ ○ ○ ○
9	○ ○ ○ ○ ○	19	○ ○ ○ ○ ○	29	○ ○ ○ ○ ○	39	○ ○ ○ ○ ○	49	○ ○ ○ ○ ○
10	○ ○ ○ ○ ○	20	○ ○ ○ ○ ○	30	○ ○ ○ ○ ○	40	○ ○ ○ ○ ○	50	○ ○ ○ ○ ○

SAMPLE TEST 1
(CBEST)

This test is similar to the California Basic Educational Skills Test (CBEST) used in California and Oregon. The Reading, Mathematics, and Writing sections of this test can also be used to practice for the Pre-Professional Skills Test (PPST) used in Delaware, Kansas, Minnesota, Nebraska, Nevada, and Wisconsin. They are useful, too, in preparing for teacher certification tests administered by Colorado, Connecticut, Illinois, Michigan, and South Carolina.

Format of the CBEST

Reading	50 questions	65 minutes
Mathematics	50 questions	70 minutes

———————————————— *Break* ————————————————

Writing	two essays	60 minutes

Scoring the test

Raw scores for Reading and Mathematics sections are determined by totaling the number of questions answered correctly. There is no penalty for incorrect answers. Each of the two essays is scored on a scale of one (fail) to four (pass). Passing scores for both California and Oregon are set at a total scaled score of 123 for all three sections with no section below a scaled score of 37.

READING

65 Minutes—50 Questions

Directions: **Choose the best answer for each question and blacken the corresponding space on the Answer Sheet for Sample Test 1. The correct answers and explanations follow the test.**

Questions 1 to 4

Halley's comet has been known as the "evil star" since ancient times. It heralds death and disaster. In fact, the word "disaster" evolved from "evil star" or "bad star," which comets were often called. A chronological study shows that there is a correlation between the appearance of comets and waves of epidemics and suicides.

Halley's comet appeared over Jerusalem in 66 A.D., foreshadowing its destruction by the Romans. Mass suicides are recorded at this time, including 960 in Masada. When two comets appeared in 1347, the Black Death swept through Europe, killing 25 million, and a series of mass suicides occurred.

Recordings of associations between comets and mass suicides have been made every time Halley's comet has neared Earth since the sixteenth century. There was clear evidence of a connection between the comet and suicides, particularly among children, in 1910. Waves of suicides were recorded at the time in Japan, Italy and Spain. In 1985–1986, a wave of teen-age suicides and airline crashes coincided with the return of Halley's comet.

The appearance of the comet Kahoutek in 1973 coincided with the Watergate scandal, President Nixon's fall, the assassination of Spanish Premier Luis Carrero Blanco, earthquakes in Mexico and Pakistan, which killed 5,500, and droughts in Africa and India, which left 200,000 dead.

Comet Halley frames these events, but does not cause them. Other spectacular comets seem to have influenced some people, resulting in their suicide. Further research of these phenomena continues.

1. The earliest date linking Halley's comet with disaster is

   (A) 66 A.D.
   (B) 960 A.D.
   (C) 1347 A.D.
   (D) 1910 A.D.
   (E) 25,000,000 years ago

2. The comet Kahoutek caused

   (A) the Watergate scandal and President Nixon's fall
   (B) the assassination of Spanish Premier Luis Carrera Blanco
   (C) earthquakes in Mexico and Pakistan
   (D) droughts in Africa and India
   (E) none of the above

3. The central idea of the passage is

   (A) Halley's comet causes suicides
   (B) comet Kahoutek causes political and natural disasters
   (C) comets cause disasters
   (D) some comets influence some people
   (E) when two comets appear, they cause series of mass suicides

4. From reading the passage, it can be deduced that a meaning of "distemper" is

   (A) not tempered
   (B) absence of temper
   (C) expelling temper
   (D) deprived of temper
   (E) bad temper

Questions 5 to 7

Most of us hold jobs most of our lives, yet how many of us really enjoy that work and gain feelings of accomplishment, confidence, fulfillment and serenity from it? No job is perfect. Regardless of how successful we are, at some time or another we all experience feelings of doubt, inferiority, disgust or boredom with what we are doing. To gain perspective and add variety to our lives, we need to get away from our work at times.

Usually people in staid, secure jobs tend to pursue exciting hobbies or competitive sports, while those in dangerous or insecure jobs are content to choose quiet hobbies such as reading, art or music. Some presidents are known to have read westerns or mysteries for relaxation, while Nathaniel Hawthorne wrote *The Scarlet Letter* during his career as a customshouse inspector.

We may wonder that some people's hobbies seem more important to them than their work. Perhaps this is because the hobby makes use of an aptitude the person possesses that is not used in work. If a woman has an aptitude for music, but does not make music her career, joining a band may satisfy her need to express herself musically. Despite a considerable investment of money and many hours of practice, she considers the activity worthwhile because she enjoys it and it makes use of her musical talent. If she does not use her musical aptitude in some way, she might become frustrated. In addition to providing a salary, her job makes use of some of her aptitudes; her hobby makes use of other aptitudes.

In this way, a person can lead a fulfilled and balanced life.

5. From the passage, it can be assumed that Nathaniel Hawthorne

    (A) poured great mental energy into his hobby
    (B) was a boring writer
    (C) wrote westerns and mystery stories
    (D) had an insecure and dangerous job
    (E) revealed his inner feelings only in his writing

6. A hobby

    (A) requires considerable investment of time and money
    (B) has value because of the enjoyment we derive from it
    (C) is monetarily rewarding
    (D) should be related to work in order to be of benefit
    (E) uses aptitudes we do not possess

7. From reading the passage we can conclude that

    (A) the person who is deeply interested in her hobby is not leading a balanced life
    (B) we should get away from our jobs as often as possible, or we will lose perspective
    (C) most of us don't have careers that use all of our abilities
    (D) it is essential that everyone have a hobby in order to live a balanced life
    (E) if you have a dangerous job, you should not go white-water rafting

8. This past winter pilots reported changes in the mighty jet stream, the "rivers" of wind in the upper atmosphere. The weather has deviated considerably from normal: severe snow storms, thunderstorms, tornadoes in unlikely places, exceptionally cold weather, greater amounts of snow and rainfall than usual.

From this information, one can conclude that

    (A) the weather affects the jet stream
    (B) the jet stream affects the weather
    (C) there will be no more unusual weather
    (D) the weather will return to normal shortly
    (E) it will be an unusually hot summer

9. After members of the Japanese Alpine Club reached the top of Mount Everest, Y. Muira, one of Japan's foremost skiers, skied nearly two miles down a seventy-degree slope. High winds buffeted him, and during the run he fell, losing his right ski. He skied the rest of the distance on one ski, terminating his run just short of a crevasse.

Muira did not continue his run because

    (A) he was at the bottom of the mountain
    (B) it was too windy
    (C) he couldn't continue skiing on one ski
    (D) it was too difficult to breathe at that altitude
    (E) there was a deep crack in the ice

Questions 10 and 11

We think of musicals as pure entertainment, but some have explored social issues that were not generally discussed at the time. The messages were slipped in between the singing and dancing. For example, *Showboat* and *South Pacific* both addressed racial prejudice. In *South Pacific* there were parallel stories, each emphasizing a certain aspect of racial prejudice.

10. The above passage

    (A) is racially prejudiced
    (B) is informative without bias
    (C) advocates musicals portraying social issues
    (D) opposes musicals portraying social issues
    (E) is inflammatory

11. The people who wrote the words and music for the musicals

    (A) did not intend to explore racial prejudice
    (B) deliberately explored racial prejudice
    (C) had strong feelings against racial prejudice
    (D) were unconcerned about racial prejudice
    (E) not enough information to make a judgment

12. Two-year colleges received a larger share of their total financial support from state funds and a smaller share from local governments in 1983–84 than they did in the previous year.

    From this we can conclude that

    (A) state governments will increase their influence on two-year colleges

    (B) state governments will decrease their influence on two-year colleges
    (C) local governments will increase their influence on two-year colleges
    (D) two-year colleges will have increased funding
    (E) two-year colleges will have decreased funding

13. Scotland is a kingdom united with England and Wales in Great Britain.

    We can conclude that

    (A) England is the same as Great Britain
    (B) Wales and England make up Great Britain
    (C) Scotland is part of England
    (D) Scotland is part of Great Britain
    (E) Scotland is not part of Great Britain

Questions 14 and 15

Quicksand pits are found in virtually every part of the world, but falling into one is seldom as horrible as it is depicted in stories.

14. Quicksand is found

    (A) practically everywhere
    (B) here and there
    (C) seldom
    (D) only in stories
    (E) in horrible parts of the world

15. The stories mentioned

    (A) have pictures of quicksand
    (B) have illustrations of quicksand
    (C) describe quicksand experiences
    (D) explain what quicksand is
    (E) give a realistic account of experiences with quicksand

Questions 16 to 21

COMPARISON OF AUTO INSURANCE COSTS		
	With Usual Deductible	*With Higher Deductible*
Deductible	$150.00	$500.00
Monthly premium	$125.00	$100.00
Total coverage	$5,000.00	$5,000.00

One way to hold down the cost of auto insurance is to raise the amount of deductible costs you are willing to pay before the insurance company assumes financial responsibility. This can lower monthly premiums without risking the basic purpose of auto insurance—to cover losses you can't afford to absorb.

16. *Besides* lower premium payments, what effect does a higher deductible have?

(A) You pay less if there is damage.
(B) You must pay more if there is damage.
(C) You will have more total insurance.
(D) Your insured amount will be more.
(E) Your insured amount will be less.

17. How much will be saved in premiums over one year by taking a higher deductible?

(A) $1,200.00
(B) $300.00
(C) $150.00
(D) $125.00
(E) $500.00

18. Sam chooses the higher deductible and has an accident with total damages of $1,000.00 after one year. You conclude that

(A) he saves money with the higher deductible
(B) he should have kept the usual deductible
(C) the results would be the same with both policies
(D) the policies cannot be compared
(E) Sam should change insurance companies

19. What is Sam's total cost for insurance and repair of the accident in question 18 compared with what he would have paid on the usual deductible?

(A) $350 more
(B) $50 less
(C) $350 less
(D) $400 more
(E) $50 more

20. If Sam (who has the higher deductible policy) has an accident that causes $7,000 damage to his car, he will have to pay

(A) $7,000
(B) $5,000
(C) $2,500
(D) $2,000
(E) $500

21. Who will benefit the most from the policy he or she has chosen as opposed to the other policy?

	Person	Deductible	Repair costs per accident	Accidents per year
(A)	John	usual	$400	4
(B)	Harry	usual	$500	1
(C)	Sam	higher	$400	2
(D)	Betsy	higher	$4,000	1
(E)	Barbara	higher	$650	4

22. "Counting their toes and counting candles on birthday cakes are some of the ways that children can learn math." How can you use this information in the classroom?

(A) Tell children that math can be used in everyday situations.
(B) Teach more math in class.
(C) Start teaching math at a higher level because children already know math.
(D) Show how math can be used in everyday situations.
(E) None of the above.

Questions 23 and 24

"Growth in state funds for colleges is expected to slow further in 1987."

23. This statement means that state funds for colleges

(A) will increase in 1987
(B) will decrease in 1987
(C) will increase in 1987, but at a lower rate
(D) will decrease in 1987, but at a lower rate
(E) decreased during 1987

24. What action would you expect a college to consider because of the statement above?

    I. decreasing enrollment
    II. seeking other sources of funding
    III. decreasing services to students

    (A) I only
    (B) II only
    (C) III only
    (D) I and III only
    (E) I, II and III

25. "There have been significant increases in four other types of health insurance provided by insurance companies." A logical conclusion is that

    (A) some types of health insurance have decreased
    (B) the previous sentence discussed a type or types of health insurance
    (C) all types of health insurance have increased
    (D) only four types of health insurance have increased
    (E) only insurance companies provide health insurance

26. Complete this sentence:

    "Students cannot learn to write and compute well unless they first learn how to think; therefore,

    (A) we need to teach students to think."
    (B) writing and computing should be delayed."
    (C) students need to stay home until they can think."
    (D) students need to stay in school longer."
    (E) students who don't learn to think cannot learn to write and compute."

27. Driven by a high wind, dunes creep across deserts, forming a relentless tide of sand.

    Sand in the desert

    (A) can be controlled by planting shrubbery
    (B) stays in the same place
    (C) looks like waves
    (D) goes back and forth like a tide
    (E) cannot be controlled

28. "The Star-Spangled Banner" was written by F.S. Key in 1814. President Wilson ordered it played at military services in 1916. It was designated the national anthem by Act of Congress in 1931.

    (A) "The Star-Spangled Banner" was played at President Wilson's inauguration.
    (B) "The Star-Spangled Banner" became the national anthem under President Wilson.
    (C) President Wilson thought "The Star-Spangled Banner" should be our national anthem.
    (D) "The Star-Spangled Banner" was written more than 100 years before being designated the national anthem.
    (E) F.S. Key and President Wilson were acquaintances.

29. The coming of the railroads proved a boon to California agriculture.

    We can conclude that

    (A) the railroads were a problem for California farmers
    (B) the railroads brought more people to California
    (C) without the railroads, California agriculture would not have increased as rapidly as it did
    (D) the railroads made products cheaper
    (E) the railroads made products more expensive

30. "Not a ship escaped heavy damage" means

    (A) no ship had damage
    (B) every ship had heavy damage
    (C) all ships had some damage, but not all had heavy damage
    (D) some ships had heavy damage
    (E) some ships had damage

31. "Students learn more when they are praised." If you applied this statement in the classroom, you would

    (A) praise each student for everything she does
    (B) praise each student when he has done a good job

(C) praise at least one student every day

(D) praise each student at least once a week

(E) make the praise valuable by praising only in exceptional circumstances

Questions 32 and 33

When a cold air layer lies below a warm layer, mirage images appear above the real object. When the layers are reversed, the image is inverted below the real object.

32. Which drawing illustrates the above information?

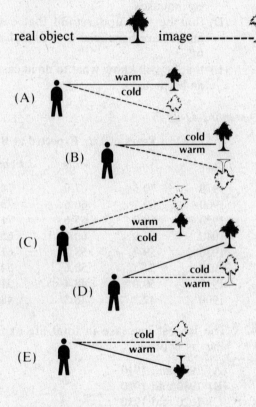

real object ——— image - - - - -

33. A mirage is

(A) an inversion
(B) an air layer
(C) a reversion
(D) an image
(E) an object

34. "People can have clean air if they demand it. The remedies for most forms of air pollution are known; they need only be applied."

This statement would be most strengthened by which of the following statements?

(A) The death rate has decreased in some cities.

(B) Pollution-control regulations have been passed.

(C) Smog-control devices are required in some states.

(D) Environmental lessons have been added to the curriculum in many schools.

(E) In several cities air-pollution-control programs are in effect with striking improvement of the air quality.

Questions 35 to 38

Knowledge of words has become our most valuable tool today. With a good vocabulary we can better understand others and communicate our thoughts to them. There is a high correlation between a large precise vocabulary and achievement in worldly success, earnings and management status.

Frustration over the inability to express thoughts in words often results in physical aggressiveness. For some years the nation's vocabulary level has been decreasing every year, while crime has been steadily increasing. A limited vocabulary is a serious handicap. Hard working people can advance only so far, before they reach a plateau beyond which they are hampered by their lack of vocabulary. As a result of being stymied in their employment, these people change jobs frequently. By middle-age many low-vocabulary people are stuck in routine jobs. When companies reduce personnel due to mergers or economic constraints, it's often the low-vocabulary people who are left without jobs.

35. We can conclude that people with a low level of vocabulary

(A) all have routine jobs

(B) have difficulty expressing themselves in words

(C) are unemployed most of the time

(D) are physically aggressive

(E) are laid off when companies merge

36. There is a high correlation between

    (A) a large vocabulary and job success
    (B) size of vocabulary and the crime rate
    (C) low vocabulary and retention rate upon the merger of two companies
    (D) size of vocabulary and lack of communication
    (E) lack of advancement and extent of vocabulary

37. All of the following are mentioned as disadvantages of a limited vocabulary except

    (A) lack of opportunity to be promoted to higher paid positions
    (B) difficulty in understanding others
    (C) more apt to be let go from job
    (D) less apt to have interesting work
    (E) lack of opportunity to use manual dexterity

38. Developing a large vocabulary enables one to

    I. be promoted
    II. change jobs easily
    III. understand others easily

    (A) III only
    (B) II and III only
    (C) I and II only
    (D) I and III only
    (E) I, II and III

39. What probable effect will a decreasing birthrate have on education?

    I. Fewer teachers will be needed.
    II. Fewer schools will be needed.
    III Fewer students will enroll.

    (A) I only
    (B) II only
    (C) III only
    (D) II and III only
    (E) I, II and III

40. "Moderation in all things, including moderation" leads one to think that

    (A) one should always be moderate
    (B) one should sometimes be immoderate
    (C) it is mediocre to be moderate
    (D) moderation is dull
    (E) moderation is modern

41. Earthquakes cause damage and loss of life, but scientists point out that they are vital to the continued development of our earth. Mountains are constantly eroding, and if they were not raised again, the world would become a place of stagnant seas and swamps.

    The likely effect of the above information on a reader is

    (A) no change in attitude
    (B) that he will understand the benefits of earthquakes
    (C) that he will be better prepared for earthquakes
    (D) that he will understand that earthquakes are beneficial as well as harmful
    (E) that he will know what to do in case of an earthquake

Questions 42 to 46

Years of Life Expected at Birth

Year	Total	Male	Female
1970	70.5	67.0	74.3
1960	69.7	66.6	73.1
1950	68.2	65.6	71.1
1940	62.9	60.8	65.2
1930	59.7	58.1	61.6
1920	54.1	53.6	54.6
1910	50.0	48.4	51.8
1900	47.3	46.3	48.3

42. The largest increase in total life expectancy is between

    (A) 1900 and 1910
    (B) 1910 and 1920
    (C) 1920 and 1930
    (D) 1930 and 1940
    (E) 1940 and 1950

43. What is the last census year in which a person who is still living in 1985 could have been born and outlived his or her expected life span?

    (A) 1900
    (B) 1910
    (C) 1920
    (D) 1930
    (E) 1940

44. A man born in 1950 can expect to live to the year

    (A) 2015
    (B) 2000
    (C) 2018
    (D) 2021
    (E) 2026

45. Which of the following are true, according to the chart?

    I. Women live longer than men.
    II. Life expectancy has increased every reporting period.
    III. Women have increased their life expectancy more than men.

    (A) I only
    (B) I and II only
    (C) I and III only
    (D) I, II and III
    (E) II only

46. Projecting the information into the future, the following conclusion can be made:

    I. Life expectancy will increase, but at a slower rate.
    II. There will be an increasing number of older people.
    III. The life expectancy of men will decrease.

    (A) I only
    (B) II only
    (C) III only
    (D) I and II only
    (E) I, II and III

Questions 47 to 49

Vocabulary is acquired, not innate. Vocabulary grows faster in the first year of life than at any other time. At age ten vocabulary is learned twice as fast as a few years later and three times as fast as at college age. Contrary to public belief, vocabulary test scores rarely improve because of formal learning. Children of high vocabulary parents have a head start. Parents are urged to start a child's vocabulary building at an early age. A limited vocabulary leads to school problems, leaving the young person with feelings of failure.

Many people view vocabulary building as a formidable task, but they already know many words. Only about 3,500 words separate the high and low vocabulary person, and spell the difference between success and failure. English is based on Anglo-Saxon word order but the words of subtlety and precision are Latin. The number of years a person studies Latin correlates with a large and exact English vocabulary, which in turn correlates with earnings. Vocabulary building requires both patience and effort, but the rewards are worthwhile.

47. Learning vocabulary

    (A) is done most readily before a child's first birthday
    (B) is an inherited ability
    (C) is fastest at age ten
    (D) is easiest during the college years
    (E) depends on how many years of Latin you study

48. The passage states that parents should begin vocabulary building for their child

    (A) during the first year
    (B) at age ten
    (C) at age thirteen
    (D) during the college years
    (E) not specified

49. Only about 3,500 words is

    (A) the number of words known by a person of low vocabulary level
    (B) the number of words known by a person of high vocabulary level
    (C) the difference between the number of words known by a high vocabulary and a low vocabulary person.
    (D) the number of words known before age ten
    (E) the average number of words learned during college

50. Nuclear plants use large amounts of water for cooling. One likely effect of this is

    (A) a shortage of water
    (B) contamination of water
    (C) higher water temperatures downstream
    (D) fewer nuclear plants near water
    (E) higher humidity

MATHEMATICS
70 Minutes—50 Questions

Directions: **Choose the best answer for each question and blacken the corresponding space on the Answer Sheet for Sample Test 1. The correct answers and explanations follow the test.**

1. The 7 in 1234.5678 represents

    (A) ones
    (B) tens
    (C) tenths
    (D) hundredths
    (E) thousandths

2. Round off 76,569 to the nearest thousand.

    (A) 76
    (B) 77
    (C) 76,000
    (D) 76,500
    (E) 77,000

3. $7/9$ lies between each of the following pairs of numbers except

    (A) $2/3$ and $3/2$
    (B) $7/11$ and $9/7$
    (C) $1/2$ and 1
    (D) 0.7 and 0.9
    (E) $7/8$ and $8/9$

4. To check whether $\dfrac{x^2 - 4}{x + 2} = x - 2$, you could

    (A) multiply $x - 2$ by $x^2 - 4$
    (B) multiply $x - 2$ by $x + 2$
    (C) multiply $x - 2$ by x
    (D) multiply $x + 2$ by x
    (E) multiply $x - 2$ by 2

5.
    $$16,752 \div 3 =$$

    When James tried to solve this problem, he found that it

    (A) has a remainder of 1
    (B) has a remainder of 2
    (C) has no remainder
    (D) cannot be divided
    (E) is smaller than 5,500

6.
    Jessica has 7 bills totaling $135.00 in $50.00, $20.00, $10.00, and $5.00 denominations. How many $20.00 bills does she have?

    When Jeremy began to solve this problem, he started with five $20.00 bills. After he tried that, he knew that

    (A) he was right
    (B) there were more than five $20.00 bills
    (C) there were four $5.00 bills
    (D) there was one $50.00 bill
    (E) there were four $20.00 bills

7. Harlan paid $45.05, including sales tax, for a pair of tennis shoes. If the rate of sales tax was 6%, how much tax did he pay?

    (A) $2.55
    (B) $2.70
    (C) $42.50
    (D) $45.59
    (E) $47.75

8. Which fraction is smallest?

    (A) $2/3$
    (B) $4/9$
    (C) $1/2$
    (D) $5/11$
    (E) $3/7$

9. For which problem would you use $1/2 \times 1/3$ to get the answer?

    (A) Jerry wants a third less than half of a pie.
    (B) Jeffrey wants to divide a third by a half.
    (C) Jeremy wants to find a half less than a third.
    (D) Jurgen wants to divide a half by a third.
    (E) Jerome wants half of a third of a pie.

10. Muriel worked part time at a drug store. She worked 5 hours Monday, 4 hours on

Tuesday, 3 hours Wednesday, 2 hours Thursday and 6 hours on Friday. What were her average dollar earnings per day?

(A) 3
(B) 4
(C) 5
(D) 20
(E) not enough information

11. Which pair of numbers has a ratio of 4 to 11?

(A) 49, 110
(B) 16, 33
(C) 77, 28
(D) 28, 77
(E) 110, 49

12. On an assignment, Sidney did 18 problems correctly and 6 incorrectly. The ratio of problems attempted to problems solved incorrectly is

(A) 1:4
(B) 4:3
(C) 4:1
(D) 3:4
(E) 18:6

13. The scale on a house plan is 1:36. This means that

(A) 1 in. = 36 yds
(B) 1 ft = 6 yds
(C) 1 ft = 3 yds
(D) 1 in. = 1 yd
(E) 1 in. = 3 yds

14. To get a B (80%) on a test, Susan had to answer at least 104 questions correctly. The number of questions on the test was

(A) 140
(B) 130
(C) 107
(D) 100
(E) 64

15. In a dominoes tournament, each player plays every other player once. The winner is the person who wins the greatest number of games. What is the total number of games played if 8 people participate?

(A) 8
(B) 15
(C) 28
(D) 32
(E) 64

16.

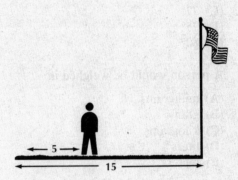

A man 6 feet tall casts a shadow 5 feet long. The flagpole nearby casts a 15-foot shadow. How tall is the flagpole?

(A) 11 ft
(B) 15 ft
(C) 18 ft
(D) 21 ft
(E) 26 ft

17. Brenda earns six times as much as Marvin. Marvin earns

(A) $6.00
(B) one-sixth of their combined income
(C) six divided by Brenda's earnings
(D) six times Brenda's earnings
(E) Brenda's earnings divided by six

18. The prime factors of 60 are

(A) 1, 2, 3, 5
(B) 2, 3, 5
(C) 1, 3, 4, 5
(D) 12, 5
(E) 6, 10

19. $\sqrt{4725}$ is closest to

(A) 65
(B) 68
(C) 69
(D) 75
(E) 225

20. The temperature in Kevin's room has been fluctuating between 65° and 80°. The average temperature for the past five days has been 72°. What is the lowest average temperature the room can have for the week?

    (A) 65°
    (B) 70°
    (C) 72°
    (D) 75°
    (E) 80°

21. A person would be weighed in

    (A) milligrams
    (B) grams
    (C) kilograms
    (D) liters
    (E) meters

22. Convert 35° Celsius to Fahrenheit.

    (A) 7°F
    (B) 20°F
    (C) 52°F
    (D) 67°F
    (E) 95°F

23. The basic rate for a telephone is $6.00 per month. Each call is charged at 30¢. How much will Nancy pay for March if she made 25 calls?

    (A) $6.55
    (B) $13.50
    (C) $15.30
    (D) $15.75
    (E) $18.25

24. Sidney is baking 50 muffins. How many muffin tins will he need if there are 8 muffin cups in each tin?

    (A) 6
    (B) 6.25
    (C) 7
    (D) 8
    (E) 9

25. Tammy is the owner of a lamp store. A $50.00 lamp has been marked down 10% but hasn't sold. She decides to mark it down another 20%. What price will she put on it?

    (A) $20.00
    (B) $30.00
    (C) $35.00
    (D) $36.00
    (E) $40.00

26. Gudelia is five years older than Francis. Five years ago she was twice as old as Francis. How old is Francis?

    (A) 5
    (B) 10
    (C) 15
    (D) 20
    (E) none of these

27. The difference between a two-digit number and the number reversed is 36. The sum of the digits is 10. What is the number?

    (A) 56
    (B) 64
    (C) 73
    (D) 82
    (E) 91

28. Margaret borrowed $2,700 from the credit union to be paid back at the end of three years at 12% annual simple interest. How much will she pay back?

    (A) $972.00
    (B) $2,700.00
    (C) $3,105.00
    (D) $3,672.00
    (E) $3,780.00

29. David filled a container that was 12 inches long by 8 inches wide, to a depth of 6 inches. How should he determine the number of cubic inches of water in the container?

    (A) 2(12 + 8 + 6)
    (B) 8(6 + 12)
    (C) 6(8 + 12)
    (D) 12(6 + 8)
    (E) 6 × 8 × 12

30. Diane is going to put fringe around a tablecloth that is 3 feet by 5 feet. How many yards of fringe will she need to buy?

    (A) 16 yds

(B) 2⅔ yds
(C) 5 yds
(D) 5⅓ yds
(E) 10 yds

31. (b − 4)(b + 3) =

(A) $b^2 - 12$
(B) $2b - 1$
(C) $b^2 - 1$
(D) $b^2 - b - 12$
(E) $b^2 - b + 12$

32.

> You can buy eight tapes for $60.00 at Tape World upon presentation of a $4.00 discount certificate. Under these terms, how much does one tape cost?

Which formula would you use to solve this problem?

(A) 8t = 60
(B) 8t + 4 = 60
(C) 8t − 4 = 60
(D) 8t + 60 = −4
(E) 4 − 8t = 60

33. $3k^2 - 4k + 7 - 2k^2 =$

(A) $k^2 - 4k + 7$
(B) $-4k + 7$
(C) $6k^2 - 4k + 7$
(D) $-6k^4 - 4k + 7$
(E) $-3k^5 + 7$

34. What is the area of a rectangular chart that is $3a^2$ wide and $4a^3$ long?

(A) $7a^5$
(B) $12a^5$
(C) $7a^6$
(D) $144a^6$
(E) $72a$

35. 678 + K − M − 401 = 385; K = 5M. Find the value of M.

(A) 27
(B) 108
(C) 277
(D) 18
(E) 411

36. x° + y° =

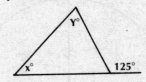

(A) 55°
(B) 62.5°
(C) 90°
(D) 125°
(E) 180°

37.

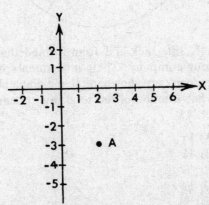

The coordinates of point A are

(A) X = 3, Y = 2
(B) X = −3, Y = 2
(C) X = 2, Y = −3
(D) X = −2, Y = −3
(E) none of the above

38.

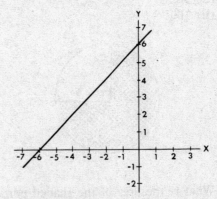

The equation for the above line is

(A) X − Y = 6
(B) X + Y = 6
(C) X = 6
(D) Y = 6
(E) Y − X = 6

Questions 39 and 40

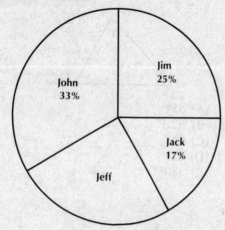

39. Jeff, Jill, Jack and John formed the Jay-Four company. Their investments in the company are shown in the pie graph above. What fraction of the total investment was Jeff's?

    (A) ⅓
    (B) ¼
    (C) ⅕
    (D) ⅙
    (E) ²/₇

40. How many degrees does Jim's investment represent?

    (A) 25°
    (B) 50°
    (C) 75°
    (D) 90°
    (E) 100°

41.

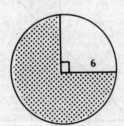

What is the area of the shaded portion of the circle above?

    (A) 3π
    (B) 9π
    (C) 12π
    (D) 27π
    (E) 36π

42. The formula for the area of a circle is $A = \pi r^2$. Find the area of a circle with a radius of 4.

    (A) 8
    (B) 4π
    (C) 16π
    (D) 8π
    (E) 16

43. Jason paid $11.60 for a shirt that was marked down by 20%. How much money did he save by buying at the sale price rather than the original price?

    (A) $2.00
    (B) $2.90
    (C) $2.32
    (D) $14.50
    (E) $11.60

44. Ken has a drawer full of marker pens. Four are black, three are red, two are green and six are blue. If he pulls out one pen at random, what are his chances of pulling out a red one?

    (A) 1 in 15
    (B) even
    (C) 1 in 5
    (D) 2 in 15
    (E) 4 in 6

45. If the area of a square is ⅓ more than the area of a triangle with a base of 12 and a height of 8, what is length of one side of the square?

    (A) 8
    (B) 15
    (C) 48
    (D) 64
    (E) 96

46. James is arranging a display of coffee tins on a table 40 inches wide and 42 inches long. How many tins, each 6 inches in diameter, can be placed on the surface of the table without stacking the tins?

(A) 42
(B) 46
(C) 47
(D) 182
(E) 186

47. There were 180 parents and students at graduation. At least a third of the audience consisted of students. How many students attended?

(A) 60–179
(B) 60–180
(C) 61–180
(D) 120–179
(E) 121–180

Questions 48 to 50

The community swimming pool was being filled at a steady rate. The depth of the water was measured every 15 minutes and recorded in inches and centimeters.

Time	Inches	Centimeters
9:00 a.m.	7	17.92
9:15 a.m.	14	35.84
9:30 a.m.	21	53.76
9:45 a.m.	28	71.86
10:00 a.m.	35	89.60
10:15 a.m.	42	107.52

48. At which time was an incorrect measurement logged?

(A) 9:15
(B) 9:30
(C) 9:45
(D) 10:00
(E) at no time

49. At the same rate, when will the water in the pool be 7 feet deep?

(A) 10:30
(B) 11:00
(C) 11:15
(D) 11:45
(E) 12:00

50. How deep will the water be at noon?

(A) 6 ft
(B) 7 ft
(C) 7 ft 7 in.
(D) 8 ft
(E) more than 8 ft

WRITING
60 Minutes—Two Essays

Directions: **You have 60 minutes in which to write two essays. The essay topics are intended to measure how well you write, given limitations on time and subject. Quality is more important than quantity. Spend some of your time organizing your thoughts. Use specific examples to support your opinions. Write only on the assigned topic. Write legibly and within the lines provided. Space for notes is provided below.**

Topic A

John Molloy found that students reacted differently when he dressed casually from the way they reacted when he dressed more formally. From your observations and experiences, relate how what you wear affects you and others and how you would use this information.

Topic B

Do you agree or disagree with the statement, "Good teachers are born, not made"? Support your position with examples from your experience with teachers you have met.

TOPIC A

_____

_____

_____

_____

_____

_____

_____

_____

_____

_____

_____

_____

_____

_____

_____

_____

_____

_____

_____

_____

_____

_____

_____

TOPIC B

_____

_____

_____

_____

_____

_____

_____

_____

_____

_____

_____

_____

_____

_____

_____

_____

_____

_____

_____

_____

ANSWERS TO SAMPLE TEST 1

READING

1. A	11. B	21. A	31. B	41. D
2. E	12. A	22. D	32. B	42. C
3. D	13. D	23. C	33. D	43. C
4. E	14. A	24. E	34. E	44. A
5. A	15. C	25. B	35. B	45. D
6. B	16. B	26. A	36. A	46. D
7. C	17. B	27. E	37. E	47. A
8. B	18. B	28. D	38. D	48. E
9. E	19. E	29. C	39. E	49. C
10. B	20. C	30. B	40. B	50. C

MATHEMATICS

1. E	11. D	21. C	31. D	41. D
2. E	12. C	22. E	32. C	42. C
3. E	13. D	23. B	33. A	43. B
4. B	14. B	24. C	34. B	44. C
5. C	15. C	25. D	35. A	45. A
6. D	16. C	26. B	36. D	46. A
7. A	17. E	27. C	37. C	47. A
8. E	18. B	28. D	38. E	48. C
9. E	19. C	29. E	39. B	49. D
10. E	20. B	30. D	40. D	50. C

SCORING OF SAMPLE TEST 1

Each institution or state decides on the passing score. In general, 35 correct on the reading and 33 correct on the mathematics sections will be passing.

How to score the writing. The writing section is scored holistically, which makes it difficult to grade. You may want to have someone else score it and make suggestions on how to improve your writing, or you may want or need to score it yourself.

Here is a suggestion for scoring the essay yourself. Start with a total of 50 points for each essay. Then subtract as follows for errors.

Subtract

- 1½ points for every line that you wrote over the limit
- 1 point for every punctuation, spelling or minor grammatical error
- 3 points for each major grammatical error, incorrectly used word or failure to paragraph correctly
- 5 points for low vocabulary level or jargon
- 10 points if your arguments don't support your statement
- 10 points if you didn't fill more than the first page
- 10 points if you did not have a conclusion
- 25 points if you didn't stay on the topic

This will give you a raw score for each essay. Add the two raw scores together to get your total. You need a total score of 75 points to pass.

EXPLANATION OF ANSWERS TO SAMPLE TEST 1

READING

1. **A** The second paragraph states the earliest date mentioned.

2. **E** The comet did not cause these events.

3. **D** The last paragraph states this.

4. **E** *Disaster* means *evil* or *bad* star; similarly *distemper* means *bad temper*.

5. **A** In paragraph two, Hawthorne is contrasted to presidents who have very demanding jobs. He probably had a job which did not tax his mental ability and, therefore, had a hobby which did.

6. **B** As stated in paragraph 3, a hobby is for enjoyment.

7. **C** The other statements are too extreme.

8. **B** Rivers of wind have widespread effects on weather.

9. **E** A crevasse is a deep cut in ice or rock.

10. **B** No advocacy or bias is shown.

11. **B** "The messages were slipped in," but we don't know what opinions they expressed.

12. **A** Who pays, says. No other statement is logical.

13. **D** England, Scotland and Wales make up Great Britain.

14. **A** *Virtually* means *practically*.

15. **C** *Depict* means *describe*.

16. **B** A higher deductible means that you pay more for repairs before the insurance company starts paying.

17. **B** $25.00 per month or $25 × 12 = $300.00 per year.

18. **B** He saves $300.00 in premiums, but pays $500.00 − $150.00 = $350.00 more deductible, for a loss of $50.00.

19. **E** See 18, above.

20. **C** He pays the first $500.00. He is insured for $5,000.00, so he will have to pay any amount over that: $7,000.00 − $5,000.00 = $2,000.00. Altogether he will have to pay $2,500.00

21. **A** Best bets are the usual policy and several accidents, or higher deductible and few accidents. Eliminate B, C and E. This is a time-consuming problem, so if you're short of time, choose A or D and move on.

Check A:

Usual

Premiums	$125 × 12 =	$1,500
Deductible	$150 × 4 =	600
Total Cost		$2,100

Higher

Premiums	$100 × 12 =	$1,200
Deductible	$400 × 4 =	1,600
Total Cost		$2,800

$700 savings.

Check D:

Usual

Premiums	$125 × 12 =	$1,500
Deductible	$150 × 1 =	150
Total cost		$1,650

Higher

Premiums	$100 × 12 =	$1,200
Deductible	$500 × 1 =	500
Total Cost		$1,700

$50 savings.

22. **D** *Show* beats *tell*.

23. **C** Growth has decreased, but it's still growth.

24. **E** They will *consider* all three, but perhaps act only on II.

25. **B** *Other* is the key word.

26. **A** E is the only other logical choice to consider. Notice however, that the passage says, "write and compute WELL."

27. **E** *Relentless* means steady and persistent; unremitting. The implication is that the movement of the sand cannot be stopped.

28. **D** 1931 − 1814 = 117 years.

29. **C** A *boon* is a benefit.

30. **B** If no ships escaped heavy damage, then every ship had heavy damage.

31. **B** Students sense when praise is not deserved.

32. **B** Both drawings below are correct.

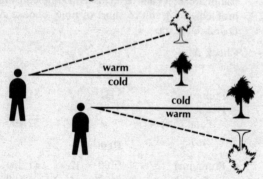

33. **D** The passage refers to *mirage images.*

34. **E** Only E illustrates the argument.

35. **B** The second sentence states, "With a good vocabulary we can better . . . communicate our thoughts. . . ." Conversely, people without a good

vocabulary would have difficulty expressing themselves.

36. **A** Sentence 3 states this.

37. **E** All the others are listed as disadvantages.

38. **D** I and III are mentioned. II is possible but not mentioned.

39. **E** If there are fewer children, there will be fewer students, and fewer teachers and schools will be needed.

40. **B** Even moderation has to be tempered, which means that sometimes one should not be moderate.

41. **D** Choice A is possible, but D is more likely.

42. **C** Look for a large difference.

    (A) about 3   (D) about 3
    (B) about 4   (E) about 5
    (C) about 5
    Work out C and E.

43. **C** Underline *last.* Add the year and life expectancy. It has to be less than 1985.

44. **A** 1950 + 65.6 = 2015.6

45. **D** All are true.

46. **D** I and II are valid. III is doubtful.

47. **A** The second sentence gives this information.

48. **E** Beginning vocabulary development is suggested "at an early age" but no age is specified.

49. **C** The second sentence of the second paragraph contains the answer.

50. **C** Choice C is the most logical. Using the water for cooling means the water will be heated.

MATHEMATICS

1. **E** See page 46.

2. **E** 76,569

   ↑   5 or more, round up.

   1,000
   ───────
   77,000

3. **E** Compare by cross-multiplication.

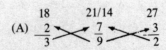

(B) $\begin{array}{ccc} 63 & 77/49 & 81 \\ \dfrac{7}{11} & \dfrac{7}{9} & \dfrac{9}{7} \end{array}$

(C) $\begin{array}{ccc} 9 & 14/7 & 9 \\ \dfrac{1}{2} & \dfrac{7}{9} & \dfrac{1}{1} \end{array}$

(D) $\begin{array}{ccc} 63 & 70/70 & 81 \\ \dfrac{7}{10} & \dfrac{7}{9} & \dfrac{9}{10} \end{array}$

(E) $\begin{array}{ccc} 63 & 56/63 & 72 \\ \dfrac{7}{8} & \dfrac{7}{9} & \dfrac{8}{9} \end{array}$ $\dfrac{7}{9}$ is smaller than both $\dfrac{7}{8}$ and $\dfrac{8}{9}$.

4. **B** To check $\dfrac{12}{3} = 4$, you would multiply 3 by 4.

Similarly, you would multiply (x + 2) by (x − 2) to check $\dfrac{x^2 - 4}{x + 2} = x - 2$.

5. **C** 1 + 6 + 7 + 5 + 2 = 21, which is divisible by 3; therefore, 16,752 is divisible by 3 and has no remainder.

6. **D** Try the various answer choices.
   - (A) 5 × 20 = 100. You have $35.00 to make up with two bills; this isn't possible.
   - (B) 6 × 20 = 120; you need one $15.00 bill, not possible.
   - (C) You need an odd number of $5.00 bills.
   - (D) 3 × 20 = 60. This leaves $75.00 to be made up with four bills; 50 + 10 + 10 + 5 = 75.
   - (E) 4 × 20 = 80. This leaves $55.00 to be made up with three bills; not possible.

7. **A** Your sales tax will be less than $3.00; eliminate C, D and E.

$$\begin{array}{cc} \$ & \% \\ \dfrac{x}{\$45.05} = & \dfrac{6}{106} \end{array}$$

$$106x = (45.05)(6)$$
$$x = 270.3 \div 106$$
$$x = \$2.55$$

8. **E** Compare by cross-multiplication.

$\begin{array}{cc} 18 & 12 \\ \dfrac{2}{3} & \dfrac{4}{9} \end{array}$ $\dfrac{4}{9}$ is smaller.

$\begin{array}{cc} 8 & 9 \\ \dfrac{4}{9} & \dfrac{1}{2} \end{array}$ $\dfrac{4}{9}$ is smaller.

$\begin{array}{cc} 44 & 45 \\ \dfrac{4}{9} & \dfrac{5}{11} \end{array}$ $\dfrac{4}{9}$ is smaller.

$\begin{array}{cc} 28 & 27 \\ \dfrac{4}{9} & \dfrac{3}{7} \end{array}$ $\dfrac{3}{7}$ is smallest.

With this type of question, first check to determine whether there are any answers you can eliminate, e.g., ⅔ is 0.67, ½ is 0.50.

9. **E** You need to try out the choices.
   - (A) ½ − ⅓
   - (B) ⅓ ÷ ½
   - (C) ⅓ − ½
   - (D) ½ ÷ ⅓
   - (E) ½ × ⅓

10. **E** You need to know how much she earned per hour. There's not enough information.

11. **D** Look for the smaller number to be placed first. Eliminate C and E. Next, is the first number divisible by 4? Eliminate A. Is the second number divisible by 11? "When the first number is divided by 4 and the second number is divided by 11, are the quotients (answers) the same?" Try B: $^{16}/_4 = 4$; $^{33}/_{11} = 3$; no. Try D: $^{28}/_4 = 7$; $^{77}/_{11} = 7$; yes.

12. **C** Problems attempted : incorrect answers
$$18 + 6 : 6$$
$$24 : 6$$
$$4 : 1$$

13. **D** Convert to same measure.
   - (A) 1 in. = 36 × 36 in.
   - (B) 1 ft = 6 × 3 ft
   - (C) 1 ft = 3 × 3 ft
   - (D) 1 in. = 36 in.
   - (E) 1 in. = 3 × 36 in.

14. **B** $$\dfrac{80\%}{100\%} = \dfrac{104}{n}$$
$$80n = 104(100)$$
$$n = \dfrac{104(100)}{80} = 130$$

15. **C** Player 1 plays players 2, 3, 4, 5, 6, 7, 8 = 7 games
Player 2 plays players 3, 4, 5, 6, 7, 8 = 6 games
Player 3 plays players 4, 5, 6, 7, 8 = 5 games
Player 4 plays players 5, 6, 7, 8 = 4 games
Player 5 plays players 6, 7, 8 = 3 games
Player 6 plays players 7, 8 = 2 games
Player 7 plays player 8 = 1 game
Total number of games played = 28

Each player plays the others only once. Player 1 plays player 2, therefore that game is not counted in player 2's number of games. Player 8 has already played each of the others.

16. **C**

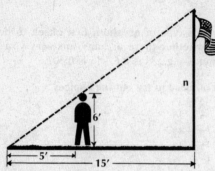

$$\frac{man}{shadow} = \frac{flagpole}{shadow}$$

$$\frac{6}{5} = \frac{n}{15}$$

$$6 \times 15 = 5n$$

$$\frac{6 \times 15}{5} = n$$

$$18 = n$$

17. **E** Brenda = 6 Marvin

Marvin = $\frac{Brenda}{6}$ or ⅙ Brenda

If Brenda earns 6 times what Marvin earns, then Marvin earns ⅙ of what Brenda earns.

18. **B**

$$
\begin{array}{r|r}
2 & 60 \\
2 & 30 \\
3 & 15 \\
5 & 5 \\
\end{array}
$$

(A) 1 is not prime.
(C) 1 and 4 are not prime.
(D) 12 is not prime.
(E) 6 and 10 are not prime.

19. **C** $\sqrt{47\,25}$

1. 2 places in answer; eliminate E.
2. square root closest to 47 is 6 ($6^2 = 36$); eliminate D.
3. 47 is close to 49, so try 68 or 69.
   $68^2 = 4624$ $69^2 = 4721$ (closest)

20. **B** The lowest temperature will be less than 72; eliminate C, D, E.

$$
\begin{array}{r}
5 \times 72 = 360 \\
2 \times 65 = 130 \\
\hline
490
\end{array}
\qquad \frac{490}{7} = 70
$$

21. **C** Pounds is the equivalent measure to kilograms.

22. **E** C ➡ F larger; eliminate A, B.

Approximation	Formula
$2C + 30° = F$	$9/5C + 32° = F$
$2 \times 35° + 30° = 100°$	$9/5(35)° + 32° = 95°$

23. **B** $6.00 + 25 \times 0.30 = 6.00 + 7.50 = \$13.50$

24. **C** $50 \div 8 = 6¼$ He'll need 7.

25. **D** 10% off = 90% $\$50 \times 0.9 = \$45$
    20% off = 80% $\$45 \times 0.8 = \$36$

26. **B** A. Five years ago Francis was less than a year old; eliminate.
    B. Substitute 10 for Francis.

    Now: G = 15, F = 10
    5 years ago: $15 - 5 = 2(10 - 5)$
                   $10 = 2 \times 5$

27. **C** Is the sum of the digits 10? Eliminate A. Subtract the digits reversed. Look for 36.

$$
\begin{array}{cc}
(B)\quad 64 & (C)\quad 73 \\
\underline{-46} & \underline{-37} \\
18 & 36 \\
\end{array}
$$

28. **D** Total to be repaid is more than amount borrowed; eliminate A and B.
    Total   = Principal + Interest
    Interest = Principal × Rate × Time

$$= \$2,700 \times \frac{12}{100} \times 3 = \$972$$

    Total = $\$2,700 + \$972 = \$3,672$

29. **E** Volume = $1 \times w \times h$
              = $12 \times 8 \times 6$

30. **D** Perimeter = $2(l + w)$
              = $2(3 + 5)$
              = $2(8) = 16$ ft
    16 ft ÷ 3 = 5⅓ yds

31. **D**

$$b^2 \qquad -12$$
$$(b - 4)\qquad(b + 3) \qquad = b^2 - b - 12$$
$$-4b$$
$$+3b$$
$$-b$$

32. **C** You don't need to solve the problem.
    8 tapes − \$4.00 = \$60.00

33. **A** $3k^2 - 4k + 7 - 2k^2 =$
           $3k^2 - 2k^2 - 4k + 7 =$
           $k^2 - 4k + 7$

34. **B** Area = length × width
    $$= 4a^3 \times 3a^2$$
    $$= 12a^5$$

35. **A** Estimate:
    $$700 + 4M - 400 = 400$$
    $$300 + 4M = 400$$
    $$4M = 100$$
    $$M = 25$$

    Eliminate B, C and E.
    Now solve the problem
    $678 + K - M - 401 = 385$; $K = 5M$
    Substitute $678 + 5M - M - 401 = 385$
    Combine $678 - 401 + 4M = 385$
    $$277 + 4M = 385$$
    Subtract 277 $\underline{-277 \qquad\qquad -277}$
    $$4M = 108$$
    Divide by 4 $M = 27$

36. **D** The exterior angle equals the sum of the two opposite interior (inside) angles. The three inside angles of a triangle add up to 180°.

    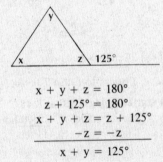

    $$x + y + z = 180°$$
    $$z + 125° = 180°$$
    $$x + y + z = z + 125°$$
    $$\underline{-z = -z}$$
    $$x + y = 125°$$

37. **C**

    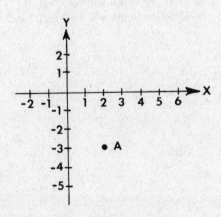

    The X direction is listed first, then Y.
    A is 2 units to the right (+) along X, hence X = 2.
    A is 3 units down (−) along Y, hence Y = −3.

38. **E**

    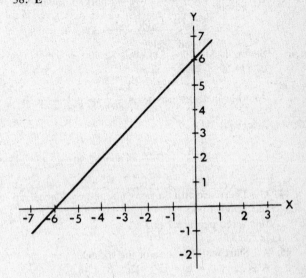

    When X is 0, Y is 6.
    When Y is 0, X is −6.
    Try out the choices.
    (A) Cover X with your finger (0)
    $$-Y = 6 \text{ or } Y = -6$$
    Cover Y with your finger (0)
    $$X = 6; \text{ no}$$
    (B) When X = 0   Y = 6
    When Y = 0   X = 6; no
    (C) vertical
    (D) horizontal
    (E) When Y = 0, −X = 6 or X = −6
    When X = 0, Y = 6; yes

39. **B**   33%
        17%   100%
      <u>+25%</u>   <u>−75%</u>
      75% others   25% Jeff = ¼

40. **D** $\dfrac{25\%}{100\%} = \dfrac{d°}{360°}$

    $$\frac{25 \times 360}{100} = d° = 90°$$
    or 25% is ¼
    $$¼ \times 360° = 90°$$

41. **D** Area of a circle $a = \pi r^2$
    You want ¾ of the area.
    $$¾\pi r^2 = ¾\pi 6^2 = 27\pi$$

42. **C** $A = \pi r^2$
    $$= \pi 4^2$$
    $$= 16\pi$$

43. **B** $\dfrac{\text{part}}{\text{whole}} = \dfrac{\$11.60}{p} = \dfrac{80\%}{100\%}$ (marked down 20%)

$$\dfrac{\$11.60 \times 100}{80} = p = \$14.50$$

Saving is $14.50 − $11.60 = $2.90
or $14.50 × 20% = $2.90

Another method: Saving is $\dfrac{20\%}{80\%} = \dfrac{p}{\$11.60}$ or ¼

of $11.60

$$\dfrac{\$20 \times 11.60}{80} = p = \$2.90$$

44. **C** There are fifteen pens altogether. Three are red. 3 out of 15 = $^3/_{15}$ = $^1/_5$. The chances of getting a red pen are 1 in 5.

45. **A** Start with the area of the triangle.
$A = ½ \times b \times h = ½ \times 12 \times 8 = 48$
The area if the square is ⅓ more than 48.
⅓ × 48 = 16.
The area of the square is 48 + 16 = 64.

$A = s^2 = 64$
$s = \sqrt{64} = 8$; One side of the square = 8.

46. **A**

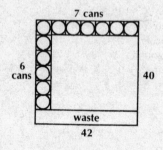

42 ÷ 6 = 7 tins in a row.
40 ÷ 6 = 6⅔ rows.
Number of cans = 6 × 7 = 42.
(You can't put ⅔ of a tin on the table.)

47. **A** 180 ÷ 3 = 60
There were at least 60 students. There was at least one parent. The number of students was 60 to 179.

48. **C** Look for a discrepancy. There is none in time or inches, but there is one in centimeters. The error occurred at 9:45.

Time	Change	In	Change	Centi-meters	Change
9:00		7		17.92	
	15		7		17.92
9:15		14		35.84	
	15		7		17.92
9:30		21		53.76	
	15		7		18.10
9:45		28		71.86	
	15		7		17.74
10:00		35		89.60	
	15		7		17.92
10:15		42		107.52	
	15				

49. **D** It fills at 28 inches per hour.
$$\dfrac{7 \text{ ft} \times 12}{28} = 3 \text{ hours to fill to 7 feet.}$$
The pool started being filled at 8:45
Add $\dfrac{3:00}{11:45}$ hours

50. **C** Refer to question 49.
At 11.45 the depth will be 7 feet.
At 12:00 the depth will be 7 feet 7 inches.

ANSWER SHEET FOR SAMPLE TEST 2

READING

	A B C D E		A B C D E		A B C D E		A B C D E		A B C D E
1	○○○○○	11	○○○○○	21	○○○○○	31	○○○○○	41	○○○○○
2	○○○○○	12	○○○○○	22	○○○○○	32	○○○○○	42	○○○○○
3	○○○○○	13	○○○○○	23	○○○○○	33	○○○○○	43	○○○○○
4	○○○○○	14	○○○○○	24	○○○○○	34	○○○○○	44	○○○○○
5	○○○○○	15	○○○○○	25	○○○○○	35	○○○○○	45	○○○○○
6	○○○○○	16	○○○○○	26	○○○○○	36	○○○○○	46	○○○○○
7	○○○○○	17	○○○○○	27	○○○○○	37	○○○○○	47	○○○○○
8	○○○○○	18	○○○○○	28	○○○○○	38	○○○○○	48	○○○○○
9	○○○○○	19	○○○○○	29	○○○○○	39	○○○○○	49	○○○○○
10	○○○○○	20	○○○○○	30	○○○○○	40	○○○○○	50	○○○○○

MATHEMATICS

	A B C D E		A B C D E		A B C D E		A B C D E		A B C D E
1	○○○○○	11	○○○○○	21	○○○○○	31	○○○○○	41	○○○○○
2	○○○○○	12	○○○○○	22	○○○○○	32	○○○○○	42	○○○○○
3	○○○○○	13	○○○○○	23	○○○○○	33	○○○○○	43	○○○○○
4	○○○○○	14	○○○○○	24	○○○○○	34	○○○○○	44	○○○○○
5	○○○○○	15	○○○○○	25	○○○○○	35	○○○○○	45	○○○○○
6	○○○○○	16	○○○○○	26	○○○○○	36	○○○○○	46	○○○○○
7	○○○○○	17	○○○○○	27	○○○○○	37	○○○○○	47	○○○○○
8	○○○○○	18	○○○○○	28	○○○○○	38	○○○○○	48	○○○○○
9	○○○○○	19	○○○○○	29	○○○○○	39	○○○○○	49	○○○○○
10	○○○○○	20	○○○○○	30	○○○○○	40	○○○○○	50	○○○○○

SAMPLE TEST 2
(CBEST)

Here is another test similar to the California Basic Educational Skills Test (CBEST) used in California and Oregon. The Reading, Mathematics, and Writing sections of this test can also be used to practice for the Pre-Professional Skills Test (PPST) used in Delaware, Kansas, Minnesota, Nebraska, Nevada, and Wisconsin. They are useful, too, in preparing for teacher certification tests administered by Colorado, Connecticut, Illinois, Michigan, and South Carolina.

Format of the CBEST

Reading	50 questions	65 minutes
Mathematics	50 questions	70 minutes

——————————————— *Break* ———————————————

Writing	two essays	60 minutes

Scoring the test

Raw scores for Reading and Mathematics sections are determined by totaling the number of questions answered correctly. There is no penalty for incorrect answers. Each of the two essays is scored on a scale of one (fail) to four (pass). Passing scores for both California and Oregon are set at a total scaled score of 123 for all three sections with no section below a scaled score of 37.

READING

65 Minutes—50 Questions

Directions: **Choose the best answer for each question and blacken the corresponding space on the Answer Sheet for Sample Test 2. The correct answers and explanations follow the test.**

Questions 1 to 3

The number of first-aid information classes for children ages four to fourteen is increasing. Because of the rising maternal employment rate, growing numbers of children are spending part of the day alone or with foreign-speaking housekeepers. This increases the likelihood that children will have to deal with emergencies partially or entirely on their own. The first-aid programs are designed to help prevent household and other accidents, home fires, child abuse, and kidnapping. Children can choose among courses such as first aid, fingerprinting and photo identification, fire safety, emergency telephone calling, personal safety and babysitting safety. Children ten or older can also attend an hour-long cardiopulmonary resuscitation class.

Children practice emergency calling know-how and the use of the 911 number, but only after they have learned that this number should be called only when a police officer, firefighters or an ambulance is needed quickly. Children learn about such things as wearing seat belts and the do's and don'ts for treating burns and broken bones. They learn not to put butter on burns, because it insulates the burn and retains heat. They also learn that they should not try to straighten broken bones but to leave that for the doctor to do.

1. A child who is nine can participate in which of the following programs?

   (A) fingerprinting and photo identification
   (B) how to deal with broken bones
   (C) cardiopulmonary resuscitation
   (D) all of the above
   (E) A and B only

2. The underlying cause of the increasing number of children's first-aid programs is

   (A) increased crime rate
   (B) better health awareness
   (C) more mothers working
   (D) federal funding for the programs
   (E) increase in the number of emergency situations

3. According to the passage, children can learn all of the following *except*

   (A) how to call the emergency number
   (B) what to put on a burn
   (C) how to straighten a broken bone
   (D) how to prevent household accidents
   (E) how to prevent kidnapping

Questions 4 to 7

A new nationwide study may shatter the widely held notion that a mother's employment is detrimental to her children. It states that school-age children of working mothers outscore children of mothers who do not work outside the home in math and reading. They have a lower absentee rate from school and have significantly higher IQ scores. The new study also found that children of employed mothers are more self-reliant than children of nonworking mothers. This supports earlier studies which showed a higher sense of self-esteem and greater skill in handling personal relationships among children of working mothers. Employed mothers participate in significantly more recreational activities with their children than do their nonworking counterparts. All significant social and academic criteria favor children of employed mothers. Working mothers were shown to rely more heavily on babysitters and relatives for evening childcare than mothers who are not employed. Families of nonworking mothers were more likely to have more members of the family present at the evening meal. Nonworking mothers expressed higher satisfaction with their own parenting, and their children also reported better mother–child relations.

4. According to the study, mothers working outside the home

    (A) had more family members at the evening meal
    (B) were more satisfied with their parenting than nonworking mothers
    (C) felt more guilty about their work
    (D) did more recreational things with their children
    (E) stayed home more in the evenings

5. Who reported higher satisfaction with parenting and mother–child relationships?

    (A) employed mothers
    (B) children of employed mothers
    (C) mothers staying home
    (D) children of mothers who stay at home
    (E) C and D

6. We can infer from the passage that it was previously believed that

    (A) a mother's work had detrimental effects on her children
    (B) children of working mothers had a high sense of self-esteem
    (C) children of nonworking mothers had a high absentee rate from school
    (D) working mothers had a high sense of satisfaction with their parenting
    (E) children of working mothers were left alone a great deal

Questions 7 and 8

Why and how did Europeans, alone among the peoples of the world, disperse around the globe? For most of human history, oceans were unbreachable barriers to the movement of people from one continent to another. As a result, Asians are principally in Asia, Africans are primarily in Africa, Arabs are mainly in the Middle East, Polynesians in the islands of the Pacific, Indians in India and so forth. But Europeans are everywhere—Greenland, Iceland, Australia, North and South America and parts of Africa. Why is this?

One reason which has been put forth is technology. The Renaissance gave European seamen ships that could cross oceans, and sufficient seamanship and navigational skills to make such voyages possible. It also gave them tools and weapons to conquer stone-age civilizations with dispatch. Why only Europeans had this technology is yet another question.

Another approach to the spread of European influence is that rather than technology, it was the plants and microbes that the Europeans brought with them that enabled them to conquer many of the lands they surveyed. Among the living things they brought with them, which included plants and animals, were the diseases that gave them the upper hand. In Europe, periodic smallpox epidemics wiped out large numbers of people, but conferred immunity on those who survived. In the New World the native people had no such diseases and no such immunity. As a result, the natives of America and Australia were almost defenseless against the onslaught of microbes brought in by the Europeans. Measles could wipe out an entire native population.

7. "The Europeans dispersed all over the world and readily conquered native civilizations primarily because of the diseases they brought with them and their immunity to most of them." This statement is

    (A) factual
    (B) a supposition
    (C) a conclusion based on interpretation of facts
    (D) unrelated to the passage
    (E) based on technical knowledge

8. Why were the Europeans able to spread to all areas of the world?

    (A) because there were too many of them
    (B) because they had navigational knowledge
    (C) because they had superior armies
    (D) because they had superior medical knowledge
    (E) though several theories have been presented, we still don't know

9. There has long been a tradition of Native American firefighters. Although they fight fires all over the United States, most of

them come from the Southwest. They follow in their fathers' footsteps. They have all been trained to protect the reservations but are eager to help elsewhere. They have a natural dedication to preserving the land because of their strong ties to the earth. Natural resources mean more to Native Americans than to most other groups. They make up some of the better firefighting crews, and have a high rate of endurance. In areas where jobs are scarce, the firefighting forces readily attract applicants.

Native American firefighters

(A) feel strongly about preserving nature
(B) are able to withstand the vigors of firefighting
(C) fight fires over a large area
(D) view the job as a good livelihood
(E) all of the above

10. The most prominent piece of sculpture in a city-center mall has disappeared. Various persons have tried to figure what happened to it. Outstanding in the investigation is that most people didn't even notice the sculpture was missing. There is speculation as to what happened to it. It may have been bulldozed accidentally or on purpose.

What is the central idea of the passage?

(A) The sculpture was too small to be noticed.
(B) The sculpture wasn't important to begin with.
(C) The sculpture wasn't noticed to begin with.
(D) Everyone hated it.
(E) People wanted to get rid of it.

Questions 11 to 15

It is too late to start thinking about your retirement on the day you pick up your gold watch, if you are lucky enough to get a gold watch. Regardless of your age, now is the time to figure out how much you will need in order to make your retirement secure, and where that money will come from. When you are in your thirties, start setting priorities for your spending so that your major expenses will be paid off when you retire. For example, buy a house or apartment so that your mortgage will be paid off by the time you leave your job. Try to save at least 5% of your pay, and build an emergency fund equal to three to six months of your living expenses. When you reach 45, try to invest 10% of your income and, if possible, try not to switch jobs until you are fully vested in your pension plan. If you anticipate large college expenses for your children, start savings and investment accounts in their names. In your fifties, try to save ten to fifteen percent of your income. When you reach 60, you may already be collecting your pension. Many companies are encouraging employees to take early retirement. Do your research carefully before deciding to take advantage of this option. Early retirees' pension checks are considerably less than the checks for those who retire at 65. The difference in payments can be substantial. In some cases, retiring at 55, may entitle you to only 25% of the pension you would have received, had you worked until age 65. If you decide to retire early, figure out what you want to do, and whether you can afford to do it. Most retirees need at least 60 to 70 percent of their preretirement salary to maintain their standard of living. Your needs may fall at the lower end of that range if your major outlays such as housing, children's education expenses and medical bills are under control or taken care of. If not, you will need more. If the combination of your pension and social security falls short of your requirements, you will have to make up the difference through savings and investments or a second career.

11. The amount of money you will need for retirement

(A) is the same for everyone
(B) is covered by social security
(C) depends on what your expenses are
(D) can be projected in your thirties
(E) is inflation-proof because it's tax free

12. The amount of money recommended to be set aside for retirement

(A) varies with your age
(B) depends on how much you earn
(C) doesn't take into consideration people's varying retirement expenses
(D) is too conservative
(E) does not allow for inflation

13. The factors which affect your retirement income are

    (A) whether your house is paid for or not
    (B) whether your children are self-suffi-
        cient
    (C) whether you have paid medical insur-
        ance or not
    (D) whether you are vested in your pen-
        sion plan or not
    (E) all of the above

14. The passage could be classified as

    (A) informative
    (B) persuasive
    (C) factual
    (D) biased
    (E) cause and effect

15. According to the passage, early retirement

    (A) should be taken advantage of because
        it extends your enjoyable life span
    (B) affords you the opportunity of a sec-
        ond career
    (C) makes the best use of your earning
        power
    (D) should be carefully checked out
    (E) gives you the option of investing your
        retirement income at your discretion

Questions 16 to 19

A subject that generally is not discussed before marriage is money and how it should be
handled. Many divorced couples will agree that
the way money is handled can break up a marriage. Do happily married couples and those later
divorced differ in how they decide to spend
money? Researchers say, "Yes." A ten-year
study in which couples were regularly inter-
viewed to determine their marital satisfaction and
financial decision-making and consumer behavior agrees. At the end of the ten-year period, one-
sixth of the couples had divorced, while another
one-sixth were happily married. The rest of the
group was dropped from the study because they
did not agree on the status of their relationship.
Allocation of financial responsibility at the beginning of marriage was strongly related to sub-
sequent marital satisfaction. Happily married
couples tend to develop areas of specialization
and greater joint influence or joint decision-

making than couples who were later divorced.
Divorced couples showed more dominance by
the husband and less influence by the wife. Couples who later divorced spent more money on
items such as stereos and color television sets,
while happily married couples spent more money
for homes, furniture, appliances and recreational vehicles—purchases that reflect family
commitment.

16. The factor that did not seem to make a dif-
    ference between happily married couples
    and those who divorced was

    (A) the allocation of fiscal duties
    (B) extent of joint influence on spending
    (C) the extent of dominance in spending
        decisions
    (D) the total amount of income
    (E) the proportion of spending on elec-
        tronic entertainment

17. A factor which is not mentioned as one
    leading to marital satisfaction is

    (A) early decision about which partner will
        be responsible for which expenses
    (B) the extent to which decisions are made
        jointly
    (C) the proportion of money spent on a
        home
    (D) the extent of spending on home enter-
        tainment
    (E) equal dominance of the partners in fis-
        cal decisions

18. What part of the original study group was
    used to draw the conclusions from?

    (A) one-sixth
    (B) one-third
    (C) two-thirds
    (D) five sixths
    (E) all

19. Mabel and Eric have been married for fif-
    teen years. They own a house, a stereo, a
    color television and just put new carpeting
    in their home. Mabel pays for all the gro-
    ceries, her children's clothes, gifts and
    outings. Eric takes care of the rest. Last
    year Eric bought a car without discussing
    it with Mabel, as all major decisions are

made by him. From this we can conclude that

(A) Eric and Mabel are divorced and in the study
(B) Eric and Mabel are happily married and in the study
(C) Eric and Mabel are not in the study because they can't agree on their status
(D) Eric and Mabel will not be married much longer
(E) The information is inconclusive

Questions 20 to 22

Thousands of Americans who return from vacation suffer from a disease known as post-vacation depression. It usually lasts for only one to three weeks. Symptoms include feeling blue, not being able to sleep at night, short-temperedness, and not being able to get going in the morning. What should be done about it? Nothing. There are many theories about the cause of the depression. One psychologist speculates that people feel let down because they had such a good time on vacation and now they find themselves back at work doing something they don't like. Another psychologist says post-vacation depression stems from not being able to complete things before leaving on vacation. Yet another psychologist thinks that many people assume incorrectly that a vacation will resolve problems. Upon returning home, they are disappointed to find the problems are still there.

A vacation can refresh you and improve your outlook, but it can seldom resolve problems which were there before vacation time. Not only are the problems still there, but it will be an extended time before you can get away again. To prevent this, people should try to resolve their problems and get their lives in order before leaving on vacation, and use their vacations as a reward and celebration.

20. The number of theories advanced on the causes of post-vacation depression is

(A) none
(B) one
(C) two
(D) three
(E) four

21. Post-vacation depression is caused by

(A) the contrast between vacation and work
(B) not tying up loose ends before leaving on vacation
(C) disappointment that unresolved problems remain
(D) all of these things
(E) none of these things

22. A vacation can accomplish all of the following *except*

(A) be a reward for hard work
(B) give you rest and relaxation
(C) refresh your outlook on life
(D) be a change of pace and scenery
(E) eliminate problems in your life

Questions 23 and 24

Ancient Greece had a democratic form of government, with all citizens voting on many issues. One issue decided by popular vote was whether or not a person should be banished. Citizens cast their ballots by writing the names of those they thought should be banished on pieces of tile or pottery or oyster shell fragments, called ostrakons. The term of exile was determined by the number of votes cast. Because the names of the people to be banished were written on ostrakons, the people were said to be ostracized.

The modern-day Amish in Pennsylvania have a similar form of punishment, called "shunning." A person who is shunned is not to be acknowledged or spoken to by any member of the community, including immediate family, for the period of time decided upon by the group. Shunning can last from one week to more than a year.

23. Currently, a person who is ostracized is considered to be

(A) voted out of office
(B) socially excluded
(C) unpopular
(D) exiled from the country
(E) a collector of tile, pottery or oyster shell fragments

24. The Amish custom of shunning is

(A) a strong form of peer pressure

(B) considered illegal in the United States
(C) a custom copied from the Greeks
(D) cruel and unusual punishment
(E) a form of brainwashing

Question 25

When you switch your television set to watch a classic movie, like "Casablanca" or "Citizen Kane," you may be surprised to find that the film is in color, courtesy of a new computerized process called colorization. The use of this process is growing, to the chagrin of a large number of people who denounce the vulgarization of some of the best films ever made. The day may come when you will be able to see them only in color. What future generations, growing up only dimly aware that anything but color movies ever existed, will miss is an art form that, as employed by its most skillful directors, conveyed a sense of time, place and mood in a way that color rarely achieves.

25. According to the passage, what is an advantage of black-and-white movies being shown in black and white as opposed to colorized?

(A) They convey a sense of time appropriately.
(B) They set the stage in a special manner.
(C) They interpret the emotions involved sensitively.
(D) all of the above
(E) none of the above

Questions 26 to 28

Where the New Jobs Will Be
(Shown in thousands)

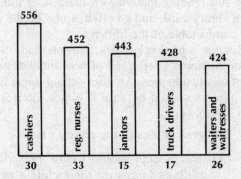

Percent change from 1985

26. What conclusion can be drawn from the graph?

(A) Many more people will need college education.
(B) There will be fewer restaurants and food outlets.
(C) Many jobs will become obsolete due to robotization.
(D) The level of education needed for the majority of new jobs is low.
(E) More people will be sick.

27. Which of the occupations listed already has the largest group of people employed?

(A) cashiers
(B) registered nurses
(C) janitors
(D) truck drivers
(E) waitresses and waiters

28. From the graph what projections can you make about business in 1995?

(A) There will be an increase in the number of retail stores.
(B) The trucking industry will diminish.
(C) The increase in restaurants will be primarily in cafeteria and fast-food types.
(D) Many of the jobs currently done by registered nurses will be taken over by licensed vocational nurses.
(E) Scanners will affect the number of grocery store cashiers.

Questions 29 to 31

Students headed toward many of the state universities this fall were picked from a record number of applicants despite higher tuition and tougher entrance requirements. Many students are driven to state colleges by spiraling private college costs. A student mirrored the current thinking when he said, "I figure I can get as good an education here, and the cost is far less." Out-of-state students also have been hard hit by rising tuition. One state university tripled its out-of-state tuition. Quality is also a lure at many state colleges.

In recent years, thirty-six states have raised their entrance requirements, requiring more English, science, math and language courses. "Since we are a state-supported college with limited enrollment, we have no choice but to increase standards," stated an admissions officer. The average SAT scores for entering freshmen has gone up considerably as a result.

29. To what does the passage attribute the increase in average SAT scores of entering freshmen at state colleges?

   (A) High schools are doing a better job of preparing students for college.
   (B) There are more students trying to get into state colleges, and since the enrollment can't be raised, the competition for the number of places available is more intense.
   (C) The increased costs of attending private schools has made many students change their focus.
   (D) The education at public colleges was poor for many years, but now it is improving.
   (E) Out-of-state tuition has been increased, thereby lessening competition

30. Students are attending state-supported colleges in increasing numbers because of

   I. higher tuition at private colleges
   II. higher out-of-state tuition
   III. quality of the education available at state colleges
   IV. higher SAT scores needed for entrance to state colleges
   V. increase in subject requirements needed for entrance to state colleges

   (A) I, II and III only
   (B) I, II and IV only
   (C) I, IV and V only
   (D) II, IV and V only
   (E) III and V only

31. Based upon the information provided, we can assume that fourteen states

   (A) have lowered their entrance requirements
   (B) have not increased their entrance requirements
   (C) have not changed their entrance requirements
   (D) require lower SAT scores
   (E) require higher SAT scores

Questions 32 to 35

Here are some tips on creating a favorable environment for schoolwork your child must do at home. Be a good role model for your child. Do chores that require thinking in front of your child, such as balancing your checkbook, reading, writing letters or working on a home computer.

A child needs a quiet setting for studying, preferably away from television or other distractions; therefore, you should create a special place for studying. Children should be discouraged from studying in bed.

Keep good research sources handy for your child. It is easier for a child to do homework and check facts if the parents keep a good dictionary, altas, encyclopedia and almanac in the house.

Check your child's homework. Though a child may not bring homework home every night, you should be suspicious if he or she never brings any home.

Show interest in your child's learning by staying in contact with his or her teacher. Ask questions about what he or she is learning at school. The dinner table is an excellent setting for these chats.

Let your child know you're proud of his or her accomplishments, but that mistakes are human. Acknowledge your child's efforts to learn in order to teach that the act of learning is worthwhile. Try not to let your child get too uptight or too relaxed about schoolwork. If a child is overwhelmed or overly anxious, he or she may give up. If he or she is overconfident, the child may not exert the effort necessary to master the subject. Teach self-discipline. Your child needs to learn that work comes before play.

Start reading to your child when he or she is young. When your child is able to read alone, have fun reading material on hand. Get him or her a library card, and go often, so he or she will feel comfortable at the library.

Monitor school schedules. Parents with older children should keep track of how much time is spent on outside jobs. An after-school job is fine, but parents should be sure it is not interfering with schoolwork.

32. The central idea of the passage is

   (A) that parents should follow prescribed outlines to ensure their child's progress

(B) that parents play an important role in their child's educational progress

(C) that parents should be involved in every aspect of their child's life

(D) that parents should read to their child as often as possible

(E) that parents need to invest a lot of money in their children's education

33. In order to create a good atmosphere for a child's learning environment, parents

(A) should follow the suggestions which are appropriate for their family

(B) must follow all the suggestions in the passage

(C) should plan the child's day so there is no free time to get into trouble.

(D) should not let their child have an outside job, as that interferes with studies

(E) should join a parents' support group

34. The format of this passage is

(A) premise and a number of reasons to support it

(B) cause and effect

(C) premise and a listing of examples

(D) chronological sequences

(E) thesis and disproof of antithesis

35. In which area does the passage suggest that parents should try to keep a balance?

(A) self-discipline

(B) study settings

(C) learning efforts

(D) reading

(E) inquiry about schoolwork

36. "The symphony will give a performance tonight at 8 P.M. through Sunday." This sentence

(A) is a concise and accurate statement

(B) is misleading because it gives the impression that the performance will last from 8 P.M. tonight until Sunday.

(C) is misleading because it gives the impression that the symphony will perform at 8 P.M. every evening through Sunday

(D) clarifies that the performance starts at 8 P.M. tonight and goes on until Sunday

(E) makes it clear that the performance is at 8 P.M. each night through Sunday

Questions 37 to 42

Plague in the United States? It's unthinkable! The plague killed millions of people in the Orient, Western Europe and the Americas during the three great pandemics of history. During the second pandemic in the fourteenth century, it was called the Black Plague because the disease darkened the victims' skin just before they died.

There has hardly been a time when the world has been without plague, but there are some areas of the world that have been plague-free so far. It may be that the rodents that carry the plague fleas do not live there. Plague tends to thrive in cool, high altitudes. In the United States it's found in the West and the Southwest. Plague flourishes in host rodents such as rats, squirrels and chipmunks until they die of it, then the fleas move to other living hosts, like cats. Humans usually contract plague by means of a fleabite. Much of the danger comes from the increasing intimacy between creatures and humans. For example, ground squirrels populate parks and accept treats from people, and in the mountains marmots sneak into summer cabins to nest. Since 1970, there have been twenty-five deaths from plague in California. Most deaths occur because victims wait too long to seek medical help and doctors diagnose the disease too late. Plague's symptoms are fever, chills, headache, muscle aches, feeling of weakness, swollen and tender lymph nodes. It is essential to contact a doctor if any of these symptoms develop within seven days of possible exposure to plague.

To avoid plague, the Department of Public Health suggests that you avoid dead or sick animals, especially cats. Deny rodents food and shelter. Put a bell on your cat's collar to minimize its contact with rodents. When camping with pets, confine or leash them to reduce their exposure to rodents. Use flea powder liberally on them. Don't feed rodents in campgrounds and picnic areas. Spray insect repellent on socks and pants' cuffs and tuck trousers into boot tops to reduce exposure to fleas.

37. People can contract plague from

(A) contact with rodents

(B) fleabites

(C) other people who have plague

(D) all of the above

(E) none of the above

38. The first pandemic occurred

 (A) during fourteen hundred B.C.
 (B) before thirteen hundred A.D.
 (C) before fourteen hundred A.D.
 (D) during the fourteen hundreds A.D.
 (E) before fourteen hundred B.C.

39. The third pandemic

 (A) spread over a wide geographic area and affected a high proportion of people
 (B) spread over a small geographic area and affected a high proportion of people
 (C) spread over a small geographic area and affected a small proportion of people
 (D) spread over a wide geographic area and affected a small proportion of people
 (E) caused pandemonium over a wide geographical area

40. To avoid contracting plague, it is suggested that one adhere to all of the following suggestions *except*

 (A) keep your cat on a leash when you take her along camping
 (B) put out feed for the squirrels in your back yard
 (C) don't bury the cat that was killed on the mountain road
 (D) don't feed the chipmunks who come to your picnic table in the park
 (E) use insecticide liberally

41. Rodents mentioned include all of the following *except*

 (A) rats
 (B) squirrels
 (C) lemmings
 (D) chipmunks
 (E) marmots

42. Plague could be found in all of these areas *except*

 (A) China
 (B) Cuba
 (C) Chile

(D) France

(E) Colorado

Questions 43 and 44

More and more women are being elected to political office. Does it really make a difference when a woman, rather than a man, holds office? One woman officeholder said that women have different life experiences that affect them. This means they gravitate toward female, child and family-oriented issues. They learn negotiating skills early and are inclined to avoid conflict and seek amicable solutions to issues. However, a female officeholder can be vulnerable if she does not appear to be strong and decisive. In the seventies, feminist meant ERA and right-to-choose on abortion. Today, post-feminist politics is emerging. The issues are broader—domestic violence, abuse, sexual harassment, comparable worth, pay equity and pension reform. As smart politicians, women increasingly stress mainstream concerns, but they carry with them a special quality of sensitivity to human issues and idealism about how government should work.

43. According to the passage, female politicians are interested in

 (A) issues limited only to their own concerns
 (B) issues limited only to their constituents' concerns
 (C) issues limited only to feminism
 (D) issues limited only to idealisms of government
 (E) issues limited only by their own and their constituents' concerns

44. The main idea of this passage is that

 (A) women officeholders have different views on and stress different issues than men officeholders
 (B) women officeholders and men officeholders approach problems differently
 (C) women officeholders and men officeholders are concerned about different issues
 (D) women and men officeholders represent different constituencies
 (E) women officeholders limit their concern to female-oriented issues

45. Too little fluoride can deprive children of protection against cavities, but too much can cause discoloration of tooth enamel.

Based on the above information, what action should be taken?

(A) Children should not be given fluoride at all.
(B) Children should be given only a moderate amount of fluoride.
(C) Children should be given a generous amount of fluoride.
(D) Children should be given as much fluoride as they can handle.
(E) None of these actions should be taken.

Questions 46 and 47

Thirteen percent of American adults are illiterate. As a result, about nineteen million Americans have difficulty reading want ads, filling out employment applications and reading job instructions.

46. From the above information we can conclude that these people

(A) don't want to work
(B) don't want to learn to read
(C) have a high unemployment rate
(D) are immigrants
(E) are illegal aliens

47. People who are illiterate

(A) learn to compensate for their lack of reading ability
(B) have below-average intelligence
(C) are not willing workers
(D) have not had an opportunity to learn to read
(E) are opposed to education

Questions 48 to 50

One psychologist equates SAT scores with the size of families. As families become larger, the children tend to be less mature intellectually. For the twenty years leading up to 1980, test scores dropped. Since then they have increased, a reflection of the size of the test-takers' families. This trend is expected to continue until the year 2000.

48. Based on the passage, family size

(A) will remain stable over a forty-year period

(B) will start to decrease in 2000
(C) started to decrease in 1960
(D) will decrease until the year 2000
(E) started to decrease in 1975

49. Based upon the information in the passage, SAT test-takers of the year 2000 will

(A) come from a large family and be intellectually mature
(B) come from a small family and be intellectually mature
(C) come from a small family and be intellectually immature
(D) come from a large family and be intellectually immature
(E) have a lower SAT score regardless of family size

50. If the information in the passage were charted, it would look like this.

(A) SAT Scores

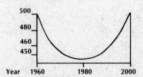

(B) SAT Scores

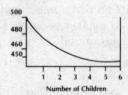

(C) SAT Scores

(D) SAT Scores

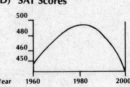

(E) SAT Scores

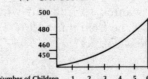

MATHEMATICS

65 Minutes—50 Questions

Directions: **Choose the best answer for each question and blacken the corresponding space on the Answer Sheet for Sample Test 1. The correct answers and explanations follow the test.**

1. What is x if $4x + 7 < -9$?

   (A) $x < 4$
   (B) $x > 4$
   (C) $x < -4$
   (D) $x > -4$
   (E) $x < -\frac{1}{2}$

2. The prime factors of 2310 are

   (A) $10 \times 5 \times 7 \times 11$
   (B) $2 \times 3 \times 5 \times 77$
   (C) $2 \times 15 \times 7 \times 11$
   (D) $2 \times 3 \times 5 \times 7 \times 11$
   (E) $1 \times 2 \times 3 \times 5 \times 7 \times 11$

3. If K represents an odd number and M represents an even number, which of the following statements are odd?

   I. $2K^3 + 3K^2 + K$
   II. $2M^3 + 3M^2 + M$
   III. $M^2 K^2 + MK + K$

   (A) I only
   (B) II only
   (C) III only
   (D) I and III only
   (E) I and II only

4. $7 - 4(3 - 6) =$

   (A) -11
   (B) -9
   (C) 1
   (D) 5
   (E) 19

5. When Richard wanted to find out what percent 32 is of 45, he tried it five different ways. Which one is correct?

   (A) $^{32}/_{45}$

   (B) $^{45}/_{32} \times 100$

   (C) $\dfrac{45 \times 32}{100}$

   (D) $\dfrac{45}{32 \times 100}$

   (E) $\dfrac{32 \times 100}{45}$

6. When public service channel EDUC held its auction, one company offered to match funds with donors. For every $15.00 a donor pledged, the company would donate $13.00. How much did the company give when Paul donated $105.00?

   (A) $13.00
   (B) $28.00
   (C) $90.00
   (D) $91.00
   (E) $120.00

7. If $x^2 = \sqrt{y}$ then $y =$

   (A) x^4
   (B) x
   (C) x^2
   (D) $\sqrt{2}^x$
   (E) y

8. If $P = 7$, find the value of
   $2P^3 + 3P^2 - 4P + 5 =$

   (A) 61
   (B) 180
   (C) 810
   (D) 866
   (E) 3,162

9. $7 \times 10^6 + 6 \times 10^5 + 8 \times 10^4 + 5 \times 10^3 =$

   (A) 7,685
   (B) 76,850
   (C) 768,500
   (D) 76×10^3
   (E) 7.685×10^6

10. $\dfrac{4}{10,000}$ would be written

    (A) 40,000
    (B) 2,500
    (C) 0.004
    (D) 0.0004
    (E) 0.00004

11. $0.0146 \div 0.125 =$

    (A) 0.0117
    (B) 0.117
    (C) 0.8506
    (D) 1.170
    (E) 8.506

12. $8\tfrac{5}{8} \div 6\tfrac{4}{7} =$

    (A) $^{28}/_{1587}$
    (B) $^{16}/_{21}$
    (C) $1^{5}/_{16}$
    (D) $1^{5}/_{56}$
    (E) $9\tfrac{1}{3}$

13. $5a^2 (2a^3 + 6a^2 - a) =$

    (A) $35a^6$
    (B) $10a^6 + 30a^4 + 5a^3$
    (C) $10a^6 + 30a^4 - 5a^2$
    (D) $10a^5 + 30a^4 + 5a^3$
    (E) $10a^5 + 30a^4 - 5a^3$

14. If $2x + y = 9$ and $3x - y = 1$ what is the value of x?

    (A) $^{8}/_{5}$
    (B) 10
    (C) 2
    (D) −4
    (E) 5

Questions 15 and 16

Before the sluice gates of the dam were opened, the level of the reservoir was 8 feet below the normal water level. After the gates had been open for 5 hours, the level was 7 feet above the normal level.

15. How much did the level of the reservoir rise?

    (A) 1 ft
    (B) 5 ft
    (C) 7 ft
    (D) 8 ft
    (E) 15 ft

16. How many feet per hour did the water in the reservoir rise?

    (A) $1\tfrac{3}{5}$ ft per hour
    (B) $\tfrac{5}{7}$ ft per hour
    (C) $1\tfrac{2}{5}$ ft per hour
    (D) $1\tfrac{1}{7}$ ft per hour
    (E) 3 ft per hour

Questions 17 and 18

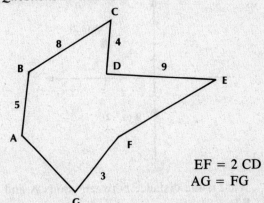

EF = 2 CD
AG = FG

17. What is the perimeter of the enclosed area?

    (A) 40
    (B) 36
    (C) 37
    (D) 32
    (E) 29

18. What is the area of the enclosed figure?

    (A) 58
    (B) 37
    (C) 64
    (D) 40
    (E) not enough information

19.

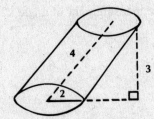

The volume of a cylinder is $\pi r^2 \times$ altitude. What is the volume of the cylinder on the bottom of p. 125?

(A) 12π
(B) 16π
(C) 18π
(D) 24π
(E) 32π

20.

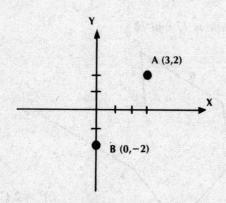

What is the distance between points A and B?

(A) 5
(B) 4
(C) 0
(D) 3
(E) −5

21.

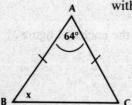

ABC is an isosceles triangle with AB = AC.

What is the measurement of angle x?

(A) 64°
(B) 60°
(C) 58°
(D) 116°
(E) 32°

22.

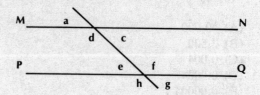

Lines MN and PQ are parallel. Which angles are equal?

(A) a, b and c
(B) a, c, e and g
(C) a, d, e, and h
(D) a, c, f and g
(E) b, d, e and f

23.

S	M	T	W	Th	F	S
9	10	11	12	13	14	15
16	17	18	19	20	21	22

Susan can see only part of her calendar. On which day of the week was the first of the month shown?

(A) Wednesday
(B) Thursday
(C) Friday
(D) Saturday
(E) Sunday

Questions 24 and 25

$$\tfrac{1}{3} \times \tfrac{4}{9} \times \tfrac{7}{6} \times \tfrac{18}{21} \times \tfrac{15}{24} =$$

24. When Sharon tried to do this problem, she found the multiplication difficult. She thought there might be an easier way. Is there?

(A) Yes, add the numerators and divide by the sum of the denominators.
(B) No, you must multiply the numerators and divide by the product of the denominators.
(C) Yes, numerators and denominators can be canceled.
(D) Yes, multiply the first two fractions, then multiply that product by the next fraction, and so on.

(E) Yes, find a common denominator, add the first two fractions, reduce, then add it to the next fraction, and so on.

25. The answer to the problem in the box is

    (A) $^{44}/_{63}$
    (B) $^{5}/_{81}$
    (C) $^{28}/_{39}$
    (D) $^{1}/_{9}$
    (E) $^{5}/_{54}$

26. To determine what part 18 is of 81, you would use which of the following expressions?

    (A) $18 \div 81$
    (B) $81 \div 18$
    (C) $(18 \div 81) \times 100$
    (D) $(81 \div 18) \times 100$
    (E) none of these

27. $\dfrac{\sqrt{1600}}{\sqrt{64}} =$

    (A) 5
    (B) 7
    (C) 25
    (D) 50
    (E) cannot be solved

28. A right triangle may have

    (A) three right angles
    (B) two right angles
    (C) all sides of equal length
    (D) two angles of equal measure
    (E) one angle greater than a right angle

29. $^{3}/_{5}$ changed to a decimal is

    (A) 3.5
    (B) 0.60
    (C) 0.06
    (D) 5.3
    (E) 0.35

30. Jill and two friends bought a lottery ticket together. Jill's share was 28%. When the ticket won, she got $70.00. What was the full amount of the winnings?

    (A) $19.60
    (B) $196.00

(C) $142.00
(D) $98.00
(E) $250.00

31.

(not drawn to scale)

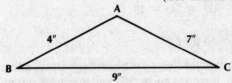

The smallest angle is

    (A) $\angle ABC$
    (B) $\angle CBA$
    (C) $\angle BCA$
    (D) $\angle BAC$
    (E) $\angle CAB$

32. $^{1}/_{8} + ^{1}/_{6}$

The least common denominator for the above problem is

    (A) 24
    (B) 48
    (C) 8
    (D) 6
    (E) $^{7}/_{24}$

33. Grandfather gave the children a riddle. "I am 60 years old. I am 4 years younger than 8 times Sally's age. How old is Sally?" What is the answer to the riddle?

    (A) 7
    (B) 7.5
    (C) 8
    (D) 15
    (E) 30

34. $10 - 6 [3 \times 4 - (7 - 3)^2 + 12 \div 6] =$

The first step in this problem would be

    (A) $10 - 6 [12 - (7 - 3)^2 + 12 \div 6] =$
    (B) $10 - 6 \times 3 \times 4 - (7 - 3)^2 + 2 =$
    (C) $4 [3 \times 4 - (7 - 3)^2 + 12 \div 6] =$
    (D) $10 - 6 [12 - 4^2 + 2] =$
    (E) $10 - 6 [3 \times 4 - 4^2 + 12 \div 6] =$

35. $(4a + 6)(2a + 3) =$

    (A) $6a + 18$
    (B) $6a^2 + 18$
    (C) $8a^2 + 12a + 18$
    (D) $8a^2 + 18$
    (E) $8a^2 + 24a + 18$

Questions 36 and 37

Jonathan bought items at the grocery store, some of which were taxed at 5% and some of which were not taxed. He bought a candy bar for 35 cents (taxable), two pencils at 20 cents each (taxable), three apples at 17 cents each (nontaxable) and a note pad (taxable) for $1.69.

36. How much tax did Jonathan pay?

    (A) 11 cents
    (B) 12 cents
    (C) 13 cents
    (D) 14 cents
    (E) 15 cents

37. How much did Jonathan pay altogether?

    (A) $2.53
    (B) $2.56
    (C) $2.86
    (D) $3.07
    (E) $3.10

38. $3K^2 - 4K + 7 - 2K^2 =$

    (A) $K^2 - 4K + 7$
    (B) $-4 + 7$
    (C) $6K^2 - 4K + 7$
    (D) $-6K^4 - 4K + 7$
    (E) $-3K^5 + 7$

39.

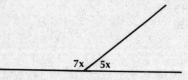

How big is the larger angle?

    (A) $10°$
    (B) $52°$
    (C) $56°$
    (D) $105°$
    (E) $120°$

40. The temperature on Sunday rose from 51°F to 86°F. What was the high temperature in Centigrade?

    (A) 16°C
    (B) 30°C
    (C) 35°C
    (D) 51°C
    (E) 86°C

41. 84, 81, 85, 87, 86, 89, 79, 93, 89

Of the above list of numbers, 86 is the

    (A) mode
    (B) range
    (C) median
    (D) mean
    (E) deviation

42. Eggs are packed in crates which hold 7 rows of 6 eggs in each layer, with a total of 5 layers. If the average breakage rate is 1.9%, on the average how many eggs are broken per crate?

    (A) 2
    (B) 4
    (C) 5
    (D) 6
    (E) 7

43. Paul bought 2½ lbs. of candy at 69 cents per pound and 2½ pounds at 89 cents per pound. How much did he pay for all of the candy?

    (A) $1.73
    (B) $2.23
    (C) $3.55
    (D) $3.95
    (E) $4.45

44. Brian had lost one test, but has scores of 76, 78, 81 and 96 on the others. His teacher says his average on the five tests is 83. When he tried to figure out the score on the missing test

    (A) he got an answer of 81
    (B) he got an answer of 82
    (C) he got an answer of 83
    (D) he got an answer of 84
    (E) he found it couldn't be done

45. It was discount day at Great Day Market. Mrs. Swanson bought $69.50 of groceries, on which she got a 12% discount. How much did she pay for her groceries?

    (A) $8.34
    (B) $61.16
    (C) $69.50
    (D) $68.67
    (E) $77.84

46. Twelve posters can be purchased for $13.80. How many posters can Shannon buy if she has $5.00?

    (A) one
    (B) two
    (C) three
    (D) four
    (E) five

47. An elementary school's enrollment of 300 consisted of 45% girls. Then 150 more girls were enrolled. Which of the following cannot be calculated from this information?

    (A) the total percentage of boys after the addition of 150 girls
    (B) the original number of boys
    (C) the total number of girls
    (D) how many students were first graders
    (E) the percentage of girls after the 150 girls enrolled

48. Rob holds a compass pointing NW. If he rotates it 225° clockwise, in which direction will it point?

    (A) S
    (B) SE

(C) E
(D) NE
(E) SW

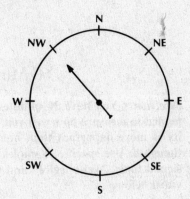

49. Sean took out a $10,000.00 loan at the credit union to buy a new car. The loan was for six years at 11.5% interest. What is the total interest paid by Sean?

    (A) $1,150.00
    (B) $6,900.00
    (C) $10,000.00
    (D) $11,000.00
    (E) $16,900.00

50. Sean had a chance to get the same $10,000 loan for the car at 10.5% interest for eight years. Which of the two loans would result in the least total interest paid?

    (A) same
    (B) 11.5% for six years
    (C) 10.5% for eight years
    (D) not enough information
    (E) 11.5% for eight years

WRITING
60 Minutes—Two Essays

Directions: You have 30 minutes for each of two essays. The essay topics are intended to measure how well you write, given limitations on time and subject. Quality is more important than quantity. Spend some of your time organizing your thoughts. Use specific examples to support your opinions. Write only on the assigned topic. Write legibly and within the lines provided. Space for notes is provided below.

Topic A
A good teacher needs more than a teaching credential and knowledge of his subject. Good teachers have special qualities that make them stand out. What special quality or qualities do you have which make you a good teacher? Tell about these qualities and how your having them makes you a better teacher.

Topic B
An increasing number of states are requiring that candidates pass teacher competency tests to get a teaching credential. It has been suggested that the same test should be used in each state. State why you agree or disagree with this suggestion.

TOPIC A

TOPIC B

ANSWERS TO SAMPLE TEST 2

READING

1.	E	11.	C	21.	D	31.	B	41.	C
2.	C	12.	A	22.	E	32.	B	42.	B
3.	C	13.	E	23.	B	33.	A	43.	E
4.	D	14.	B	24.	A	34.	C	44.	A
5.	E	15.	D	25.	D	35.	C	45.	B
6.	A	16.	D	26.	D	36.	B	46.	C
7.	C	17.	D	27.	C	37.	D	47.	A
8.	E	18.	B	28.	A	38.	B	48.	D
9.	E	19.	E	29.	B	39.	A	49.	B
10.	C	20.	D	30.	A	40.	B	50.	A

MATHEMATICS

1.	C	11.	B	21.	C	31.	C	41.	C
2.	D	12.	C	22.	B	32.	A	42.	B
3.	C	13.	E	23.	D	33.	C	43.	D
4.	E	14.	C	24.	C	34.	E	44.	D
5.	E	15.	E	25.	E	35.	E	45.	B
6.	D	16.	E	26.	A	36.	B	46.	D
7.	A	17.	A	27.	A	37.	D	47.	D
8.	C	18.	E	28.	D	38.	A	48.	A
9.	E	19.	A	29.	B	39.	D	49.	B
10.	D	20.	A	30.	E	40.	B	50.	B

EXPLANATIONS OF ANSWERS TO SAMPLE TEST 2

READING

1. **E** Cardiopulmonary resuscitation is for children ten or older.

2. **C** Higher maternal employment rate.

3. **C** Last sentence.

4. **D** "Participated in more recreational activities."

5. **E** Last sentence.

6. **A** First sentence.

7. **C** That Europeans brought communicable disease with them is factual, but the conclusion is an interpretation of that fact.

8. **E** The passage mentions several possible reasons but does not settle upon one answer.

9. **E** All are mentioned in the passage.

10. **C** If people didn't notice the loss of the sculpture, they probably didn't notice it before it was gone.

11. **C** If your house and other major expenses are taken care of, you will need less money for retirement.

12. **A** The passage suggests setting aside 5% of your income at age 30, 10% at age 45, and 10–15% at age 55.

13. **E** All are mentioned in the passage.

14. **B** The article is trying to persuade you to save money for retirement.

15. **D** Early retirement may give you considerably less income.

16. **D** Amount of income is not mentioned.

17. **D** Divorced couples spend a larger amount on television and stereos.

18. **B** One-sixth of the group was divorced and one-sixth was happily married, making a total of one-third of the original group.

19. **E** The information doesn't point strongly one way or another.

20. **D** Three theories are given.

21. **D** All three causes are mentioned in the passage.

22. **E** Problems you left behind will still be there. The others are all listed as benefits.

23. **B** Currently, the banishment is social.

24. **A** The punishment is decided on and carried out by one's peers.

25. **D** All reasons are listed in the passage.

26. **D** Of the jobs shown, only nursing requires college education.

27. **C** Janitors will increase almost as much as cashiers, but only represents a 15% increase, compared to a 30% increase in cashiers.

28. **A** Since the greatest increase in jobs will be in cashiers, that must mean that there will be more stores.

29. **B** Last paragraph.

30. **A** IV and V are not reasons for attending state-supported colleges.

31. **B** Thirty-six states have increased their requirements.

32. **B** All of the suggestions discuss the parents' involvement. A is too rigid; C is overdoing it.

33. **A** Common sense leads to A.

34. **C** The passage is a list of suggestions on how

parents can improve their child's learning environment.

35. **C** "Try not to let your child get too uptight or too relaxed about schoolwork."

36. **B** The sentence is unclear. It seems that the symphony will put on a marathon performance, which isn't likely.

37. **D** All are possible sources of contagion.

38. **B** If the second pandemic was in the fourteenth century, the first occurred before that.

39. **A** A pandemic is spread over a wide geographic area and affects a high proportion of its people.

40. **B** Don't feed rodents.

41. **C** Lemmings live in the Arctic.

42. **B** Cuba is not cool and does not have high altitudes.

43. **E** There are no particular limits to their concerns.

44. **A** Because of a difference in their perspective, women officeholders have views different from those of men officeholders.

45. **B** Some fluoride is fine, but not too much.

46. **C** If the people have difficulty reading want ads, and application forms, they have difficulty getting into the job market. Eliminate the others.

47. **A** They compensate so well that most people are unaware that they know illiterates. Eliminate the others.

48. **D** Scores will continue to go up; therefore, families will decrease in size according to the reasoning expressed in the passage.

49. **B** Families will have fewer but more intellectually mature children.

50. **A** Graph (A) mirrors the information in the passage.

MATHEMATICS

1. **C**
$$4x + 7 < -9$$
$$\underline{\quad -7 \quad -7 \quad}$$
$$4x \quad < \quad -16$$
$$\frac{4x}{4} < -\frac{-16}{4}$$
$$x < -4$$

2. **D** Eliminate before factoring.
   (A) 10 is not a prime number.
   (B) 77 is not a prime number.
   (C) 15 is not a prime number.
   (D) All are primes.
   (E) 1 is not a prime.

   The answer must be (D).

3. **C.** Remember: $E \times O = E \qquad E + O = O$
   $$O \times O = O \qquad E + E = E$$
   $$E \times E = E \qquad O + O = E$$

   I. $\underset{\text{Even}}{E \times O \times O \times O} + \underset{\text{Odd}}{O \times O \times O} + \underset{\text{Odd}}{O} = \text{Even}$

   II. $\underset{\text{Even}}{2 \times E \times E \times E} + \underset{\text{Even}}{O \times E \times E} + \underset{\text{Even}}{E} = \text{Even}$

   III. $\underset{\text{Even}}{O \times O \times E \times E} + \underset{\text{Even}}{O \times E} + \underset{\text{Odd}}{O} = \text{Odd}$

4. **E** $7 - 4(3 - 6) =$
   $7 - 4(-3) =$
   $7 - (-12) =$
   $7 + 12 = 19$

5. **E** $\dfrac{\text{is}}{\text{of}} \times 100 = \dfrac{32}{45} \times 100$

6. **D** It will be close to, but less than what Paul donated. This eliminates A and B (too small) and E (too big).
   $$\frac{13}{15} = \frac{x}{105}$$
   $$13 \times 105 = 15x$$
   $$\frac{13 \times 105}{15} = x$$
   $$\$91.00 = x$$

7. **A** $x^2 = \sqrt{y}$

   To find y, square $\sqrt{y}$
   $(\sqrt{y})^2 = (x^2)^2$
   $y = x^4$

8. **C** $2(7)^3 + 3(7)^2 - 4(7) + 5 =$
   $2(343) + 3(49) - 28 + 5 =$
   $686 + 147 - 28 + 5 = 810$

9. **E**
$$7 \times 10^6 = 7,000,000$$
$$6 \times 10^5 = 600,000$$
$$8 \times 10^4 = 80,000$$
$$5 \times 10^3 = \underline{5,000}$$
$$7,685,000$$

A, B and C are too small. Check E $7.685 \times 10^6 = 7,685,000$

10. **D** $\dfrac{4}{10} = .4$

$\dfrac{4}{100} = .04$

$\dfrac{4}{1,000} = .004$

$\dfrac{4}{10,000} = .0004$

11. **B** $0.125\overline{)0.0146}$
Move decimals three places to the right.

$$
\begin{array}{r}
.117 \\
125\overline{)14.600} \\
\underline{125} \\
210 \\
\underline{125} \\
850 \\
875
\end{array}
$$

12. **C**   Estimate $9 \div 7 = 1+$. Eliminate A, B and E.
$$8\tfrac{5}{8} \div 6\tfrac{4}{7} =$$

$\dfrac{69}{8} \div \dfrac{46}{7} =$

$\dfrac{69}{8} \times \dfrac{7}{46} =$

$\dfrac{3}{8} \times \dfrac{7}{2} = \dfrac{21}{16} = 1\tfrac{5}{16}$

13. **E** $5a^2(2a^3 + 6a^2 - a) =$
$5a^2(2a^3) + 5a^2(6a^2) + 5a^2(-a) =$
$10a^5 + 30a^4 - 5a^3$

14. **C**
$$
\begin{array}{r}
2x + y = 9 \\
\text{Add } \underline{3x - y = 1} \\
5x = 10 \\
x = 2
\end{array}
$$

15. **E**   It was 8 feet to the normal level plus 7 feet above the normal level for a total of 15 feet.

16. **E** $\dfrac{15 \text{ ft.}}{5 \text{ hrs.}} = 3$ ft. per hour

17. **A**
$$
\begin{array}{rl}
AB &= 5 \\
BC &= 8 \\
CD &= 4 \\
DE &= 9 \\
EF &= 8 \ (2 \times 4) \\
FG &= 3 \\
GA &= \underline{3} \\
& 40
\end{array}
$$

18. **E**   There is not enough information.

19. **A**   3 is the altitude.
$$V = \pi r^2 h$$
$$V = \pi 2^2 \cdot 3$$
$$V = \pi 4 \cdot 3$$
$$V = 12\pi$$

20. **A**   Distance is always positive. Eliminate C, E. This is simply a right triangle problem. Construct a right triangle. The distance between A and B is the hypotenuse of the triangle. Use the Pythagorean Theorem to find its length.

$$a^2 + b^2 = c^2$$
$$4^2 + 3^2 = c^2$$
$$16 + 9 = c^2$$
$$25 = c^2$$
$$5 = c$$

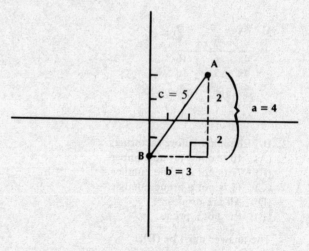

21. **C** $\angle B = \angle C$ (in an isosceles triangle, angles opposite equal sides are equal.)
$\angle B + \angle C = 2x$

$2x + 64° = 180°$
(The sum of the angles in a triangle = $180°$)
$2x = 180° - 64°$
$2x = 116°$
$x = 58°$

22. **B** a = c = e = g
            b = d = f = h

23. **D**

S	M	T	W	Th	F	S
						1
2	3	4	5	6	7	8
9	10	11	12	13	14	15
16	17	18	19	20	21	22

24. **C**

$$\frac{1}{\cancel{3}} \times \frac{\cancel{4}}{\cancel{9}_{3}} \times \frac{\cancel{7}}{\cancel{8}} \times \frac{\cancel{18}^{\cancel{3}}}{\cancel{21}_{3}} \times \frac{\cancel{15}^{5}}{\cancel{24}_{6}} =$$

25. **E** $^{5}/_{54}$

26. **A** $\dfrac{is}{of} = \dfrac{18}{81}$ or $18 \div 81$

27. **A** $\dfrac{\sqrt{1600} = 40}{\sqrt{64} = 8} = \dfrac{40}{8} = 5$

28. **D**

Eliminate.

29. **B** .60
            5)3.00

30. **E**
% $
$$\frac{28}{100} = \frac{70}{x}$$

28x = 7,000

x = $250.00

31. **C** The sizes of the angles of a triangle correspond to their opposite sides. The largest angle is opposite the largest side and the smallest angle is opposite the smallest side. Since side AB is smallest, the angle at C ($\angle$BCA) is smallest.

32. **A** The LCD is the least number both denominators, 8 and 6, will divide into evenly. Eliminate E.

8 = 2 × 2 × 2
6 = 2 × 3
LCD = 2 × 2 × 2 × 3 = 24
Or you can try each of the answers.

33. **C** 8S − 4 = 60
            + 4   +4
            8S =   64
             S =   8

34. **E** The first step in multiple operations is to do the operation in the innermost bracket.
$(7 - 3)^2 = 4^2$

$10 - 6[3 \times 4 - (7 - 3)^2 + 12 \div 6] =$
$10 - 6[3 \times 4 - 4^2 + 12 \div 6]$

35. **E**
          4a + 6
          2a + 3
        12a + 18
       8a² + 12a
    8a² + 24a + 18

36. **B**

Candy bar	$ .35
Pencils	.20
	.20
Note pad	1.69
	$2.44
Tax	× .05
	$.1220 = 12 Cents

37. **D** See the solution for question 36.

Candy, Pencils, Note Pad	$2.44
Tax	.12
3 Apples × 17 Cents	.51
	$3.07

38. **A** 3K² − 4K + 7 − 2K² =
            3K² − 2K² − 4K + 7 =
            K² − 4K + 7

39. **D** 7x + 5x = 12x
            12x = 180°
            x = 15°
            7x = 105°

40. **B** °F → °C is smaller
$\frac{5}{9}(°F - °32) = C$
$\frac{5}{9}(86 - 32) =$
$\frac{5}{9}(54) = 5 \times 6 = 30°C$
or approximately $\dfrac{°F - 30}{2} = \dfrac{86 - 30}{2} = \dfrac{56}{2} = 28°C$

41. **C** When the numbers are arranged according to size, the median is the middle number.

42. **B** $6 \times 7 \times 5 = 210$ Total Eggs Per Crate
$210 \times 0.019 = 3.99 = 4$ Eggs Broken
—or estimate

43. **D**   He bought the same of each, so it's the same as if he had bought 5 pounds at the average price.
$\dfrac{(69 + 89)}{2} = 79$ Cents Per Pound
$5 \times 79 = \$3.95$
or $2\frac{1}{2} \times 69 = \$1.725$
$2\frac{1}{2} \times 89 = \underline{\quad 2.225}$
$\overline{\$3.950} = \$3.95$
approximate $5 \times 80 = \$4.00$

44. **D** $\qquad 5 \times 83 = 415$ Total Points
$76 + 78 + 81 + 96 = \underline{331}$
Subtract $415 - 331 = \overline{\quad 84}$ The Missing Score

45. **B** $\$69.50 \times .12 = \$8.34$ discount
$\$69.50 - \$8.34 = \$61.16$

46. **D** $\$13.80 \div 12 = \$1.15$ Each
$\$5.00 \div 1.15 = 4^{40}/_{115}$
Estimate—It costs more than $1.00 per poster, so she can't buy 5.

47. **D**   Underline "CANNOT be calculated." Grade enrollment is not mentioned. All the others can be worked out.

48. **A**   There are 360° in a circle, and it is divided into 8 parts.
$360 \div 8 = 45°$ in each section
$225 \div 45 = 5$
5 sections clockwise to the South.

49. **B**   Estimate: $11\% \times 6 = 66\%$ of $10,000.00 equals more than half of $10,000.00, which is more than $5,000.00.
Interest = Principal × Rate × Time
$I = \$10,000 \times .115 \times 6 = \$6,900.00$

50. **B** $I = P \times R \times T$
$= \$10,000 \times 10.5\% \times 8$
$= \$10,000 \times .105 \times 8$
$= \$8,400.00$

Sean will pay $1,500 less in total interest at 11.5% for 6 years.

ANSWER SHEET FOR SAMPLE TEST 3

SECTION I. READING

1 Ⓐ Ⓑ Ⓒ Ⓓ Ⓔ	8 Ⓐ Ⓑ Ⓒ Ⓓ Ⓔ	15 Ⓐ Ⓑ Ⓒ Ⓓ Ⓔ	22 Ⓐ Ⓑ Ⓒ Ⓓ Ⓔ	29 Ⓐ Ⓑ Ⓒ Ⓓ Ⓔ	36 Ⓐ Ⓑ Ⓒ Ⓓ Ⓔ
2 Ⓐ Ⓑ Ⓒ Ⓓ Ⓔ	9 Ⓐ Ⓑ Ⓒ Ⓓ Ⓔ	16 Ⓐ Ⓑ Ⓒ Ⓓ Ⓔ	23 Ⓐ Ⓑ Ⓒ Ⓓ Ⓔ	30 Ⓐ Ⓑ Ⓒ Ⓓ Ⓔ	37 Ⓐ Ⓑ Ⓒ Ⓓ Ⓔ
3 Ⓐ Ⓑ Ⓒ Ⓓ Ⓔ	10 Ⓐ Ⓑ Ⓒ Ⓓ Ⓔ	17 Ⓐ Ⓑ Ⓒ Ⓓ Ⓔ	24 Ⓐ Ⓑ Ⓒ Ⓓ Ⓔ	31 Ⓐ Ⓑ Ⓒ Ⓓ Ⓔ	38 Ⓐ Ⓑ Ⓒ Ⓓ Ⓔ
4 Ⓐ Ⓑ Ⓒ Ⓓ Ⓔ	11 Ⓐ Ⓑ Ⓒ Ⓓ Ⓔ	18 Ⓐ Ⓑ Ⓒ Ⓓ Ⓔ	25 Ⓐ Ⓑ Ⓒ Ⓓ Ⓔ	32 Ⓐ Ⓑ Ⓒ Ⓓ Ⓔ	39 Ⓐ Ⓑ Ⓒ Ⓓ Ⓔ
5 Ⓐ Ⓑ Ⓒ Ⓓ Ⓔ	12 Ⓐ Ⓑ Ⓒ Ⓓ Ⓔ	19 Ⓐ Ⓑ Ⓒ Ⓓ Ⓔ	26 Ⓐ Ⓑ Ⓒ Ⓓ Ⓔ	33 Ⓐ Ⓑ Ⓒ Ⓓ Ⓔ	40 Ⓐ Ⓑ Ⓒ Ⓓ Ⓔ
6 Ⓐ Ⓑ Ⓒ Ⓓ Ⓔ	13 Ⓐ Ⓑ Ⓒ Ⓓ Ⓔ	20 Ⓐ Ⓑ Ⓒ Ⓓ Ⓔ	27 Ⓐ Ⓑ Ⓒ Ⓓ Ⓔ	34 Ⓐ Ⓑ Ⓒ Ⓓ Ⓔ	
7 Ⓐ Ⓑ Ⓒ Ⓓ Ⓔ	14 Ⓐ Ⓑ Ⓒ Ⓓ Ⓔ	21 Ⓐ Ⓑ Ⓒ Ⓓ Ⓔ	28 Ⓐ Ⓑ Ⓒ Ⓓ Ⓔ	35 Ⓐ Ⓑ Ⓒ Ⓓ Ⓔ	

SECTION II. MATHEMATICS

1 Ⓐ Ⓑ Ⓒ Ⓓ Ⓔ	8 Ⓐ Ⓑ Ⓒ Ⓓ Ⓔ	15 Ⓐ Ⓑ Ⓒ Ⓓ Ⓔ	22 Ⓐ Ⓑ Ⓒ Ⓓ Ⓔ	29 Ⓐ Ⓑ Ⓒ Ⓓ Ⓔ	36 Ⓐ Ⓑ Ⓒ Ⓓ Ⓔ
2 Ⓐ Ⓑ Ⓒ Ⓓ Ⓔ	9 Ⓐ Ⓑ Ⓒ Ⓓ Ⓔ	16 Ⓐ Ⓑ Ⓒ Ⓓ Ⓔ	23 Ⓐ Ⓑ Ⓒ Ⓓ Ⓔ	30 Ⓐ Ⓑ Ⓒ Ⓓ Ⓔ	37 Ⓐ Ⓑ Ⓒ Ⓓ Ⓔ
3 Ⓐ Ⓑ Ⓒ Ⓓ Ⓔ	10 Ⓐ Ⓑ Ⓒ Ⓓ Ⓔ	17 Ⓐ Ⓑ Ⓒ Ⓓ Ⓔ	24 Ⓐ Ⓑ Ⓒ Ⓓ Ⓔ	31 Ⓐ Ⓑ Ⓒ Ⓓ Ⓔ	38 Ⓐ Ⓑ Ⓒ Ⓓ Ⓔ
4 Ⓐ Ⓑ Ⓒ Ⓓ Ⓔ	11 Ⓐ Ⓑ Ⓒ Ⓓ Ⓔ	18 Ⓐ Ⓑ Ⓒ Ⓓ Ⓔ	25 Ⓐ Ⓑ Ⓒ Ⓓ Ⓔ	32 Ⓐ Ⓑ Ⓒ Ⓓ Ⓔ	39 Ⓐ Ⓑ Ⓒ Ⓓ Ⓔ
5 Ⓐ Ⓑ Ⓒ Ⓓ Ⓔ	12 Ⓐ Ⓑ Ⓒ Ⓓ Ⓔ	19 Ⓐ Ⓑ Ⓒ Ⓓ Ⓔ	26 Ⓐ Ⓑ Ⓒ Ⓓ Ⓔ	33 Ⓐ Ⓑ Ⓒ Ⓓ Ⓔ	40 Ⓐ Ⓑ Ⓒ Ⓓ Ⓔ
6 Ⓐ Ⓑ Ⓒ Ⓓ Ⓔ	13 Ⓐ Ⓑ Ⓒ Ⓓ Ⓔ	20 Ⓐ Ⓑ Ⓒ Ⓓ Ⓔ	27 Ⓐ Ⓑ Ⓒ Ⓓ Ⓔ	34 Ⓐ Ⓑ Ⓒ Ⓓ Ⓔ	
7 Ⓐ Ⓑ Ⓒ Ⓓ Ⓔ	14 Ⓐ Ⓑ Ⓒ Ⓓ Ⓔ	21 Ⓐ Ⓑ Ⓒ Ⓓ Ⓔ	28 Ⓐ Ⓑ Ⓒ Ⓓ Ⓔ	35 Ⓐ Ⓑ Ⓒ Ⓓ Ⓔ	

SECTION III. WRITING

1 Ⓐ Ⓑ Ⓒ Ⓓ Ⓔ	9 Ⓐ Ⓑ Ⓒ Ⓓ Ⓔ	17 Ⓐ Ⓑ Ⓒ Ⓓ Ⓔ	25 Ⓐ Ⓑ Ⓒ Ⓓ Ⓔ	33 Ⓐ Ⓑ Ⓒ Ⓓ Ⓔ	41 Ⓐ Ⓑ Ⓒ Ⓓ Ⓔ
2 Ⓐ Ⓑ Ⓒ Ⓓ Ⓔ	10 Ⓐ Ⓑ Ⓒ Ⓓ Ⓔ	18 Ⓐ Ⓑ Ⓒ Ⓓ Ⓔ	26 Ⓐ Ⓑ Ⓒ Ⓓ Ⓔ	34 Ⓐ Ⓑ Ⓒ Ⓓ Ⓔ	42 Ⓐ Ⓑ Ⓒ Ⓓ Ⓔ
3 Ⓐ Ⓑ Ⓒ Ⓓ Ⓔ	11 Ⓐ Ⓑ Ⓒ Ⓓ Ⓔ	19 Ⓐ Ⓑ Ⓒ Ⓓ Ⓔ	27 Ⓐ Ⓑ Ⓒ Ⓓ Ⓔ	35 Ⓐ Ⓑ Ⓒ Ⓓ Ⓔ	43 Ⓐ Ⓑ Ⓒ Ⓓ Ⓔ
4 Ⓐ Ⓑ Ⓒ Ⓓ Ⓔ	12 Ⓐ Ⓑ Ⓒ Ⓓ Ⓔ	20 Ⓐ Ⓑ Ⓒ Ⓓ Ⓔ	28 Ⓐ Ⓑ Ⓒ Ⓓ Ⓔ	36 Ⓐ Ⓑ Ⓒ Ⓓ Ⓔ	44 Ⓐ Ⓑ Ⓒ Ⓓ Ⓔ
5 Ⓐ Ⓑ Ⓒ Ⓓ Ⓔ	13 Ⓐ Ⓑ Ⓒ Ⓓ Ⓔ	21 Ⓐ Ⓑ Ⓒ Ⓓ Ⓔ	29 Ⓐ Ⓑ Ⓒ Ⓓ Ⓔ	37 Ⓐ Ⓑ Ⓒ Ⓓ Ⓔ	45 Ⓐ Ⓑ Ⓒ Ⓓ Ⓔ
6 Ⓐ Ⓑ Ⓒ Ⓓ Ⓔ	14 Ⓐ Ⓑ Ⓒ Ⓓ Ⓔ	22 Ⓐ Ⓑ Ⓒ Ⓓ Ⓔ	30 Ⓐ Ⓑ Ⓒ Ⓓ Ⓔ	38 Ⓐ Ⓑ Ⓒ Ⓓ Ⓔ	
7 Ⓐ Ⓑ Ⓒ Ⓓ Ⓔ	15 Ⓐ Ⓑ Ⓒ Ⓓ Ⓔ	23 Ⓐ Ⓑ Ⓒ Ⓓ Ⓔ	31 Ⓐ Ⓑ Ⓒ Ⓓ Ⓔ	39 Ⓐ Ⓑ Ⓒ Ⓓ Ⓔ	
8 Ⓐ Ⓑ Ⓒ Ⓓ Ⓔ	16 Ⓐ Ⓑ Ⓒ Ⓓ Ⓔ	24 Ⓐ Ⓑ Ⓒ Ⓓ Ⓔ	32 Ⓐ Ⓑ Ⓒ Ⓓ Ⓔ	40 Ⓐ Ⓑ Ⓒ Ⓓ Ⓔ	

SAMPLE TEST 3
(PPST)

This test is similar to the Pre-Professional Skills Tests (PPST) used in Delaware, Kansas, Minnesota, Nebraska, Nevada, and Wisconsin. The Reading, Mathematics, and Essay sections are also useful practice for the California Basic Educational Skills Test (CBEST) required for teacher certification in California and Oregon. The PPST can also help to prepare candidates for the teacher certification tests administered by Colorado, Connecticut, Illinois, Michigan, and South Carolina.

Format of the PPST

Reading	40 questions	40 minutes
Mathematics	40 questions	50 minutes

——————————————— *Break* ———————————————

Writing	40 questions	30 minutes
	one essay	30 minutes

Scoring the test

Separate scores are reported for each of the three tests. Reading and Mathematics scores are based on the number of questions answered correctly. No deductions are made for incorrect answers, so it pays to answer every question even if you have to take a wild guess. The Writing score is a composite score which is scaled to give equal weight to the multiple-choice and the essay sections. Currently, PPST scores are reported on a scale of 150 to 190.

SECTION I. READING
40 Minutes—40 Questions

Directions: **Each statement or passage is followed by one or more questions based on its content. After reading the statement or passage, choose the best answer for each question and blacken the corresponding space on the Answer Sheet for Sample Test 3. The correct answers and explanations follow the test.**

Questions 1 to 3

Who has the better memory, men or women? The answer depends on what is being recalled. Women excel in verbal memory—the recall of words, information, writing and faces. Men excel in spatial memory—in recalling landmarks, maps and positions of objects. As observers, men are more accurate in remembering men or cars, while women are more accurate at recalling what people wore, for example.

1. Based on the passage, a woman at the scene of an accident would probably be more accurate in recalling

   (A) the make of the car
   (B) the direction of the street
   (C) the license-plate number of the car
   (D) where the impact occurred
   (E) the weather conditions

2. The passage might explain why

   (A) a man misplaces things in a house
   (B) a woman has difficulty with travel directions
   (C) a woman forgets a person's name but not his face
   (D) a man remembers names
   (E) a man can quote passages from a book

3. From the information given, it may be inferred that a woman might have trouble remembering each of the following items *except*

   (A) where she left her car keys

   (B) the turn-off in driving to an acquaintance's house
   (C) what was on her shopping list
   (D) which fender of her car was dented
   (E) what Nick, the garage mechanic, looks like

Questions 4 to 6

A group of boys went to the doughnut shop and bought doughnuts, which they then consumed. Alex ate fewer doughnuts than Charlie. Bob ate fewer doughnuts than Fred. Dan ate more doughnuts than Alex. Elmer ate more doughnuts than Dan. Fred ate fewer doughnuts than Alex, and Charlie ate fewer doughnuts than Dan.

4. Who ate the most doughnuts?

   (A) Alex
   (B) Bob
   (C) Charlie
   (D) Dan
   (E) Elmer

5. Who ate the fewest doughnuts?

   (A) Bob
   (B) Charlie
   (C) Dan
   (D) Elmer
   (E) Fred

6. Charlie ate more doughnuts than

   (A) Elmer, Fred and Bob
   (B) Elmer, Dan and Alex
   (C) Dan, Fred and Bob
   (D) Alex, Fred and Bob
   (E) Dan, Alex and Bob

Questions 7 to 13

Most people have never heard of the mathematical achievements that affect their everyday lives. Nor are they aware that mathematics has

144

progressed in quantum leaps over the last thirty-five years. It is generally believed that mathematicians work in an abstract world no lay person can understand and that mathematics has no practical purposes.

It is true that most of us don't understand a great deal of mathematics, and that mathematics is an abstract field in which things must be discovered, invented or created. It is also difficult to comprehend. As with other technical fields, even understanding the language of mathematics is difficult. When mathematicians discuss their science it sounds so abstract and esoteric that the lay person feels hopelessly lost. Mathematicians are the first to admit that their work is almost impossible to discuss with non-mathematicians. However, they do acknowledge that they have been reluctant to discuss their work with people outside their field.

Mathematicians, unlike other experimental scientists, do most of their work alone, without teams of assistants and experimental apparatus. Most mathematicians do their work without direct regard to the application of the results; mathematical research is seldom concerned with solving a specific practical problem. Surprisingly enough, the abstract mathematical concepts thus developed are often the very tools needed and used to solve specific problems—in mathematics or other fields. Godfrey Hardy developed a number theory and proclaimed that it would not have any effect on the world. His work is now the basis for constructing secret codes, which is central to national security issues. Many mathematical developments that were once thought to be too abstract to have practical application have astonished physicists as being the exact tool needed to explain ideas about nature. Mathematics has become so important in physics, astronomy and economics that it is hard to tell where mathematics leaves off and the other sciences begin. Mathematics has made fundamental improvements in the design of computer software. Many recent technological developments such as supersonic aircraft wings and medical scanners would not have been possible without the recently evolved mathematical tools.

7. Based on the passage which of the following statements is (are) correct?

    I. Mathematics is an abstract science with no practical applications.

    II. Mathematics has many practical applications

    III. Mathematics has been instrumental in opening a world of new technological advances.

    (A) I only
    (B) II only
    (C) III only
    (D) I and III only
    (E) II and III only

8. The author's purpose in the passage is to

    (A) inform people about the role of math in their lives
    (B) criticize mathematicians for not communicating with lay people
    (C) let people know about the importance of mathematics
    (D) encourage more people to pursue mathematics
    (E) enhance people's concept of mathematics

9. The author's tone in the passage is

    (A) informative, without bias
    (B) anti-mathematicians
    (C) supercilious
    (D) critical of people who don't understand mathematics
    (E) not written for lay people

10. Most people

    (A) are unaware of current mathematical thinking
    (B) think mathematics is worthless
    (C) know that mathematics is important, but not why
    (D) think mathematical research is a waste of funding and resources
    (E) think of mathematics as an experimental science

11. A high school teacher could use this information to

    (A) interest students in mathematics
    (B) let students know that mathematics has useful applications
    (C) encourage students to enter the fields of mathematics

(D) show students that math is in the forefront of technological advances

(E) all of the above

12. The main idea of the passage is that

(A) mathematicians don't communicate well with lay people

(B) mathematics is an abstract field with practical application

(C) mathematics is not developed to solve specific problems

(D) the abstract concepts of mathematics are not easy to comprehend

(E) mathematicians developed supersonic aircraft wings

13. The author would probably be in favor of

(A) less mathematical research

(B) better communication by mathematicians regarding the benefits of mathematics

(C) more research by mathematicians

(D) separation of mathematics and other experimental fields

(E) mathematicians keeping to themselves

Questions 14 to 17

A recent study showed that leading scholars in the humanities and social sciences have strongly critized the scholarly journals in their fields. Many of those surveyed think the peer-review system of deciding what gets published in the journals is biased in favor of established researchers, scholars from prestigious institutions, and those who use currently fashionable approaches to a subject. About one-third say they rarely find articles of interest in their discipline's primary journal. One scholar claimed that the leading journal in his field was controlled by a small group that shut out any challenges to the theories on which they have made their reputations, resulting in stagnation. Nearly one-fourth of the respondents regard prepublication material by their colleagues to be at least as important as articles published in the journals. About one-third of those surveyed expressed dissatisfaction with the length of time it takes for articles to appear in print after they have been accepted for publication.

14. Of those surveyed regarding scholarly publications what portion were critical?

(A) all

(B) many

(C) one-third

(D) one-fourth

(E) nearly one-fourth

15. The survey showed dissatisfaction with all of the following *except*

(A) the peer-review system of deciding what gets published

(B) the lack of articles of interest

(C) too much variety in journals

(D) the control of journals by a coterie

(E) not enough new information relevant to their field

16. The greatest dissatisfaction with journals was expressed by

(A) history professors

(B) new Ph.D.'s

(C) administrators

(D) editors of journals

(E) none of the above

17. The passage

(A) draws conclusions from a survey

(B) recommends change in how articles should be reviewed

(C) furnishes data from a survey

(D) is biased in favor of the journalist

(E) is biased in favor of the scholars

Questions 18 to 21

This is the sixth consecutive year in which college costs have risen at a rate higher than inflation. At public colleges and universities, the rate of increase has slowed. At two-year public colleges, tuition is up four percent, while at four-year public colleges and universities, it is up six percent. At private institutions tuition has risen eight percent. The most common reasons for the higher charges are increases in faculty pay, increased student aid, higher insurance costs, and the need for more computers and new facilities.

Students who live on campus at four-year public colleges will pay slightly more than half the amount paid by students at private colleges. Students who live at home and commute to college save almost $1,200.00 per year.

18. According to the passage, tuition at public institutions

    (A) has decreased
    (B) has increased more than the inflation rate
    (C) has increased the same as the inflation rate
    (D) has increased less than the inflation rate
    (E) has increased

19. The least expensive education would be

    (A) living on campus at a private college
    (B) commuting to a private college
    (C) living on campus at a public university
    (D) commuting to a public university
    (E) not enough information to decide

20. From the passage, we can conclude that the current rate of inflation is

    (A) less than four percent
    (B) less than five percent
    (C) less than six percent
    (D) less than seven percent
    (E) less than eight percent

21. Reasons for higher college costs include all of the following except the

    (A) need for more computers
    (B) need to raise salaries
    (C) rise in financial aid costs
    (D) rise in insurance costs
    (E) rise in housing costs

Questions 22 to 24

Some state leaders are critical of a national report which calls for the elimination of undergraduate education programs. The report advocates that prospective teachers complete an undergraduate degree in liberal arts and then continue to a master's degree in education. It states that too many graduates of education programs lack adequate knowledge of the subjects they teach. State officials critical of the report say that the proposed changes would cost too much and that the report focuses attention on the wrong issues. Some states are already shifting toward the recommended program, but others call it an easy out and impractical. Many more teachers will be needed in the next five to ten years. Taking an extra year to complete a credential program would delay the entry of many into the ranks of much-needed teachers.

22. "All states will be required to offer education programs at the graduate, rather than the undergraduate level." Based on the information in the passage, how should you respond to this statement?

    (A) agree
    (B) disagree
    (C) not in passage
    (D) not enough information
    (E) agree partially

23. The report _____ that teachers have an undergraduate degree in liberal arts before pursuing a master's degree in education.

    (A) mandates
    (B) recommends
    (C) rules
    (D) requires
    (E) cautiously suggests

24. We can assume that the purpose of the report was to

    (A) improve education
    (B) improve the caliber of new teachers
    (C) increase departments of education
    (D) save money on educational programs
    (E) provide more teachers in the next five to ten years

Questions 25 and 26

In order to be admitted to North State Community College, a resident needs to have a high school diploma, a General Education Diploma, have passed the state high school equivalency test or be eighteen years of age. An out-of-state student needs to have a high school diploma and have finished in the upper half of his or her graduating class. Service personnel are considered the same as instate students.

25. According to the guidelines above, which of the following applicants is (are) admissible to North State Community College?

    I. Carrie, who is 17, lives in North State and dropped out of school after she passed the high school equivalency test
    II. Sean, who ran away from his home in Lincoln State at 15, joined the service, and has finished his 3 year tour of duty
    III. Hillary, who lives in South State and was valedictorian of her class

    (A) I only
    (B) II only
    (C) III only
    (D) I and II only
    (E) I, II and III

26. Ruth, who lives in North State and is sixteen, dropped out of high school. What will enable her to enroll in North State Community College?

    (A) waiting two years
    (B) joining the service
    (C) getting the General Education Diploma
    (D) A and C
    (E) A or C

27. Despite persistent claims that the SAT is unfair and unnecessary, the widely used test seems to be as entrenched as ever at selective colleges and universities.

    From the above statement we can conclude that the SAT

    (A) is used more frequently than ever across the nation
    (B) is used less frequently across the nation
    (C) will be eliminated
    (D) is used as much as ever at certain colleges
    (E) is unfair and unnecessary

Questions 28 and 29

Computers and software are increasingly being used in higher education. Some colleges have software development programs in which professors are given time off from teaching in order to write software programs for their classes. One professor developed a program that allows his students to experiment with ways of staging various Shakespearean scenes. With the advent of the software development programs, some administrators worried that faculty members would not be willing to use materials developed on other campuses; however, professors look for good software just as they look for good textbooks. Another area of concern was whether the developer of a program would have to spend all his time answering questions about the software. This fear, too, has proven false. Actually faculty members are increasingly computer-literate and less likely to need help. The problem that has yet to be solved is incompatibility of hardware. New questions which must be addressed are how students can use the materials and whether they can get access to the necessary computers.

28. A fear which proved unfounded was

    (A) professors wasting time answering questions about the program
    (B) incompatibility of hardware
    (C) getting the program to the ultimate user
    (D) not enough computers
    (E) the students not knowing how to use the programs

29. A continuing problem is

    (A) professors spending time answering questions about programs
    (B) incompatibility of hardware
    (C) getting the programs to the ultimate user
    (D) professors not using other programs
    (E) professors not looking for other programs

30. In one state, student aid work-study funds have been appropriated to pay college students to teach illiterate adults to read.

    The concept in the statement could be

    (A) young learning from old
    (B) illiterates teaching college students
    (C) college students teach illiteracy
    (D) multiple benefits from one program
    (E) waste not, want not

31. In Midway County, all high school graduates have been offered full-tuition scholar-

ships to attend the local community college. The foundation granting the scholarships is trying to stimulate the economy by encouraging people to stay in the area. "The ripple effect is tremendous," said the president of the foundation. Every student who takes advantage of this offer stays in the community. This is $10,000.00 per year that doesn't leave Midway.

As used in this passage, "ripple effect" refers to

(A) a wavy effect
(B) an irregular effect
(C) an up and down effect
(D) an increasingly greater effect
(E) an undulating effect

Questions 32 to 35

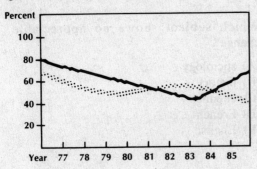

Average history scores on the senior final.

Average history scores on the junior final.

32. Senior history scores are shown to be

(A) declining steadily
(B) increasing steadily
(C) increasing after a small decline
(D) increasing after years of steady decline
(E) variable without a trend

33. The lowest senior scores were in

(A) 1982 and 44%
(B) 1983 and 44%
(C) 1984 and 44%
(D) 1982 and 55%
(E) 1983 and 55%

34. The juniors and seniors had the same scores in

(A) 1981
(B) 1984
(C) 1981 and 1984
(D) 1977 and 1986
(E) 1982 and 1983

35. The juniors had better scores than the seniors

(A) one year
(B) two years
(C) three years
(D) four years
(E) five years

Questions 36 to 40

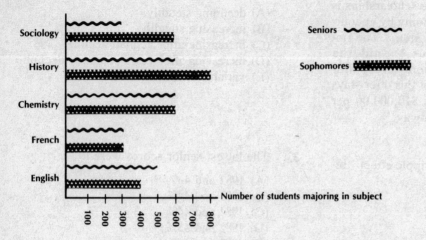

36. From the data in the graph one can project that

    (A) the overall trend is toward more students majoring in the subjects listed as a whole
    (B) English is gaining in popularity
    (C) more students are majoring in each subject
    (D) these subjects are all less popular as majors
    (E) total enrollment is declining

37. Which subject is gaining most in being chosen as a major?

    (A) sociology
    (B) history
    (C) chemistry
    (D) French
    (E) English

38. Which subject is decreasing as a major choice?

    (A) sociology

    (B) history
    (C) chemistry
    (D) French
    (E) English

39. Which subject shows no appreciable change?

    (A) sociology
    (B) history
    (C) chemistry
    (D) French
    (E) English

40. According to the graph, which subject has the largest total number of students majoring in it?

    (A) sociology
    (B) history
    (C) chemistry
    (D) French
    (E) English

SECTION II. MATHEMATICS

50 Minutes—40 Questions

Directions: Choose the best answer for each question and blacken the corresponding space on the Answer Sheet for Sample Test 3. Correct answers and solutions follow the test.

1. What is the remainder when 5619 is divided by 39?

    (A) $3/13$
    (B) 3
    (C) $144 1/13$
    (D) $1/39$
    (E) 144

2. $\dfrac{2x - y}{2} =$

    (A) $x - y$
    (B) $2x - y$
    (C) $x - \dfrac{y}{2}$
    (D) $2x - \dfrac{y}{2}$

    (E) $2(2x - y)$

3. Packages are delivered every fourth working day. If packages were delivered on Thursday, what is the next delivery date?

    (A) Saturday
    (B) Monday
    (C) Wednesday
    (D) Thursday
    (E) Friday

4. Which fraction is largest?

    (A) $2/3$
    (B) $3/4$
    (C) $7/11$
    (D) $3/5$
    (E) $5/9$

5. The difference between a two-digit number and the number with the digits reversed is

63. The sum of the digits is 7. What is the number?

    (A) 70
    (B) 61
    (C) 52
    (D) 43
    (E) 81

6. 3487.9652
    The 2 in the above number represents.

    (A) units
    (B) hundredths
    (C) thousandths
    (D) thousands
    (E) ten-thousandths

7. Paul's age is one year less than double Carmen's age. Seven years ago he was three times as old as Carmen. How old is Paul?

    (A) 25
    (B) 22
    (C) 18
    (D) 13
    (E) 6

8. 20 is what percent of 16?

    (A) 80%
    (B) $16/20$
    (C) 75%
    (D) 32%
    (E) 125%

9. Round off 14,494 to the nearest 100.

    (A) 14,000
    (B) 15,000
    (C) 14,400
    (D) 14,500
    (E) 14,490

10. To check $\dfrac{x^2 - 9}{x - 3} = x + 3$,

you could: I. Multiply $x - 3$ by $x + 3$
II. Substitute a number for x
III. Work the problem over again

(A) I only
(B) II only
(C) III only
(D) I and II only
(E) II and III only

11. $^9/_{20}$ changed to a decimal is

(A) .18
(B) 1.80
(C) .9
(D) .20
(E) .45

12. $^7/_9$ equals

(A) $^9/_{63}$
(B) $^{42}/_{54}$
(C) $^7/_{21}$
(D) $^{87}/_{114}$
(E) $^9/_7$

13. Henry was building a $^1/_{24}$ scale model of a boat. If the boat's width is 2 yards, how wide should the model be?

(A) ½ inch
(B) 1 inch
(C) 2 inches
(D) 3 inches
(E) 4 inches

14. Acme Rental Car Company charges $40.00 per day for a car, while Zenith Cars charges $37.50 per day. Which of the following can be answered with this information?

(A) the weekly rental charge for Acme
(B) the rental cost for half a day of use from Zenith
(C) the cost for renting a car for two days from Acme
(D) the surcharge for gasoline by both companies
(E) the difference between what Acme and Zenith charge per day

15.

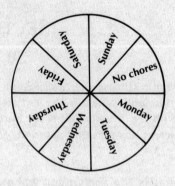

Mrs. Purden set up a wheel for her children to spin, in order to decide when each one would be responsible for washing the dishes. If Charlene spins the wheel, what are her chances of not having any chores?

(A) $^1/_6$
(B) $^1/_7$
(C) $^1/_8$
(D) $^6/_7$
(E) $^7/_8$

16. 20° Centigrade converted to Fahrenheit is

(A) −7°F
(B) 7°F
(C) 36°F
(D) 68°F
(E) 93.6°F

17. $1.025 + 30.76 + 2.087 + .1567 + 417.6 =$

(A) 1.1931
(B) 11.931
(C) 75.7887
(D) 1119.31
(E) 451.6287

18. David can complete a paper route in 3 hours, while Scott can do it in 2 hours. How long will it take if they work together?

(A) 1 hr.
(B) 1¹/₅ hrs.
(C) 2 hrs.
(D) 3 hrs.
(E) 5 hrs.

19.

> An elevator can carry six people. How many trips will it have to make to transport 26 people?

When Chris worked this problem he got an answer of 4.2. What should he do now?

(A) redo the problem
(B) choose 4 as the answer
(C) choose 5 as the answer
(D) choose 4.2 as the answer
(E) assume there is an error in the answer choices

20. A triangle's altitude is ½ of its base of 3¼ inches. What is the measurement of the altitude?

(A) ½ in.
(B) 1¼ in.
(C) 1⅝ in.
(D) 3⅓ in.
(E) 6½ in.

21. How many hours will it take a train going 78 kilometers per hour to travel 37 kilometers?

(A) 0.47 hr.
(B) 0.5 hr.
(C) 1.2 hrs.
(D) 2.0 hrs.
(E) 2.1 hrs.

22. Melissa checked the acidity level of her experiment every 10 minutes. After 10 hours, how many times had she checked it?

(A) 1
(B) 10
(C) 6
(D) 60
(E) 100

23.

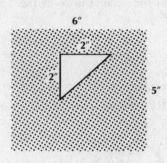

Sue cut a triangle out of a sheet of paper. How much paper did she waste?

(A) 2 sq. in.
(B) 4 sq. in.
(C) 26 sq. in.
(D) 28 sq. in.
(E) 30 sq. in.

24. Rick and Russell collect stamps and have 450 stamps between them. Rick has 50% more than Russell. How many stamps does Rick have?

(A) 180 stamps
(B) 225 stamps
(C) 270 stamps
(D) 405 stamps
(E) 675 stamps

Question 25.

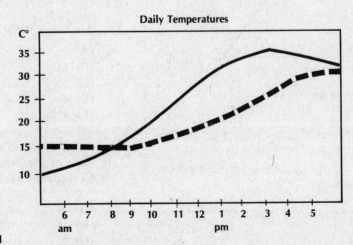

25. Based on the graph on p. 153, which of the following is true?

    I. The temperature varies more inland than at the coast.
    II. Temperatures inland and at the coast were the same at 6 P.M.
    III. At noon the temperature at the coast was 30°.

    (A) I only
    (B) II only
    (C) III only
    (D) I and II only
    (E) II and III only

26.

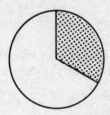

One-third of the circle is shaded. Find the shaded area if the radius is 7.

    (A) $^{49}/_3\pi$
    (B) $^{49}/_3$
    (C) 497
    (D) 49
    (E) $^7/_3\pi$

27.

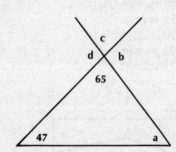

Which angle equals 115°?

    (A) a
    (B) b
    (C) c
    (D) d
    (E) b and d

28. Which fraction is the smallest?

    (A) $^7/_{11}$

(B) $^8/_{12}$
(C) $^9/_{13}$
(D) $^{10}/_{14}$
(E) $^{10}/_{15}$

29. 727,654 ÷ 9 =
    The solution to this problem

    (A) has no remainder
    (B) has a remainder of 1
    (C) has a remainder of 2
    (D) has a remainder of 3
    (E) has a remainder of 4

30. $3\frac{7}{8} + 5\frac{5}{6} - 4\frac{3}{4} =$

    (A) $4\frac{5}{6}$
    (B) $4\frac{23}{24}$
    (C) $8\frac{41}{24}$
    (D) $9\frac{17}{24}$
    (E) $14\frac{2}{3}$

31. Change $^{39}/_{24}$ to a decimal.

    (A) 0.625
    (B) 1.15
    (C) 1.58
    (D) 1.625
    (E) 2.04

32. $\frac{1}{3}$% of the kernels in popcorn do not pop. At this rate how many kernels will not pop out of 600 kernels?

    (A) 2 kernels
    (B) 6 kernels
    (C) 18 kernels
    (D) 100 kernels
    (E) 200 kernels

33. $\sqrt{236}$ is closest to

    (A) 14
    (B) 15
    (C) 16
    (D) 46
    (E) 118

34. In a class of 35 students, 15 took a test. The ratio of students who did not take the test to students who did is

    (A) $^4/_3$
    (B) $^3/_7$
    (C) $^4/_7$

(D) $\frac{3}{4}$
(E) $\frac{7}{4}$

35. What percent is 21 of 15?

 (A) 21%
 (B) 60%
 (C) 70%
 (D) 129%
 (E) 140%

36. Which of the following groups contain only prime factors?

  I. (1, 2, 3, 5)
  II. (2, 3, 4, 5)
 III. (0, 7, 11, 13)

 (A) I only
 (B) II only
 (C) III only
 (D) I and III only
 (E) none

37. Ron wants to arrange the following weights in order from largest to smallest. Which order is correct?

  I. milligram
  II. gram
 III. kilogram

(A) I, II, III
(B) II, III, I
(C) I, III, II
(D) III, II, I
(E) II, I, III

38. $3x(x - 2y) =$

(A) $3x - 6y$
(B) $3x^2 + xy$
(C) $3x^2 - 6xy$
(D) $3x^2 - 2y$
(E) $3x - 2xy$

39. $(b - 3)(b + 4) =$

(A) $b^2 - 12$
(B) $b^2 + 12$
(C) $b^2 + b - 12$
(D) $b^2 - b - 12$
(E) $b^2 - b + 12$

40. $360 - 4M + 6K + 160 = 640$

In the equation above, K = 2, find the value of M.

(A) 12
(B) 15
(C) 20
(D) 30
(E) 120

SECTION III. WRITING
30 Minutes—45 Questions

This section is designed to test your ability to recognize standard written English. Each part has its own directions.

PART A

Directions: **Some of the sentences below contain errors in grammar, word use or punctuation; others are correct. For each question, blacken the answer space that corresponds to the letter of the underlined portion that contains an error. If the sentence is correct as it stands, blacken space E on your answer sheet. No sentence contains more than one error.**

1. Every algebra teacher must make up their
   A   B   C
   own tests. No error
   D   E

2. Both the student and the teacher wants
   A   B   C
   good results. No error
   D   E

3. Neither the parents nor the teacher under-
   A   B   C   D
   stand the problem. No error
                      E

4. None of the teachers were prepared to re-
   A   B   C
   turn to school a week before the semester

   started. No error
   D   E

5. Either you or I am to blame for not re-
   A   B C   D
   winding the cassette tape. No error
                             E

6. Every teacher would be at school on time
   A   B
   if I was the principal. No error
   C D   E

7. He feels bad about having run over the dog,
   A   B   C   D
   even though it was unavoidable. No error
                                   E

8. Because he has practiced all summer, he
   A
   runs faster than any boy in school. No er-
   B   C   D   E
   ror

9. Both Cindy and Mark are tall, a character-
   A   B
   istic inherited from their father, but Mark
   C
   is the tallest. No error
   D   E

10. After having corrected test papers all eve-
    A   B
    ning, Susan decided to relax with a cup of
    C   D
    tea. No error
    E

11. Neither Jonathan nor his friends, who are
    A   B
    baseball enthusiasts also, wants to stop the
    C   D
    game to eat supper. No error
                        E

156

12. The four brothers have only one bicycle
between <u>them</u>. <u>This</u> forces them to walk <u>a</u>
     A   B   C
great deal and keeps them fit. <u>No error</u>
   D   E

13. After snowing all night, the roads were <u>im-</u>
                               A
<u>passable</u> the next morning, <u>as a result</u> the
  B   C
school buses <u>were delayed</u>. <u>No error</u>
           D   E

14. Our teachers are very <u>well</u> prepared. <u>In</u>
                    A   B
particular, <u>our</u> master teachers who <u>have</u>
        C   D
had special training. <u>No error</u>
                 E

15. Student teachers <u>benefit</u> by participating in
               A
extracurricular school activities, <u>they help</u>
                          B
provide an <u>overall</u> view of the <u>teacher's</u>
          C   D
day. <u>No error</u>
        E

16. On his vacation Benjamin wanted <u>to climb</u>
  A   B
<u>rocks</u>, to swim in the ocean and <u>scuba div-</u>
                                C
ing in the <u>Caribbean</u>. <u>No error</u>
         D   E

17. Either the counselors or Vince Johnson, the
<u>vice principal</u>, <u>makes</u> the decision <u>whether</u>
    A   B   C
to suspend students <u>or not</u>. <u>No error</u>
              D   E

18. She works very <u>hard</u> at her studies, and as
            A B
a result, she has better grades <u>than anyone</u>
                        C   D
in class. <u>No error</u>
          E

19. <u>Even though</u> she lives <u>a solitary</u> existence
    A   B
in the jungle she <u>has</u> a wonderful <u>kind of a</u>
                 C   D
<u>life</u>. <u>No error</u>
          E

20. After <u>having coped</u> with commuter traffic
          A
on the way to <u>work</u>, I did not need a bro-
              B
ken copier <u>to further</u> <u>aggravate</u> me. <u>No er-</u>
            C   D   E
ror

21. The <u>Parent Support Group</u> will have a pot-
              A
luck supper for all <u>new and returning</u>
                        B
teachers at the beginning of school. We
should all <u>try and</u> attend <u>it</u>. <u>No error</u>
          C   D   E

22. Be sure <u>to turn in</u> your <u>year-end</u> <u>attend-</u>
         A   B   C   D
ance reports on time. <u>No error</u>
                     E

23. The reason I could <u>not attend</u> the last ses-
                   A
sion of the seminar is <u>because</u> a faculty
                    B
meeting <u>was scheduled</u> <u>for</u> the same time.
          C   D
<u>No error</u>
  E

24. <u>Because</u> it is a difficult procedure, it is
  A
something <u>that should</u> <u>be done</u> by <u>myself</u>.
       B   C   D
<u>No error</u>
  E

25. This is the <u>most perfect</u> camp location <u>of all</u>
        A   B
the ones we <u>have</u> looked at. <u>No error</u>
     C   D   E

PART B

Directions: **Some of the sentences below contain errors in grammar, word choice, sentence construction and punctuation. Part or all of each sentence is underlined. Beneath each sentence are five ways of writing the underlined part. Choice A repeats the original sentence, but the other four choices are different. If you think the original sentence is the best one, select A. Otherwise, select one of the other answer choices that produces the most effective version of the original sentence. On your answer sheet, blacken the space that corresponds to your choice.**

26. Since the baby boomers have graduated from college, there are less application this year than in the past.

    (A) there are less application this year than in the past.
    (B) there are less applications this year than in the past.
    (C) there are fewer application this year than in the past.
    (D) there are fewer applications this year than in the past.
    (E) there are less applications this year than last.

27. The secretary reported that you are to call home right away.

    (A) reported that you are to call home right away.
    (B) reported that, "You are to call home right away."
    (C) reported, "You are to call home right away."
    (D) reported, you are to call home right away.
    (E) reported that, you are to call home right away.

28. He will go farther in school administration than his peers, because he has already earned his doctoral degree.

    (A) He will go farther in school.
    (B) He will succeed farther in school.
    (C) He will go farther in school.
    (D) He will go further as to school.
    (E) He will go further in school.

29. What is the latest development on the controversial education bill now before the legislature?

    (A) latest development on the controversial

    (B) late development on the controversial
    (C) recent development with the controversial
    (D) late development with the controversial
    (E) recent development on the controversial

30. The future of video tape use in the classroom is hard to predict because of the uncertainty of it's uses.

    (A) because of the uncertainty of it's uses.
    (B) because of the uncertainty of its uses.
    (C) due the uncertainty of its uses.
    (D) due the uncertainty of it's uses.
    (E) because of the uncertainty of their uses.

31. The resource teacher at our school not only does his work well, but goes out of his way to be helpful also.

    (A) but goes out of his way to be helpful also.
    (B) but goes out of his way also to be helpful.
    (C) but also goes out of his way to be helpful.
    (D) but goes out of his way to be helpful.
    (E) but goes out of his way to be helpful too.

32. As a senior, his course load was very heavy. He was taking English, Calculus, American History and Psychology I.

    (A) English, Calculus, American History and Psychology I.
    (B) English, calculus, American History and Psychology I.
    (C) English, calculus, American History and psychology I.

(D) English, Calculus, American history and psychology I.

(E) English, Calculus, American history and Psychology I.

33. "As a result of the energy <u>crisis," she stated, "we have</u> worked diligently to make our home energy-efficient."

(A) crisis," she stated, "we have
(B) crisis, she stated, we have
(C) crisis. She stated, "We have
(D) crisis," she stated, "We have
(E) crisis, she stated. "We have

34. It is very difficult to determine the detrimental affects that will result from flooding this valley.

(A) affects that will result from
(B) affects that shall result as
(C) effects that will result as
(D) effects that shall result from
(E) effects that will result from

35. I have always thought <u>these kind of mountains</u> were particularly beautiful.

(A) these kind of mountains
(B) these kinds of mountains
(C) this kinds of mountains
(D) this kind of mountains
(E) this kind of mountain

36. After I <u>observed the class for six weeks</u>, I student taught the following nine weeks.

(A) observed the class for six weeks,
(B) observed for six weeks in the classroom,
(C) had observation for six weeks in the classroom.
(D) observing the class for six weeks,
(E) had observed the class for six weeks,

37. <u>Not one of the teachers has their</u> lesson plans in on time.

(A) Not one of the teachers has their
(B) None of the teachers has their
(C) All of the teachers has their
(D) Not one of the teachers has his
(E) Not one of the teachers have their

38. <u>He is one of the staff members who teaches</u> on a provisional credential.

(A) He is one of the staff members who teaches
(B) He is one of the staff members who teach
(C) He is the only one of the staff members who teach
(D) He is one of those staff members who teaches
(E) He is the staff members who teaches

39. Harriet is <u>the only one of the teachers in that building who have</u> a classroom equipped with a sink.

(A) the only one of the teachers in that building who have
(B) the only teacher in that building who have
(C) the only one of the teachers in that building who has
(D) the only teacher in that building whose
(E) the only one in that building who has

40. <u>Each of the students in the class needs</u> a separate study plan.

(A) Each of the students in the class needs
(B) Each of the students in the class need
(C) Each of the student in the class needs
(D) Every one of the student in the class need
(E) Every student in the class need

41. <u>Waiting for the mountains to finally come into view</u>, their magnificence overwhelmed us.

(A) Waiting for the mountains to finally come into view
(B) While waiting for the mountains to finally come into view
(C) After waiting for the mountains to finally come into view
(D) Waiting for the mountains finally coming into view
(E) When the mountains finally came into view

42. The shock of the barely averted accident had her in tears. We <u>couldn't hardly blame</u> her.

    (A) barely averted accident . . . couldn't hardly
    (B) averted accident . . . couldn't hardly
    (C) barely averted accident . . . could hardly
    (D) bare averted accident . . . could hardly
    (E) averted accident . . . could hardly

43. Of all the books he had read, his favorite was *The rise and fall of athens*.

    (A) *The rise and fall of athens*.
    (B) *The Rise and Fall of Athens*
    (C) The Rise and Fall of Athens.
    (D) <u>The rise and fall of Athens.</u>
    (E) ''The Rise and Fall of Athens.''

44. Last Thursday Jeffrey and I saw the <u>blue jays flying south for the winter</u>.

    (A) blue jays flying south for the winter.
    (B) blue jays flying South for the winter.
    (C) blue jays flying South for the Winter.
    (D) blue jays flying south for the Winter.
    (E) blue jays flying south during the winter.

45. Since our exhibits paralleled each other, the award was given to <u>both you and I</u>.

    (A) both you and I.
    (B) both of us.
    (C) both I and you.
    (D) both you and me.
    (E) both me and you.

SECTION III. ESSAY

30 Minutes—Essay Topic

Directions: You have 30 minutes in which to write an essay on the topic specified. The essay section is intended to measure how well you write, given limitations on time and subject. Quality is more important than quantity. Spend some of your time organizing your thoughts. Use specific examples to support your statements. Write only on the assigned topic. Write legibly and within the lines provided. You may use the space below the topic for notes.

Topic
Describe one experience that you had in college which made you a different person from the one you were when you entered college.

SECTION III. ESSAY

(blank lined answer space)

ANSWERS TO SAMPLE TEST 3

SECTION I. READING

1.	C	11.	E	21.	E	31.	D
2.	B	12.	B	22.	B	32.	D
3.	C	13.	B	23.	B	33.	B
4.	E	14.	B	24.	B	34.	C
5.	A	15.	C	25.	E	35.	B
6.	D	16.	E	26.	E	36.	A
7.	E	17.	C	27.	D	37.	A
8.	C	18.	E	28.	A	38.	E
9.	A	19.	D	29.	B	39.	C
10.	A	20.	E	30.	D	40.	B

SECTION II. MATHEMATICS

1.	B	11.	E	21.	A	31.	D
2.	C	12.	B	22.	D	32.	A
3.	B	13.	D	23.	D	33.	B
4.	B	14.	E	24.	C	34.	A
5.	A	15.	C	25.	A	35.	E
6.	E	16.	D	26.	A	36.	E
7.	A	17.	E	27.	E	37.	D
8.	E	18.	B	28.	A	38.	C
9.	D	19.	C	29.	E	39.	C
10.	D	20.	C	30.	B	40.	B

SECTION III. WRITING

1.	C	11.	D	21.	C	31.	C	41.	E
2.	C	12.	A	22.	E	32.	B	42.	C
3.	D	13.	A	23.	B	33.	A	43.	B
4.	B	14.	B	24.	D	34.	E	44.	A
5.	E	15.	B	25.	A	35.	B	45.	D
6.	D	16.	C	26.	D	36.	E		
7.	E	17.	E	27.	C	37.	D		
8.	C	18.	D	28.	E	38.	B		
9.	D	19.	D	29.	A	39.	C		
10.	E	20.	D	30.	B	40.	A		

EXPLANATION OF ANSWERS TO SAMPLE TEST 3

SECTION I. READING

1. **C** Women recall written material well; therefore they are likely to recall license-plate numbers.

2. **B** Travel directions include landmarks and maps.

3. **C** A shopping list is written material.

4. **6** Arrange the boys in order from the one who ate most to the one who ate least, then answer all three questions from the chart.
   Elmer — Dan — Charlie — Alex — Fred — Bob
   most -- least
   4) **E**
   5) **A**
   6) **D**

7. **E** Rule out I because mathematics is abstract, but it has practical applications.

8. **C** The author does not criticize or encourage. He discusses more than mathematics' role in our lives; therefore C is the best answer.

9. **A** Eliminate all other choices.

10. **A** C is a possible answer, but A is more exact.

11. **E** The teacher could use all four points.

12. **B** A, C, and D are too specific. E is false, leaving B as the correct answer.

13. **B** He discusses problems of communication between mathematicians and lay people.

14. **B** No specific numbers were given. All is too broad, therefore B is the best choice.

15. **C** Eliminate; the four other choices were mentioned.

16. **E** The article doesn't state which category was most dissatisfied.

17. **C** The article is based on data from a survey, and neither gives opinions nor draws conclusions.

18. **E** "At public institutions the rate of increase has slowed"—but it still increased. No specific figure is given for the inflation rate.

19. **D** Attending a public university and living at home is the cheapest.

20. **E** There are two possible rankings of rising costs.
    4%—two-year college costs
    6%—public four-year college costs
       —inflation
       —average four-year college costs
    8%—private four-year college costs
    or
    4%—two-year colleges
       —inflation
       —average four-year college costs
    6%—public four-year college costs
    8%—private four-year college costs
    In each case inflation is definitely less than eight percent.

21. **E** All the others are mentioned as reasons for increased costs.

22. **B** The passage states that some states have already adopted such a program; however, the program is not mandatory.

23. **B** The report recommends (advocates).

24. **B** It is specifically geared to improving teacher education. Improved education is a hoped-for by-product.

25. **E** Carrie has passed the high school equivalency test. Sean has been in the service and is eighteen. Hillary was first in her class.

26. **E** Joining the service will not help her enter NSCC. She will be eligible at age eighteen (in two years) or after earning a General Education Diploma.

27. **D** The word "entrenched" is the key. The others are not stated in the passage.

28. **A** The words "unfounded fear" key us to the answer. "The fear has proven false."

29. **B** "The problem that has yet to be solved is incompatibility of hardware."

30. **D** Both the students and the adults who learn to read benefit.

31. **D** All the others describe wave motion.

32. **D** The seniors' scores went down for seven years before increasing.

33. **B** The low point was in 1983 and was between 40% and 50%.

34. **C** The lines cross in 1981 and 1984.

35. **B** The juniors' scores were better in 1982 and 1983.

36. **A** Eliminate the others.

37. **A** The largest increase is in sociology; 300 more sophomores than seniors.

38. **E** English is the only subject showing a decline.

39. **C** Chemistry has no change.

40. **B** Combine the numbers of sophomores and seniors.

SECTION II. MATHEMATICS

1. **B**
$$144 \text{ R } 3$$

```
      144 R 3
39)5619
   39
   ---
   171
   156
   ---
    159
    156
    ---
      3
```

The key word is "remainder."

2. **C** $\dfrac{2x - y}{2} = \dfrac{2x}{2} - \dfrac{y}{2} = x - \dfrac{y}{2}$

3. **B**

Thursday	Friday	~~Saturday~~	~~Sunday~~
Delivery	1 Delivery		

Monday	Tuesday	Wednesday
2 Delivery	3 Delivery	4 Delivery

4. **B** Underline *largest*. Are there any numbers you can eliminate immediately?

Compare: (A) $\dfrac{2}{3}$ ⤬ $\dfrac{3}{4}$ 9 is larger than 8; eliminate ⅔

(C) $\dfrac{3}{4}$ ⤬ $\dfrac{7}{11}$ Eliminate ⁷⁄₁₁

(D) $\dfrac{3}{4}$ ⤬ $\dfrac{3}{5}$ Eliminate ³⁄₅

(E) $\dfrac{3}{4}$ ⤬ $\dfrac{5}{9}$ Eliminate ⁵⁄₉

5. **A** Check: sum of digits is 7. Eliminate E. Reverse number and subtract.

   (A) $\begin{array}{r} 70 \\ -07 \\ \hline 63 \end{array}$

6. **E** $\begin{array}{r} 3\,4\,8\,7\,.\,9\,6\,5\,2 \\ 2 \\ \hline 1\,0\,0\,0\,0 \end{array}$

7. **A** The answer must fit in both equations.

$$P = 2C - 1$$
$$P - 7 = 3(C - 7)$$

Paul can't be 6, because the problem talks about "7 years ago." Eliminate E. It has to be A. Check.

$$\begin{array}{r} 25 = 2C - 1 \\ +1 \quad\quad +1 \\ \hline 26 = 2C \\ 13 = C \end{array}$$

$$25 - 7 = 3(13 - 7)$$
$$18 = 3(6)$$
$$18 = 18$$

Paul is 25.

8. **E** The question asks for percentage. Eliminate B. Estimate: 20 is more than 16, therefore it is more than 100%. Only E qualifies.

$$\dfrac{is}{of} \quad \dfrac{20}{16} \times 100 = 125\%$$

9. **D** 14,494

$$\begin{array}{r} 14{,}494 \\ \uparrow \\ \underline{100} \\ 14{,}500 \end{array}$$

number above first 0 is 5 or bigger, so add 1.

10. **D** To check division, e.g., $^{12}/_{3} = 4$, multiply 3×4, therefore I fits; eliminate B, C and E. You can also substitute a number for x; therefore II fits. The answer is D.

11. **E** Estimate: $^{9}/_{20}$ is a little less than ½.

$$\begin{array}{r} .45 \\ 20\overline{)\ 9.00} \\ -8\ 0 \\ \hline 1\ 00 \\ -1\ 00 \\ \hline 0 \end{array}$$

12. **B** The numerator is smaller than the denominator—eliminate E. The numerator must be divisible by 7. Eliminate all but B and C. Denominator must be divisible by 9. Eliminate C

$$\frac{42 \div 6}{54 \div 6} = \frac{7}{9}$$

13. **D** $\frac{\text{Model}\ \ 1}{\text{Boat}\ \ 24} = \frac{W}{2\text{ yds.}}$ Change 2 yards to inches (2 × 36)

$$\frac{1}{24} = \frac{W}{72}$$

Cross-multiply:

$24W = 72$

$W = 3$ inches

14. **E** \$40.00 − \$37.50 = \$2.50
There is not enough information to answer the rest.

15. **C** This wheel is divided into eighths. "No chores" is 1 of those 8. Her chances are 1 in 8 or ⅛.

16. **D** C ➡ F = bigger
Eliminate A and B:
$^{9}/_{5}$°C + 32 = °F
$^{9}/_{5}$ (20) + 32 =
36 + 32 = 68°F
Or Estimate:
2C + 30 =
2(20) + 30 =
40 + 30 = 70 D is closest.

17. **E** Round off all numbers and estimate:
1 + 31 + 2 + 418 = 452
E is the only possibility

18. **B** It will take less time than 2 hours. Eliminate C, D and E.
David completes route in 3 hours. In 1 hour, he does ⅓. Scott completes route in 2 hours. In 1 hour, he does ½. David and Scott complete ⅓ + ½ = $^{5}/_{6}$ in 1 hour. They complete all of it in $^{6}/_{5}$ = $1^{1}/_{5}$ hours. In estimating how long it takes for two people working together to do a job, keep in mind that it will take between one-half the time it takes each one to do the job alone. In this case, between $^{2}/_{2}$ = 1 hr. and $^{3}/_{2}$ = 1½ hours. In general, it will take less time than the faster worker, but more than ½ that time.

19. **C** The elevator will need to make five trips. The excess verbiage is only window dressing.

20. **C** 3¼ ÷ 2 =
$^{13}/_{4}$ × ½ = $^{13}/_{8}$ = 1⅝″

21. **A** It will take a little less than ½ hour. No need to work it out. 37 ÷ 78 = 0.47.

22. **D** She checked it 6 times per hour; 60 ÷ 10 = 6
In 10 hours she checked it 6 × 10 = 60 times.

23. **D** 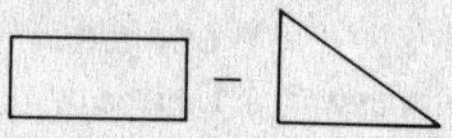 = shaded area

area of rectangle − area of triangle
(5 × 6) (½ × 2 × 2) =

wasted paper

30 − 2 = 28 square inches

24. **C** Eliminate E. Rick has 50% more than Russell. For every 100 Russell has, Rick has 150; or Rick has three for every two Russell has.

$$\frac{100}{150} = \frac{2}{3}$$

x = Russell's stamps
1.5x = Rick's stamps

$$x + 1.5x = 450$$
$$2.5x = 450$$
$$x = 180$$
$$1.5x = 270$$

There are $2 + 3 = 5$ parts
$450 \div 5 = 90$ stamps

Check: Rick has $\dfrac{3}{5} = \dfrac{x}{450}$
$$(3)(450) = 5x$$
$$270 = x$$

or estimate: Rick has more than half (225); eliminate A, B and E.

25. **A** I. Yes inland temperatures ranged from 10° to 35°
No II. Can't tell.
No III. It was 30° inland at noon.
It was 20° at the coast at noon.

26. **A** $A = \pi r^2$
$A = \pi \cdot 7^2$
$A = 49\pi$

$\frac{1}{3} A = \frac{1}{3} \times 49\pi = \frac{49}{3}\pi$

27. **E** $a = 180 - (65 + 47) = 68$
$b = 180 - 65 = 115$
$c = 65$ (opposite angle)
$d = 180 - 65 = 115$ or b

28. **A** Compare by cross-multiplication.

(B) Reduce $\frac{8}{12} = \frac{2}{3}$
(D) Reduce $\frac{10}{14} = \frac{5}{7}$
(E) Reduce $\frac{10}{15} = \frac{2}{3}$

Note that E is the same as B. Eliminate B and E.

$\dfrac{91}{11}\ \dfrac{7}{} \times \dfrac{9}{13}\ \dfrac{99}{}$ Eliminate C.

$\dfrac{49}{11}\ \dfrac{7}{} \times \dfrac{5}{7}\ \dfrac{55}{}$ Eliminate D.

29. **E** You can divide it out, which is the long way, or add the digits and divide the total by 9. The remainder is your answer.
$7 + 2 + 7 + 6 + 5 + 4 = 31$
$31 \div 9 = 3$ Remainder of 4

30. **B** Estimate $4 + 6 - 5 = 5$ It's either A or B. The common denominator is 24.

$+ 3\frac{7}{8} = \quad 3\frac{21}{24}$
$+5\frac{5}{6} = + 5\frac{20}{24}$
$\qquad\qquad 8\frac{41}{24}$
$4\frac{3}{4} = - 4\frac{18}{24}$
$\qquad\qquad 4\frac{23}{24}$

31. **D** $\frac{39}{24} = 1\frac{3}{8} = 1\frac{5}{8}$
$13 \div 8 = 1.625$

32. **A** 1% of 600 = 6
$\frac{1}{3}$% of 600 = 2

33. **B** You can try squaring the answers. Start with the middle number.

$16^2 = 256$—too big
$15^2 = 225$—too small
236 is closer to 225 than 256.

34. **A** $\dfrac{\text{Didn't Take Test}}{\text{Did Take Test}} = \dfrac{35-15}{15} = \dfrac{20}{15} = \dfrac{4}{3}$

35. **E** $\dfrac{\text{is}}{\text{of}} \times 100 = \dfrac{21}{15} \times 100 = 140\%$

or $\dfrac{21}{15} = \dfrac{x}{100}$; $x = 140\%$

36. **E** I. 1 is not a prime number.
II. 4 is not a prime number.
III. 0 is not a prime number.

37. **D**

38. **C** $3x(x - 2y) =$
$3x \cdot x - 3x \cdot 2y =$
$3x^2 - 6xy$

39. **C** $\begin{array}{r} b - 3 \\ b + 4 \\ \hline b^2 - 3b \\ + 4b - 12 \\ \hline b^2 + b - 12 \end{array}$

40. **B** $360 - 4M + 6K + 160 = 640$
$360 - 4M + 12M + 160 = 640$
$360 + 8M + 160 = 640$
$520 + 8M = 640$
$8M = 120$
$M = 15$

SECTION III. WRITING

1. **C** his—"every" is singular.

2. **C** want—"both . . . and" takes a plural verb.

3. **D** understands—With "neither . . . nor" the verb agrees with the noun closest to it.

4. **B** was—"none" is singular.

5. **E** The sentence is correct.

6. **D** were—The subjunctive of "was" is "were".

7. **E** The sentence is correct.

8. **C** "any other"—He cannot be faster than himself.

9. **D** taller—When comparing two items, use "-er" ending.

10. **E** The sentence is correct.

11. **D** want—"want" agrees with "friends," which is plural.

12. **A** among—"between" two people, "among" three or more.

13. **A** After it had snowed—The original is a dangling participle.

14. **B** prepared, in—The original is a sentence fragment.

15. **B** activities. They—The original is a run-on sentence.

16. **C** to scuba dive—The original is not parallel.

17. **E** The sentence is correct.

18. **D** anyone else—She cannot have better grades than herself.

19. **D** kind of life—"a" should be omitted.

20. **D** irritate—"aggravate" means "to make worse."

21. **C** try to attend—The infinitive is needed.

22. **E** The sentence is correct.

23. **B** that—"reason" and "because" are redundant.

24. **D** me—"myself" has to be preceded by I or me.

25. **A** omit "most"—"perfect" does not need a qualifier.

26. **D** "fewer applications"—applications can be counted, therefore "fewer."

27. **C** direct quote, delete "that."

28. **E** "further"—This is used figuratively.

29. **A** The sentence is correct.

30. **B** "its"—"it's" is the contraction for "it is;" "its" is the possessive of "it."

31. **C** "but also"—"not only" is together; "but also" should be together too.

32. **B** "calculus"—calculus is not capitalized. The other subjects are capitalized because they are the name of a language, country, or a specific course.

33. **A** The sentence is correct.

34. **E** "effect"—"effect" is a noun; "affect" is a verb.

35. **B** "these kinds"—"these" is plural, therefore needs the plural "kinds."

36. **E** "had observed"—I had observed first, then I taught. "Observed" needs to be in the past-perfect tense in order to show that the observation occurred before the teaching.

37. **D** "his"—"not one" is singular, therefore it should be "his lesson plans."

38. **B** "teach"—He is one of several who teach on a provisional credential, he is not the only one; therefore use the plural form "teach."

39. **C** "has"—Harriet is the only one (singular), and she has a classroom equipped with a sink.

40. **A** The sentence is correct.

41. **E** "When the mountains finally came into

view''—A gerundial phrase, which begins with a word ending in -ing, must refer to the subject of the main clause. The subject is "magnificence," referring to mountains; therefore the subordinate clause must refer to it also.

42. **C** "could hardly"—"hardly" and "scarcely" are negative, and should not be used with other negatives.

43. **B** *The Rise and Fall of Athens*—First and last words of a book title are capitalized, as well as nouns and verbs. Book titles are underlined or printed in italics.

44. **A** The sentence is correct.

45. **D** "me"—The indirect object uses "me," not "I."

ANSWER SHEET FOR SAMPLE TEST 4

MATHEMATICS

1 (A) (B) (C) (D)   12 (A) (B) (C) (D)   23 (A) (B) (C) (D)   34 (A) (B) (C) (D)   45 (A) (B) (C) (D)

2 (A) (B) (C) (D)   13 (A) (B) (C) (D)   24 (A) (B) (C) (D)   35 (A) (B) (C) (D)   46 (A) (B) (C) (D)

3 (A) (B) (C) (D)   14 (A) (B) (C) (D)   25 (A) (B) (C) (D)   36 (A) (B) (C) (D)   47 (A) (B) (C) (D)

4 (A) (B) (C) (D)   15 (A) (B) (C) (D)   26 (A) (B) (C) (D)   37 (A) (B) (C) (D)   48 (A) (B) (C) (D)

5 (A) (B) (C) (D)   16 (A) (B) (C) (D)   27 (A) (B) (C) (D)   38 (A) (B) (C) (D)   49 (A) (B) (C) (D)

6 (A) (B) (C) (D)   17 (A) (B) (C) (D)   28 (A) (B) (C) (D)   39 (A) (B) (C) (D)   50 (A) (B) (C) (D)

7 (A) (B) (C) (D)   18 (A) (B) (C) (D)   29 (A) (B) (C) (D)   40 (A) (B) (C) (D)   51 (A) (B) (C) (D)

8 (A) (B) (C) (D)   19 (A) (B) (C) (D)   30 (A) (B) (C) (D)   41 (A) (B) (C) (D)   52 (A) (B) (C) (D)

9 (A) (B) (C) (D)   20 (A) (B) (C) (D)   31 (A) (B) (C) (D)   42 (A) (B) (C) (D)   53 (A) (B) (C) (D)

10 (A) (B) (C) (D)   21 (A) (B) (C) (D)   32 (A) (B) (C) (D)   43 (A) (B) (C) (D)   54 (A) (B) (C) (D)

11 (A) (B) (C) (D)   22 (A) (B) (C) (D)   33 (A) (B) (C) (D)   44 (A) (B) (C) (D)   55 (A) (B) (C) (D)

READING

1 (A) (B) (C) (D) (E)   14 (A) (B) (C) (D) (E)   27 (A) (B) (C) (D) (E)   40 (A) (B) (C) (D) (E)   53 (A) (B) (C) (D) (E)

2 (A) (B) (C) (D) (E)   15 (A) (B) (C) (D) (E)   28 (A) (B) (C) (D) (E)   41 (A) (B) (C) (D) (E)   54 (A) (B) (C) (D) (E)

3 (A) (B) (C) (D) (E)   16 (A) (B) (C) (D) (E)   29 (A) (B) (C) (D) (E)   42 (A) (B) (C) (D) (E)   55 (A) (B) (C) (D) (E)

4 (A) (B) (C) (D) (E)   17 (A) (B) (C) (D) (E)   30 (A) (B) (C) (D) (E)   43 (A) (B) (C) (D) (E)   56 (A) (B) (C) (D) (E)

5 (A) (B) (C) (D) (E)   18 (A) (B) (C) (D) (E)   31 (A) (B) (C) (D) (E)   44 (A) (B) (C) (D) (E)   57 (A) (B) (C) (D) (E)

6 (A) (B) (C) (D) (E)   19 (A) (B) (C) (D) (E)   32 (A) (B) (C) (D) (E)   45 (A) (B) (C) (D) (E)   58 (A) (B) (C) (D) (E)

7 (A) (B) (C) (D) (E)   20 (A) (B) (C) (D) (E)   33 (A) (B) (C) (D) (E)   46 (A) (B) (C) (D) (E)   59 (A) (B) (C) (D) (E)

8 (A) (B) (C) (D) (E)   21 (A) (B) (C) (D) (E)   34 (A) (B) (C) (D) (E)   47 (A) (B) (C) (D) (E)   60 (A) (B) (C) (D) (E)

9 (A) (B) (C) (D) (E)   22 (A) (B) (C) (D) (E)   35 (A) (B) (C) (D) (E)   48 (A) (B) (C) (D) (E)   61 (A) (B) (C) (D) (E)

10 (A) (B) (C) (D) (E)   23 (A) (B) (C) (D) (E)   36 (A) (B) (C) (D) (E)   49 (A) (B) (C) (D) (E)   62 (A) (B) (C) (D) (E)

11 (A) (B) (C) (D) (E)   24 (A) (B) (C) (D) (E)   37 (A) (B) (C) (D) (E)   50 (A) (B) (C) (D) (E)   63 (A) (B) (C) (D) (E)

12 (A) (B) (C) (D) (E)   25 (A) (B) (C) (D) (E)   38 (A) (B) (C) (D) (E)   51 (A) (B) (C) (D) (E)

13 (A) (B) (C) (D) (E)   26 (A) (B) (C) (D) (E)   39 (A) (B) (C) (D) (E)   52 (A) (B) (C) (D) (E)

SAMPLE TEST 4
(CONNCEPT)

This test is similar to the Connecticut Competency Examination for Prospective Teachers (CONNCEPT), which is required for all students wishing to be admitted to teacher education programs in the state of Connecticut and for all candidates seeking a state teaching certificate for Connecticut. The Mathematics and Essay Tests are also useful in preparing for the CBEST required in California and Oregon and the PPST required in Delaware, Kansas, Minnesota, Nebraska, Nevada, and Wisconsin. This sample test can also help to prepare candidates for teacher certification tests administered by Arizona, Colorado, Florida, Illinois, Michigan, and South Carolina.

Format of the CONNCEPT

	Total Time	**Three hours**
Mathematics		55 questions
Reading		63 questions
Writing		one essay

The CONNCEPT has a total time limit of three hours. The individual subtests are not timed. It is suggested that you allot one hour to each of the subtests because you must pass all three subtests at one administration in order to pass the CONNCEPT.

Scoring the test

Test scores for the multiple-choice sections are based on the number of questions answered correctly. You do not lose points if you have to guess. The CONNCEPT score report will include an overall score for each of the three subtests and an indication of whether or not each subtest was passed. If you fail any one of the subtests, you must retake and pass the entire examination. You need about 39 questions right on the mathematics test and 44 on the reading test in order to pass.

SAMPLE CONNCEPT

180 Minutes—118 Questions

Directions: **Choose the best answer for each question and blacken the corresponding space on the Answer Sheet for Sample Test 4. The correct answers and the explanations follow the test.**

MATHEMATICS (55 QUESTIONS)

1. A recipe for biscuits calls for ½ cup lard to 2½ cups of flour. What is the ratio of lard to flour?

    (A) 1:2½
    (B) 5:1
    (C) 1:5
    (D) 1:6

2. 7,500 times what number is 75?

    (A) 0.01
    (B) 10
    (C) 0.1
    (D) 100

3. Kim is sent to the store with $10.00. She can spend what is left on comic books, after she has bought five packages of gelatin at $1.65 each. How much can she spend on comic books?

    (A) $8.25
    (B) $2.25
    (C) $1.75
    (D) $1.25

4. If comic books cost 57 cents each, how many can Kim buy if she has $2.25?

    (A) 2
    (B) 3
    (C) 4
    (D) 5

5. "This diet will enable you to lose up to 85% of your excess weight." From this statement, you can assume that:

    (A) everyone will lose 85% of his excess weight
    (B) 85% of the people trying the diet will lose 85% of their excess weight
    (C) some people could lose 85% of their excess weight
    (D) 85% of the people trying to diet will lose their weight

6. If Pete and Mike can rake all the leaves in six hours, how long will it take if Barbara and Karen help them, assuming that all four work at the same speed.

    (A) 3 hours
    (B) 4 hours
    (C) 6 hours
    (D) 8 hours

7. Find the Celsius (°C) reading if its equivalent Fahrenheit (°F) reading is 104°.

    $$°C = \frac{5}{9} (°F - 32)$$

    (A) 26°
    (B) 40°
    (C) 58°
    (D) 72°

8. How much ground can a worm cover in one day if it travels at a speed of 4 mm/second?

    (A) 345,600 cm
    (B) 34,560 mm
    (C) 345.6 km
    (D) 0.3456 km

9. Milk is measured in

    (A) kilograms
    (B) milligrams

176

(C) liters
(D) meters

10. ⅜ changed to a percent is equivalent to

(A) 36%
(B) 37.5%
(C) 38%
(D) 83%

11. "There is a 10% chance that the seeds will not sprout." What is the best interpretation of this statement?

(A) 10% of the seeds will not sprout.
(B) There is a 90% chance that the seeds will sprout.
(C) 1 out of 10 seeds will not sprout.
(D) 900 out of 1000 seeds will sprout.

12. The directions for making concrete call for two parts cement, four parts sand, three parts rock, and one part water. If I have 3 gallons of cement, how much water should I use?

(A) 1 gallon
(B) ½ gallon

(C) 1½ gallons
(D) 2 gallons

13. How many degrees above freezing is it on this outdoor Fahrenheit thermometer?

(A) 5°
(B) 23°
(C) 25°
(D) 55°

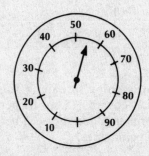

14. If every item in a store is taxable at 7%, what is the price paid for an item costing t dollars?

(A) 7t
(B) t + 7
(C) t + .07
(D) 1.07t

15.

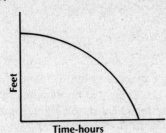

Which chart represents this graph?

(A) Time	Feet		(B) Time	Feet		(C) Time	Feet		(D) Time	Feet
0	30		0	0		0	30		0	30
1	28		1	7½		1	22½		1	17
2	24		2	15		2	15		2	6
3	13		3	22½		3	7½		3	2
4	0		4	30		4	0		4	0

16. If $\dfrac{24}{a} = \dfrac{15}{b}$, find a when b = 10.

(A) 16
(B) 62.5
(C) 15
(D) 6.25

17. When a number N is divided by a number

M that is less than 1, the result is always larger than N. Which example disproves the statement?

(A) 50 ÷ (−½) = −100
(B) 50 ÷ 0.2 = 250
(C) 50 ÷ .8 = 62.5
(D) 50 ÷ (½) = +100

18. Given the formula V = *l*wh, all the following are true *except*

    (A) $\dfrac{V}{l} = wh$

    (B) $\dfrac{V}{l w} = h$

    (C) $\dfrac{V}{l wh} = 1$

    (D) $\dfrac{1}{l w} = Vh$

19. Ken is going to paint a room with paint which covers 125 sq. ft. per gallon. What information does he need before he goes to the paint store?

    (A) the number of square feet in the room
    (B) the price per gallon of the paint
    (C) whether the paint covers well or not
    (D) nothing, he has all the information he needs

20. In a recent administration of the CST, one-fifth of the students scored above average on the verbal part and two-fifths scored above average on the math portion. Based upon this information, which of the following is a valid conclusion?

    (A) Two-fifths of the students scored below average in both math and verbal.
    (B) Three-fifths of the students scored above average in both math and verbal.
    (C) One-fifth of the students scored above average on both math and verbal.
    (D) Three-fifths of all the students are above average in math, verbal, or both.

21. 76% of $48.00 is approximately

    (A) $12.00
    (B) $36.00
    (C) $37.00
    (D) $38.00

22. A $7.50 belt is on sale for $5.50. How should the percent discount be determined?

    (A) (200 ÷ 7.50) 100

(B) (5.50 ÷ 7.50) 100
(C) 2.00 ÷ 100
(D) (2.00) (100)

23. Decide which decimal fraction is between 0.05 and .4?

    (A) .42
    (B) .049
    (C) .062
    (D) .45

24. If 40 pounds of gravel costs $2.50, how much does 3 tons of gravel cost?

    (A) $100
    (B) $125
    (C) $375
    (D) $500

25.

Word Processors	Pages Complete	Hours
Janelle	7	2
David	16	5
Ronald	10	3
Kathryn	13	4

Which word processor works most slowly?

    (A) Janelle
    (B) David
    (C) Ronald
    (D) Kathryn

26. Miss Felling's class is going to make placemats. Each placemat will be 9 inches by 12 inches. How many yards of 36-inch material will she need for 34 placemats?

    (A) 2 yds
    (B) 4 yds
    (C) 3 yds
    (D) 5 yds

27. Mr. Evarard's house payment uses up $240.50 of his monthly salary of $1850.00. What percent of his salary is his house payment?

    (A) 13%
    (B) 1.3%
    (C) 1.6%
    (D) 16%

28. In order to enroll in kindergarten, a child must be at least 5½ years old before the first day of school. Which child will be eligible to start school on September 2, 1988?

(A) Clarissa—born April 2, 1983
(B) Jamie—born February 28, 1984
(C) Margaret—born March 4, 1983
(D) Donald—born February 28, 1983

Question 29

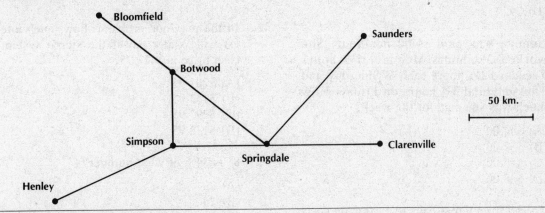

29. According to the above map, which two towns are approximately 287 kilometers apart?

(A) Bloomfield and Henley
(B) Bloomfield and Clarenville
(C) Henley and Clarenville
(D) Saunders and Henley

30. What is ⁷/₉ of ³/₁₄?

(A) ¹⁰/₂₃
(B) ¹/₆
(C) ⁹⁸/₂₇
(D) ²⁷/₉₈

31. Mark spends ⅜ of his day at work, ¼ of it sleeping, ¹/₁₂ exercising or playing sports and ⅙ on incidentals such as eating and driving to work. How much time does that leave him for his hobby of fly-tying.

(A) none
(B) 1 hour
(C) 2 hours
(D) 3 hours

32. Coriane wanted an A on her physics test. She needed 24 more points to get an A, which is 90%. What score did she get?

(A) 66%
(B) 76%
(C) 90%
(D) 114%

33. Which area is bigger?

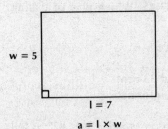
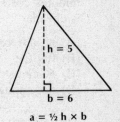

(A) the rectangle, by 50
(B) the triangle, by 15
(C) the triangle, by 35
(D) the rectangle, by 20

34. $6.7[3.2 - (0.8 \times 9 - 3.8)] =$

(A) −13.4
(B) −1.34
(C) 1.34
(D) 13.4

35. There was a large amount of poster paper in the supply room. June took ⅜ of it. Karla took ³/₅ of what was left. How much of the original supply was left when Harrison came to the storeroom?

(A) ⅝
(B) ²/₅
(C) ⅜
(D) ¼

36. Barbara had 69 on each of her first three tests and scores of 76, 79 and 82 on the rest. What is her average for these tests?

    (A) 69
    (B) 74
    (C) 76
    (D) 79

37. Geneva was paid $4.00 per hour. She worked 2⅓ hours Monday, 1½ hours Tuesday, 2¾ hours each Wednesday and Thursday and 3⅔ hours on Friday. How much was she paid for the week?

    (A) $44.00
    (B) $52.00
    (C) $50.00
    (D) $48.00

38. To call from Great Falls to Lexington costs 50 cents for the first minute and 33 cents per minute thereafter. A flat fee for 10 minutes costs $3.45. Which way of calling is cheaper?

    (A) no difference
    (B) flat fee
    (C) 50 cents and 33 cents
    (D) not enough information

39. The temperature on Monday was 87°; it fell 5° on Tuesday; rose 3° on Wednesday; warmed another 4° on Thursday and dropped 6° on Friday. What was the difference in the temperature between Monday and Friday?

    (A) −4°
    (B) +7°
    (C) +5°
    (D) +4°

40. If a car travels 532 miles on 18 gallons of gasoline, how many miles per gallon does it get?

    (A) 26
    (B) 27
    (C) 28
    (D) 29

41. Walter paid $75.00 down on a stereo sys-

tem, and will make 32 payments of $17.50 each. How much will he pay in all?

    (A) $75.00
    (B) $635.00
    (C) $560.00
    (D) $114.50

42. In the previous problem, how much interest will Walter pay if the stereo system's cash price is $427.95?

    (A) $207.05
    (B) $132.05
    (C) $297.95
    (D) $132.95

43. 85 is 34% of what number?

    (A) 29
    (B) 25
    (C) 250
    (D) 290

44. The fall enrollment at Columbia Junior College is 14,780, up from 12,890 the previous year. What is the increase in enrollment?

    (A) 1,890
    (B) 1,910
    (C) 1,980
    (D) 2,110

45. New linoleum is being put in Mr. Ketcham's classroom, which will be paid for out of special funds. The room is 42 feet by 51 feet. How many square yards of linoleum will be needed?

    (A) 79 sq yds
    (B) 238 sq yds
    (C) 714 sq yds
    (D) 2142 sq yds

46. How much will the linoleum in the above problem cost, if it costs $7.00 per square yard?

    (A) $555.00
    (B) $1,666.00
    (C) $4,998.00
    (D) $14,994.00

47. Madge's baby weighs 21 lbs. 5 oz., while her sister Joan's baby weighs 17 lbs. 7 oz. What is the difference in their weights?

    (A) 3 lbs 14 oz
    (B) 4 lbs 2 oz
    (C) 3 lbs 8 oz
    (D) 18 lbs 12 oz

48. The total of 2,839 + 62,987 + 247 + 1,755 + 487 is

    (A) 68,135
    (B) 68,315
    (C) 68,531
    (D) 6,835

49. $-9 - (-4) =$

    (A) -13
    (B) -5
    (C) $+5$
    (D) $+13$

50. $\frac{5}{7} - \frac{1}{8} =$

    (A) $\frac{3}{5}$
    (B) $\frac{1}{4}$
    (C) $\frac{47}{56}$
    (D) $\frac{33}{56}$

Questions 51 to 55

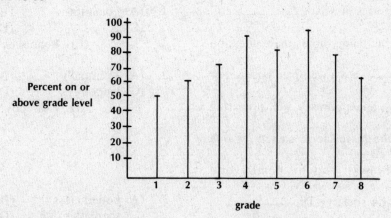

51. Which grades have the same percent of students scoring on grade level?

    (A) third and seventh
    (B) second and eighth
    (C) fifth and seventh
    (D) not enough information

52. When the percents of each grade are averaged, what is the average for the school?

    (A) 67.5%
    (B) 72.5%
    (C) 75%
    (D) 77%

53. If each student performs the same next year as this year, which class will have the highest percentage on grade level?

    (A) fourth

    (B) fifth
    (C) sixth
    (D) seventh

54. Which class has the least number of students on grade level?

    (A) first
    (B) second
    (C) eighth
    (D) not enough information

55. Which class has the smallest percentage of students below grade level?

    (A) first
    (B) fourth
    (C) sixth
    (D) eighth

READING

(63 questions)

Directions: **This test consists of reading passages with certain key words omitted. Each missing word is indicated by a numbered blank. To the right of each passage are groups of words numbered to correspond to the blanks. Choose the word that makes the best sense in each blank and indicate your answer by blackening the corresponding space on your answer sheet.**

Questions 1 to 11

There are two theories of what _____ a college education. One theory holds that education should lead _____ to a well-paid position or profession. It has, as its primary aim, preparing the student to take his place in society as one who supports himself and his family and _____ benefits society. The _____ is reflected in the instructional mode, which consists primarily of lecture, specific reading, assignments, multiple-choice tests, papers written, but not discussed, in fact little or no discussion at all. Indeed, this is a thoroughly _____ approach.

The other theory espouses that the education should train the person to think; to be able to see through the _____ of the matter and support his viewpoint of it. This graduate is groomed to make his contribution to society in _____

1.   (A) constitutes   (B) makes
      (C) is   (D) derives
          (E) behooves

2.   (A) eventually   (B) ultimately
      (C) smoothly   (D) a person
          (E) directly

3.   (A) nonetheless   (B) thereby
      (C) thereafter   (D) moreover
          (E) no doubt

4.   (A) society   (B) teaching
      (C) theory   (D) scholarship
          (E) methodology

5.   (A) mundane   (B) complete
      (C) satisfactory   (D) practical
         (E) unsatisfactory

6.   (A) basis   (B) intensity
      (C) balance   (D) base
         (E) heart

7.   (A) concrete   (B) many
      (C) intangible   (D) factual
         (E) organized

ways, by forwarding the knowledge of the past

through his _____ of it to the future. The
                8

instruction for this method of learning is impre-

cise, calling for the student to present and

_____ his interpretation of what he has
    9

heard or listened to. There are no cut and dried

answers, which may be disconcerting, but which

_____ life.
   10

Is one method superior to another, and are

they _____ exclusive?
         11

Questions 12 to 27

With would-be teachers all looking for jobs, it

may seem paradoxical that school districts in the

Southwest United States are _____ across
                                   12

the nation. By 1991, more than one million new

teachers will be _____ nationally. Then why
                     13

are there _____ teachers?
              14

The answer is that school districts are looking

for teachers in _____ fields—specifically,
                    15

bilingual teachers, teachers of math, science or

special education. Large school districts have

recruiters who travel to Canada and the North-

east because there is a _____ of teachers
                            16

there. They extol the virtues of their area and

their school district. They may even help ar-

8. (A) working   (B) knowledge
   (C) vision   (D) application
            (E) processing

9. (A) recite   (B) defend
   (C) expand   (D) persuade
            (E) conclude

10. (A) reflects   (B) are real
    (C) magnifies   (D) makes a game of
            (E) contradicts

11. (A) really   (B) only
    (C) both   (D) similarly
            (E) mutually

12. (A) closing   (B) expanding
    (C) recruiting   (D) terminating
            (E) traveling

13. (A) prepared   (B) needed
    (C) fired   (D) unemployed
            (E) unprepared

14. (A) too many   (B) excess
    (C) some   (D) unemployed
            (E) no

15. (A) particular   (B) all
    (C) some   (D) unpopular
            (E) unknown

16. (A) surplus   (B) dearth
    (C) lack   (D) supply
            (E) lot

range relocation loans and find employment for

_____ .
17

Smaller districts with _____ resources
18

urge teachers to become credentialed in the areas

needing more teachers, and promote future-

teacher clubs to encourage _____ students
19

to become teachers.

Small communities find it particularly

_____ to get and keep teachers. Many of the
20

teachers _____ from urban areas, and as
21

soon as possible, secure positions close to home.

Some small-town districts have programs that

encourage _____ to become teachers.
22

While some school districts deal with the

problems of _____ schools, others try to
23

cope with overcrowding. The methods are as

_____ as the districts. Harrison Unified has
24

put three elementary schools on an all-year

schedule. All the elementary schools in the

Whiteman District are on _____ sessions.
25

Portable classrooms are used by the Evans

School District, while the Hawkins and Wynona

Districts are building new schools. None of the

choices is _____ whether they involve in-
26

convenience or spending more money, but chil-

dren must be _____ .
27

17. (A) them   (B) others
    (C) themselves   (D) spouses
            (E)   some

18. (A) no   (B) limited
    (C) unlimited   (D) compounded
            (E)   scanty

19. (A) young   (B) willing
    (C) high school   (D) poor
            (E)   some

20. (A) new   (B) inconvenient
    (C) soon   (D) easy
            (E)   difficult

21. (A) come   (B) arrive
    (C) leave   (D) commute
            (E)   are newly

22. (A) commuters   (B) clerks
    (C) local residents (D) trainees
            (E)   newcomers

23. (A) overcrowding   (B) too many students
    (C) building   (D) renovating
            (E)   closing

24. (A) diverse   (B) similar
    (C) strange   (D) peculiar
            (E)   conventional

25. (A) break   (B) double
    (C) refresher   (D) summer
            (E)   interim

26. (A) hasty   (B) palatable
    (C) nice   (D) unpleasant
            (E)   well thought out

27. (A) cared for   (B) boarded
    (C) educated   (D) taken care of
            (E)   disciplined

Questions 28 to 35

The idea of people meeting _____ is used in
                                    28
a previously racially torn city to build

_____. Through the generosity of an anon-
   29
ymous donor, people come together for dinner

once a month. The only _____ is that each
                              30
person must bring a guest of a different race.

There is no _____, or formal discussion—
                31
just people eating, _____ every day events
                         32
and getting to know each other on a one-to-one

basis as people. This creates a _____ at-
                                      33
mosphere in which problems can be solved. The

group seeks to get at a basic need of all

_____—the need for people to get to know
   34
one another, across all lines and differences. As

one member put it, "When people get to know

each other and are friends, they're more

_____ to work things out."
   35

28. (A) people   (B) others
    (C) town officials (D) strangers
       (E) government officials

29. (A) acquiescence (B) concept
    (C) bridges   (D) fear
       (E) understanding

30. (A) charge   (B) fee
    (C) connection   (D) stipulation
       (E) reservation

31. (A) timetable   (B) menu
    (C) waiter   (D) agenda
       (E) lunch

32. (A) discussing   (B) debating
    (C) fighting over (D) rehashing
       (E) commemorating

33. (A) hothouse   (B) negative
    (C) friendly   (D) proverbial
       (E) open

34. (A) countries   (B) communities
    (C) people   (D) government
       (E) assistance

35. (A) susceptible   (B) opposed
    (C) receptive   (D) used
       (E) likely

Questions 36 to 41

The American volunteer has _____ been a
                                 36
woman, but now forty-four percent of the ninety-

two million volunteers who provide seventy bil-

lion dollars worth of services per year are men.

On every level _____ has become more
                    37
professional, mostly because people's lives are

36. (A) recently   (B) forever
    (C) traditionally (D) eternally
       (E) never

37. (A) helping   (B) fund raising
    (C) serving   (D) volunteerism
       (E) paid work

busier today. People have to decide carefully

where their ——————— will have the biggest im-
                38
pact. Men and women ages twenty-five to fifty-

four showed the ——————— increase in the per-
                    39
centage of volunteers in the last five years.

Three-fourths of all professional and business-

people volunteered, making those occupations

the largest ——————— of volunteers. There is a
              40
commitment by some volunteers to pick up the

——————— not covered by public and private
  41
sectors.

Questions 42 to 48

Working, and being successful at it, has a posi-

tive ——————— on a woman's health. Women
        42
who have multiple roles—jobs, a spouse, chil-

dren—have even better ——————— and mental
                          43
health than women who face fewer challenges.

Even single working mothers, who face many

problems, are healthier than ——————— women,
                                44
regardless of their situation. Most predictive of

a woman's ill-health is inactivity, regardless of

age. Working can even be ——————— in re-
                            45
covering from clinically diagnosed depression.

Working may offer women a sense of

——————— over their lives. However, women in
  46
jobs that combine high demands, such as cleri-

38. (A) presents   (B) commitment
    (C) proposal   (D) tradition
              (E) work ethic

39. (A) surging   (B) coming
    (C) average   (D) lowest
              (E) greatest

40. (A) contributors   (B) priorities
    (C) beneficiaries   (D) recipients
              (E) promulgators

41. (A) balance   (B) slack
    (C) benefits   (D) proposals
              (E) work

42. (A) effect   (B) affect
    (C) impaction   (D) morale
              (E) goal

43. (A) finances   (B) housing
    (C) psychological   (D) feelings
              (E) physical

44. (A) healthy   (B) sick
    (C) relaxed   (D) nonworking
              (E) rich

45. (A) negative   (B) counterproduc-
                                tive
    (C) therapeutic   (D) harmful
              (E) resourceful

46. (A) control   (B) joy
    (C) helplessness   (D) contentment
              (E) challenge

cal and secretarial work, with little personal control, are _____ to heart disease. House-
47
wives of the late 1970s were considerably healthier than those of the 1960s. The difference seemed to be that the housewives of the 1970s chose their own roles, rather than playing the role dictated by_____. The sense of con-
48
trol and freedom may be the most healthful change.

Questions 49 to 54

Children's temper tantrums occur at the most _____ times and locations. A child usually
49
outgrows the tendency toward tantrums before _____, but not always. Such behavior is not
50
unheard of at preschool. The problem is how to handle it, _____ without making a scene?
51
Often, taking the child away from the audience works wonders. But a teacher who has charge of a roomful of children can _____ do that.
52
Some children hold their breath during tantrums. This is _____ at first, but there's
53
nothing to worry about. To stop the tantrum, try blowing gently in the child's face or apply a cold, wet washcloth. Say something unusual or silly. Whispering might make a child _____ down
54
to try to hear you. Most of all, try to not let it upset you, which is easier said than done.

47. (A) apt   (B) immune
     (C) suspect   (D) vulnerable
            (E) responsive

48. (A) husbands   (B) society
     (C) chance   (D) religion
            (E) finances

49. (A) opportune   (B) awful
     (C) undesirable   (D) dangerous
            (E) challenging

50. (A) the age of two   (B) the age of three
     (C) puberty   (D) first grade
            (E) kindergarten

51. (A) mostly   (B) at all cost
     (C) preferably   (D) rarely
            (E) solely

52. (A) always   (B) never
     (C) usually   (D) seldom
            (E) consequentially

53. (A) disconcerting   (B) horrifying
     (C) annoying   (D) amazing
            (E) usual

54. (A) reach   (B) quiet
     (C) cool   (D) sit
            (E) lie

Questions 55 to 58

Tax preparation services rely on a large,

_____, and well-trained work force. For
    55

many years it consisted primarily of house-

wives, who enjoyed the temporary work and ad-

ditional income. With the _____ number of
               56

older people, tax preparation companies now

woo retired people to _____ their incomes.
          57

In doing this, tax preparation services have

joined the _____ of other businesses who
      58

have realized the value of retired people—and

their ready availability. Many employees of fast-

food services, restaurants, and doughnut shops

are no longer the pimply teenagers, but the gray-

haired grandfathers.

Questions 59 to 63

Is eye _____ the fad of the 1980s? There is
     59

a tremendous amount of television advertising

about radial keratotomy. It's as if you could go

to the _____ drugstore to get it. The sur-
     60

gery requires cutting several slits in the cornea

of the eye to temporarily ease nearsightedness.

No one knows what the _____ effects are,
      61

and some experts say it may impair vision.

About one-fourth of all _____ who have had
      62

the surgery have problems with glare, visual

functions and night driving. The effects of the

surgery in years to come are _____, yet it
       63

is being sold like breakfast cereal.

---

55. (A) permanent   (B) ubiquitous
     (C) highly paid   (D) marginal
          (E) temporary

56. (A) failing   (B) healthy
     (C) reduced   (D) stable
          (E) increasing

57. (A) use   (B) take
     (C) keep   (D) supplement
          (E) supplant

58. (A) ranks   (B) merger
     (C) group   (D) way
          (E) class

59. (A) glasses   (B) lifting
     (C) surgery   (D) vision
          (E) enhancement

60. (A) new   (B) neighborhood
     (C) super   (D) specialty
          (E) medical

61. (A) present   (B) current
     (C) reduced   (D) long-term
          (E) immediate

62. (A) elderly   (B) men
     (C) women   (D) children
          (E) patients

63. (A) unknown   (B) many
     (C) negative   (D) visible
          (E) hidden

WRITING (ONE ESSAY)

Directions: Write an essay on the assigned topic. The essay topic is intended to measure how well you write, given limitations on time and subject. Quality is more important than quantity. Before you begin to write, take some time to organize your thoughts. Use specific examples to support your statements. Write only on the assigned topic. Write legibly and within the lines provided. You may use the space below the topic for your notes.

Topic

The school district that is considering hiring you is particularly concerned that their teachers sponsor at least one extracurricular activity. Write a letter to the principal telling him about your interest, qualifications and background in one such extracurricular activity.

Write Your Essay Here:

_____

_____

_____

_____

_____

_____

_____

_____

_____

_____

_____

_____

_____

_____

_____

_____

_____

_____

_____

_____

_____

_____

_____

_____

ANSWERS TO SAMPLE TEST 4

MATHEMATICS

1.	C	12.	C	23.	C	34.	B	45.	B
2.	A	13.	B	24.	C	35.	D	46.	B
3.	C	14.	D	25.	B	36.	B	47.	A
4.	C	15.	A	26.	C	37.	B	48.	B
5.	C	16.	D	27.	A	38.	D	49.	B
6.	A	17.	A	28.	D	39.	A	50.	D
7.	B	18.	D	29.	D	40.	D	51.	B
8.	D	19.	A	30.	B	41.	B	52.	B
9.	C	20.	C	31.	D	42.	A	53.	D
10.	B	21.	B	32.	A	43.	C	54.	D
11.	B	22.	A	33.	D	44.	A	55.	C

READING

1.	A	14.	D	27.	C	40.	A	53.	A
2.	E	15.	A	28.	A	41.	B	54.	B
3.	B	16.	A	29.	E	42.	A	55.	E
4.	B	17.	D	30.	D	43.	E	56.	E
5.	D	18.	B	31.	D	44.	D	57.	D
6.	E	19.	C	32.	A	45.	C	58.	A
7.	C	20.	E	33.	C	46.	A	59.	C
8.	D	21.	D	34.	B	47.	D	60.	B
9.	B	22.	C	35.	E	48.	B	61.	D
10.	A	23.	E	36.	C	49.	C	62.	E
11.	E	24.	A	37.	D	50.	E	63.	A
12.	C	25.	B	38.	B	51.	C		
13.	B	26.	B	39.	E	52.	D		

EXPLANATION OF ANSWERS TO SAMPLE TEST 4

MATHEMATICS

1. **C**   Lard: Flour
$$\tfrac{1}{2}: 2\tfrac{1}{2}$$
$$1: 5$$

2. **A** $7500x = 75$
$$x = \frac{75}{7500}$$
$$x = \frac{1}{100} = 0.01$$

3. **C** $\$1.65 \times 5 = \$8.25$
$\$10.00 - \$8.25 = \$1.75$

4. **B** $2.25 \div .57 = 3\frac{54}{57}$

She can buy 3 comic books.

5. **C**   Key words are "lose up to 85%." Not everyone will lose the 85%. Eliminate A. Also eliminate B and D—one can't assume what percent of people will lose.

6. **A**   If twice as many people work, it will take half as long to do the job.
$$\frac{6}{2} = 3 \text{ hours}$$

7. **B** $°C = \tfrac{5}{9} (°F - 32)$
$°C = \tfrac{5}{9} (104 - 32)$
$°C = \tfrac{5}{9} (72)$
$°C = 40°$

8. **D** $4 \text{ mm} \times 60 \text{ sec} \times 60 \text{ min} \times 24 \text{ hrs}$
$345,600 \text{ mm} =$
$34,560 \text{ cm} =$
$345.6 \text{ m} =$
0.3456 km

9. **C**   Liquid is measured in liters.

10. **B** $\tfrac{3}{8} \times 100 = 37.5\%$.

11. **B**   "There is a chance . . .", but it is not for sure; eliminate A, C and D. Answer B restates the statement.

12. **C**   *Cement*   *Water*
$$\frac{2}{3} = \frac{1}{x}$$
$2x = 3 = 1\tfrac{1}{2}$ gallons
$x = \tfrac{3}{2}$

13. **B**   Reading is 55°. Freezing is 32°. Therefore, it is 23° above freezing.

14. **D** $t + .07t = 1.07t$

15. **A**   The chart starts with feet at its highest. Eliminate B. The feet fall very little at first and then faster.

16. **D** $\dfrac{24}{a} = \dfrac{15}{10}$
$24 \times 10 = 15a$
$240 = 15a$
$16 = a$

17. **A** $50 \div (-\tfrac{1}{2}) =$
$50 \times (-2) = -100$, which is less than 50.

18. **D**   If $\dfrac{1}{lw} = Vh$ then
$$\frac{1}{lwh} = V$$
but $V = l$wh, so this statement must be false.

19. **A**   B and C may be desirable, but A is essential.

20. **C**   By using "below average," no account is being taken of those whose scores are "average."

21. **B**   76% is close to 75%, which is ¾.
¾ $\times \$48 = 3 \times 12 = \$36$.

22. **A**   The sale price represents a discount of $2.00. Discount is compared to the original price, and is multiplied by 100 to find the percentage.
$(\$2.00 \div \$7.50) \times 100$

23. **C** Write the decimals 0.05 and 0.40 or move each decimal two places to the right: 5 and 40.
    (A) becomes 41—too big.
    (B) becomes 4.9—too small.
    (C) becomes 6.2—just right.
    (D) becomes 45—too big.

24. **C** Pounds
    $$\frac{40}{3 \times 2000} = \frac{\$2.50}{x}$$
    $$\frac{1}{3 \times 50} = \frac{2.50}{x}$$
    $$x = \$2.50(150)$$
    $$x = \$375.00$$

25. **B** The key phrase is "most slowly." We are looking for the person who completes the fewest pages per hour.
    Janelle—$^7/_2 = 3\frac{1}{2}$
    David—$^{16}/_5 = 3\frac{1}{5}$ (least number of pages)
    Ronald—$^{10}/_3 = 3\frac{1}{3}$
    Kathryn—$^{13}/_4 = 3\frac{1}{4}$

26. **C** She can get 3 across ($36 \div 12 = 3$) and 4 per yard ($36 \div 9 = 4$) for a total of 12 placemats per yard. Or she can get 4 across ($36 \div 9 = 4$) and 3 per yard ($36 \div 12 = 3$) for the same total of 12 placemats per yard. She'll need $34 \div 12 = 2.83$ or 3 yards.

27. **A** The payment is more than 10%. Eliminate (B) and (C). Try (A). $(240.50 \div 1850.00) \times 100 = 13\%$
    or
    $1850 \times .13 = 240.50$

28. **D**
    $$\begin{array}{rr} \text{Sept. 2, 1988} & 9 \quad 2 \quad 1988 \\ -\text{ 6 months 5 years} & -6 \qquad\quad 5 \\ \hline \text{March 2, 1983} & 3 \quad 2 \quad 1983 \end{array}$$
    (must be born before 3/2/83)

29. **D** Put the corner of your answer sheet at the first town and mark the distance to the next town along the edge, using it as a ruler. Then mark it against the scale.

30. **B** $\dfrac{\cancel{7}^{1}}{\cancel{9}_{3}} \times \dfrac{\cancel{3}^{1}}{\cancel{14}_{2}} = \dfrac{1}{6}$

31. **D** Change everything to hours:
    $^3/_8 = {}^9/_{24} = 9$ hours
    $^1/_4 = {}^6/_{24} = 6$ hours
    $^1/_{12} = {}^2/_{24} = 2$ hours
    $^1/_6 = {}^4/_{24} = 4$ hours
    Total $\quad \overline{21 \text{ hours}}$
    He has $24 - 21 = 3$ hours for his hobby.

32. **A** $90 - 24 = 66$

33. **D**
    $$\begin{array}{r} 5 \times 7 = 35 \\ -\frac{1}{2} \times 5 \times 6 = \underline{15} \\ 20 \end{array}$$

34. **B** Remove brackets from the inside out.
    $6.7 [3.2 - (0.8 \times 9 - 3.8)] =$
    $6.7 [3.2 - (7.2 - 3.8)] =$
    $6.7 [3.2 - 3.4] =$
    $6.7 (-0.2) = -1.34$

35. **D** Jane took $^3/_8$. $1 - ^3/_8 = {}^5/_8$ left.
    Karla took $^3/_5$ of $^5/_8$. $\quad ^3/_5 \times ^5/_8 = ^3/_8$
    That left $^5/_8 - ^3/_8 = ^2/_8$ or $\frac{1}{4}$

36. **B**
    $$\begin{array}{r} 69 \\ 69 \\ 69 \\ 76 \\ 79 \\ + 82 \\ \hline 444 \div 6 = 74 \end{array}$$

37. **B** $2\frac{1}{3} + 1\frac{1}{2} + 2\frac{3}{4} + 3\frac{2}{3} = 13$
    $13 \times \$4.00 = \$52.00$

38. **D** If the call is less than 10 minutes, the 50 cents + 33 cents rate is cheaper. If the call is 10 minutes or longer, the flat fee is cheaper.

39. **A** $(-5 + 3 + 4 - 6) = -4$

40. **D** $532 \div 18 = 29$

41. **B** $\$75.00 + 32 \times 17.50 =$
    $\$75.00 + 560.00 = \$635.00$

42. **A**
    $$\begin{array}{r} 635.00 \\ -427.95 \\ \hline \$207.05 \end{array}$$

43. **C** $\dfrac{85}{34} \times 100 = \dfrac{8500}{34} = 250$
    Check: $250 \times .34 = 85$

44. **A**
    $$\begin{array}{r} 14,780 \\ -12,890 \\ \hline 1,890 \end{array}$$

45. **B** The key is "square yards."
    $$\frac{42 \times 51}{9} = 238 \text{ or } \frac{42}{3} \times \frac{51}{3} = 238$$

46. **B** $238 \times \$7.00 = \$1,666.00$

47. **A**   16 oz. = 1 lb.
      21 lbs 5 oz = 20 lbs. 21 oz
      $$\begin{array}{r} 20 \text{ lbs. } 21 \text{ oz} \\ - 17 \text{ lbs. } 7 \text{ oz} \\ \hline 3 \text{ lbs. } 14 \text{ oz} \end{array}$$

48. **B**   Estimate: the answer is about 68,000. Now add the three last digits of each number:
      $$\begin{array}{r} 839 \\ 987 \\ 247 \\ 755 \\ 487 \\ \hline 315 \end{array}$$

49. **B** $-9 - (-4) =$
      $-9 + 4 = -5$

50. **D** $^5/_7 - ^1/_8 =$
      $$\frac{5 \times 8}{7 \times 8} - \frac{1 \times 7}{8 \times 7} = \frac{40 - 7}{56} = \frac{33}{56}$$

51. **B**   Second and eighth grades.

52. **B**
      $$\begin{array}{r} 50 \\ 60 \\ 70 \\ 90 \\ 80 \\ 95 \\ 75 \\ 60 \\ \hline 580 \end{array}$$
      $580 \div 8 = 72.5\%$

53. **D**   The highest scores are the sixth grade. The ones in the sixth grade this year will be in the seventh grade next year.

54. **D**   The question asks for *number* of students, but the information is given in percentages.

55. **C**   "Smallest" and "below" are important. This statement means the same as "which class has the largest percentage of students on or above grade level."

READING

Questions 1 to 11

There are two theories of what <u>constitutes</u> a college
                                    1
education. One theory holds that education should lead

<u>directly</u> to a well-paid position or profession. It has,
  2
as its primary aim, preparing the student to take his

place in society as one who supports himself and his

family and <u>thereby</u> benefits society. The theory is re-
             3   4
flected in the instructional mode, which consists pri-

marily of lecture, specific reading, assignments,

multiple-choice tests, papers written, but not dis-

cussed, in fact little or no discussion at all. Indeed, this

is a thoroughly <u>practical</u> approach.
                   5
    The other theory espouses that the education should

train the person to think; to be able to see through to

the <u>heart</u> of the matter and support his viewpoint of
      6
it. This graduate is groomed to make his contribution

to society in <u>intangible</u> ways, by forwarding the
                 7
knowledge of the past through his <u>application</u> of it to
                                        8
the future. The instruction for this method of learning

is imprecise, calling for the student to present and

<u>defend</u> his interpretation of what he has heard or lis-
  9
tened to. There are no cut and dried answers, which

may be disconcerting, but which <u>reflects life.</u>
                                     10
    Is one method superior to another, and are they

<u>mutually exclusive?</u>
  11

Questions 12 to 27

With would-be teachers all looking for jobs, it may

seem paradoxical that school districts in the South-

west United States are recruiting across the nation. By
_____
12

1991 more than one million new teachers will be

needed nationally. Then why are there unemployed
_____   _____
13   14
teachers?

The answer is that school districts are looking for

teachers in particular fields—specifically, bilingual
_____
15
teachers, teachers of math, science or special educa-

tion. Large school districts have recruiters who travel

to Canada and the Northeast because there is a sur-
                                                 ___
                                                 16
plus of teachers there. They extol the virtues of their

area and their school district. They may even help ar-

range relocation loans and find employment for

spouses.
_____
17
    Smaller districts with limited resources urge teach-
                           _____
                             18
ers to become credentialed in the areas needing more

teachers, and promote future-teacher clubs to encour-

age high school students to become teachers.
    _____
        19
    Small communities find it particularly difficult to get
                                            _____
                                               20
and keep teachers. Many of the teachers commute
                                         _____
                                            21
from urban areas, and as soon as possible, secure po-

sitions close to home. Some small-town districts have

programs that encourage local residents to become
                           _____
                             22
teachers.

While some school districts deal with the problems

of closing schools, others try to cope with over-
   _____
    23

crowding. The methods are as diverse as the districts.
                             _____
                               24
Harrison Unified has put three elementary schools on

an all-year schedule. All the elementary schools in the

Whiteman District are on double sessions. Portable
                          _____
                            25
classrooms are used by the Evans School District,

while Hawkins and Wynona Schools are building new

schools. None of the choices are palatable, whether
                                 _____
                                    26
they involve inconvenience or spending more money,

but children must be educated.
                    _____
                       27

Questions 28 to 35

The idea of people meeting people is used in a previ-
           _____
             28
ously racially torn city to build understanding.
                                _____
                                     29
Through the generosity of an anonymous donor, peo-

ple come together for dinner once a month. The only

stipulation is that each person must bring a guest of a
_____
    30
different race. There is no agenda, or formal discus-
                                              _____
                                                31
sion—just people eating, discussing every day events
                         _____
                             32
and getting to know each other on a one-to-one basis

as people. This creates a friendly atmosphere in which
                         _____
                            33
problems can be solved. The group seeks to get at a

basic need of all communities—the need for people to
                  _____
                      34
get to know one another, across all lines and differ-

ences. As one member put it, "When people get to

know each other and are friends, they're more likely
                                              _____
                                                35
to work things out."

Questions 36 to 41

The American volunteer has <u>traditionally</u> been a
                               36
woman, but now forty-four percent of the ninety-two
million volunteers who provide seventy billion dollars
worth of services per year are men. On every level
<u>volunteerism</u> has become more professional, mostly
  37
because people's lives are busier today. People have
to decide carefully where their <u>commitment</u> will have
                         38
the biggest impact. Men and women ages twenty-five
to fifty-four showed the <u>greatest</u> increase in the per-
                       39
centage of volunteers in the last five years. Three-
fourths of all professional and businesspeople volunteered, making those occupations the largest <u>contrib</u>-
                              40
<u>utors</u> of volunteers. There is a commitment by some
volunteers to pick up the <u>slack</u> not covered by public
                         41
and private sectors.

Questions 42 to 48

Working, and being successful at it, has a positive <u>ef</u>-
                              42
<u>fect</u> on a woman's health. Women who have multiple
roles—jobs, a spouse, children—have even better
<u>physical</u> and mental health than women who face
 43
fewer challenges. Even single working mothers, who
face many problems, are healthier than <u>nonworking</u>
                              44
women, regardless of their situation. Most predictive
of a woman's ill-health is inactivity, regardless of age.

Working can even be <u>therapeutic</u> in recovering from
                        45
clinically diagnosed depression.

Working may offer women a sense of <u>control</u> over
                             46
their lives. However, women in jobs that combine high
demands, such as clerical and secretarial work, with
little personal control, are <u>vulnerable</u> to heart dis-
                           47
ease. Housewives of the late 1970s were considerably
healthier than those of the 1960s. The difference
seemed to be that the housewives of the 1970s chose
their own roles, rather than playing the role dictated
by <u>society</u>. The sense of control and freedom may be
  48
the most healthful change.

Questions 49 to 54

Children's temper tantrums occur at the most <u>unde</u>-
                              49
<u>sirable</u> times and locations. A child usually outgrows
the tendency toward tantrums before <u>kindergarten</u>, but
                         50
not always. Such behavior is not unheard of at preschool. The problem is how to handle it, <u>preferably</u>
                         51
without making a scene? Often, taking the child away
from the audience works wonders. But a teacher who
has charge of a roomful of children can <u>seldom</u> do that.
                         52
Some children hold their breath during tantrums. This
is <u>disconcerting</u> at first, but there's nothing to worry
 53
about. To stop the tantrum, try blowing gently in the
child's face or apply a cold, wet washcloth. Say

something unusual or silly. Whispering might make a child <u>quiet</u> down to try to hear you. Most of all, try to
54
not let it upset you, which is easier said than done.

Questions 55 to 58

Tax preparation services rely on a large, <u>temporary,</u>
55
and well-trained work force. For many years it consisted primarily of housewives, who enjoyed the temporary work and additional income. With the increasing number of older people, tax preparation
56
companies now woo retired people to <u>supplement</u> their
57
incomes. In doing this, tax preparation services have joined the <u>ranks</u> of other businesses who have real-
58
ized the value of retired people—and their ready availability. Many employees of fast-food services, restaurants, and doughnut shops are no longer the pimply teenagers, but the gray-haired grandfathers.

Questions 59 to 63

Is eye <u>surgery</u> the fad of the 1980s? There is a tre-
59
mendous amount of television advertising about radial keratotomy. It's as if you could go to the <u>neighborhood</u> drugstore to get it. The surgery re-
60
quires cutting several slits in the cornea of the eye to temporarily ease nearsightedness. No one knows what the <u>long-term</u> effects are, and some experts say it may
61
impair vision. About one-fourth of all <u>patients</u> who
62
have had the surgery have problems with glare, visual functions and night driving. The effects of the surgery in years to come are <u>unknown,</u> yet it is being sold like
63
breakfast cereal.

ANSWER SHEET FOR SAMPLE TEST 5

1 Ⓐ Ⓑ Ⓒ Ⓓ   9 Ⓐ Ⓑ Ⓒ Ⓓ   17 Ⓐ Ⓑ Ⓒ Ⓓ   25 Ⓐ Ⓑ Ⓒ Ⓓ   33 Ⓐ Ⓑ Ⓒ Ⓓ

2 Ⓐ Ⓑ Ⓒ Ⓓ   10 Ⓐ Ⓑ Ⓒ Ⓓ   18 Ⓐ Ⓑ Ⓒ Ⓓ   26 Ⓐ Ⓑ Ⓒ Ⓓ   34 Ⓐ Ⓑ Ⓒ Ⓓ

3 Ⓐ Ⓑ Ⓒ Ⓓ   11 Ⓐ Ⓑ Ⓒ Ⓓ   19 Ⓐ Ⓑ Ⓒ Ⓓ   27 Ⓐ Ⓑ Ⓒ Ⓓ   35 Ⓐ Ⓑ Ⓒ Ⓓ

4 Ⓐ Ⓑ Ⓒ Ⓓ   12 Ⓐ Ⓑ Ⓒ Ⓓ   20 Ⓐ Ⓑ Ⓒ Ⓓ   28 Ⓐ Ⓑ Ⓒ Ⓓ   36 Ⓐ Ⓑ Ⓒ Ⓓ

5 Ⓐ Ⓑ Ⓒ Ⓓ   13 Ⓐ Ⓑ Ⓒ Ⓓ   21 Ⓐ Ⓑ Ⓒ Ⓓ   29 Ⓐ Ⓑ Ⓒ Ⓓ   37 Ⓐ Ⓑ Ⓒ Ⓓ

6 Ⓐ Ⓑ Ⓒ Ⓓ   14 Ⓐ Ⓑ Ⓒ Ⓓ   22 Ⓐ Ⓑ Ⓒ Ⓓ   30 Ⓐ Ⓑ Ⓒ Ⓓ   38 Ⓐ Ⓑ Ⓒ Ⓓ

7 Ⓐ Ⓑ Ⓒ Ⓓ   15 Ⓐ Ⓑ Ⓒ Ⓓ   23 Ⓐ Ⓑ Ⓒ Ⓓ   31 Ⓐ Ⓑ Ⓒ Ⓓ   39 Ⓐ Ⓑ Ⓒ Ⓓ

8 Ⓐ Ⓑ Ⓒ Ⓓ   16 Ⓐ Ⓑ Ⓒ Ⓓ   24 Ⓐ Ⓑ Ⓒ Ⓓ   32 Ⓐ Ⓑ Ⓒ Ⓓ   40 Ⓐ Ⓑ Ⓒ Ⓓ

SAMPLE TEST 5
(ExCET)

The Examination for the Certification of Educators in Texas (ExCET) Program consists of Professional Development Tests at three levels (elementary, secondary, all-level) and Content Specialization Tests in twenty-six different areas. Candidates for initial teacher certification in Texas must pass *both* a Professional Development Test at the appropriate level *and* a Content Specialization Test in each area for which certification is sought.

This Sample Test contains questions similar to those included on the ExCET Professional Development Tests. Each Professional Development Test contains 125 questions on assessment, evaluation, instructional methodology, classroom management, principles of education, instructional planning, and curriculum development. About three-quarters of the questions are the same for all three tests. The remaining questions are specific to elementary or secondary teaching. The test for all levels contains questions from both areas. Sample questions one through ten are elementary education questions, and sample questions eleven through twenty are representative of secondary education questions.

This Sample Test may also be used to practice for the Professional Knowledge Tests required by Alabama, Florida, and Georgia.

PROFESSIONAL DEVELOPMENT TEST

Directions: **For each question, choose the best answer and blacken the corresponding space on the Answer Sheet for Sample Test 5. There is no penalty for guessing so you should answer every question. Correct answers and explanations follow the test.**

1. Some children are ready for formal education at age four. Whether a child is ready for formal education or not depends primarily on the child's

   (A) age
   (B) maturity
   (C) home environment
   (D) physical size

2. Preparation of materials peripheral to classroom instruction such as copying, bulletin boards, supplies, guest speakers and report cards is the responsibility of the

   (A) classroom teacher
   (B) resource teacher
   (C) school secretary
   (D) teacher aide

3. If a teacher has a problem with another teacher, her first step toward resolution should be to

   (A) talk directly with the teacher involved
   (B) ask her fellow-teachers for their suggestions
   (C) ask her fellow-teachers to intercede on her behalf
   (D) discuss it with her principal

4. Discipline in the classroom is the responsibility of the

   (A) classroom teacher
   (B) principal
   (C) superintendent
   (D) board of education

5. Before a child is disciplined, the problem should be discussed with

   I. the student
   II. the parents
   III. the counselor
   IV. the principal or vice-principal
   V. the superintendent

   (A) I only
   (B) II only
   (C) I, II and III
   (D) I, II, III and IV

6. The main focus of preschool should be to

   (A) teach the children to read and to do arithmetic
   (B) ease the transition from home to school and help the child learn to get along with others
   (C) teach the child to be independent
   (D) teach the child to be competitive

7. Extracurricular activities in an elementary school, such as participating in parent-support group fund-raisers and preparing students for the Christmas play are

   (A) an imposition on teachers
   (B) at the teacher's volition
   (C) expected of teachers
   (D) part of what the teacher has contracted to perform

8. Students from foreign countries will not only have to learn English, but also have to

   (A) learn an additional language
   (B) learn a new form of mathematics
   (C) adapt to the cultural customs of their classmates
   (D) teach the language to their parents

9. Mr. Harrison has a computer with several math and spelling tutorial programs. These should be used as

(A) the primary instruction in the class
(B) reinforcement and drill in the lesson taught by Mr. Harrison
(C) an interesting amusement for students who have finished their homework
(D) a way of teaching the children to type

10. Whether a movie should be used in conjunction with a lesson or not depends mostly on

(A) whether the movie enhances the children's understanding of the lesson
(B) whether the movie is available on that date
(C) whether there is enough class time for the movie
(D) whether the movie is entertaining or not

11. The curriculum director of a new high school thinks that all students should take the same curriculum. Do you agree with this statement?

(A) Yes, because all students should graduate from high school with the same body of knowledge.
(B) No, because not all students have the same educational needs.
(C) Yes, because high school students are too young to decide what classes they need to take.
(D) No, because it would require too many teachers in the same fields, resulting in unfairness to teachers in the fields not taught.

12. To test whether a student knows what a particular word means, the teacher should ask the student to

(A) use it in a sentence
(B) define the word
(C) spell the word and identify its part of speech
(D) give the etymology of the word

13. A teacher gives the class a test on expo-

nents at the beginning of a new lesson to determine the extent of instruction needed. This illustrates

(A) assessment
(B) reinforcement
(C) awareness
(D) diagnosis

14. Mrs. Parsons has a ninth-grade career explorations class. To augment the textbook she could use

(A) movies showing ''A Day in the Life of . . .'' particular careers
(B) guest speakers from the community who would talk about their careers and the preparation needed for them
(C) information on careers from various professional organizations
(D) all of the above

15. A student marks a true–false test all ''true.'' From this the teacher can assume that

(A) the student was guessing at the answers
(B) the test was not well-constructed
(C) the student did not understand the instructions
(D) the student cheated

16. A student who is repeatedly truant is most appropriately punished by

(A) suspension
(B) extra homework
(C) detention
(E) being banned from extracurricular activities

17. Individual lesson plans are most effective

(A) with students who are of low intellect
(B) with students whose progress varies widely
(C) in classes with many students
(D) in classes with few students

18. A teacher wants to encourage creative thinking. She poses a question and

    (A) tells the students to come up with creative answers
    (B) accepts what the students consider creative answers
    (C) accepts all suggested answers
    (D) accepts only creative answers

19. With an increasing variety of family situations, a teacher needs to

    (A) be careful not to inadvertently offend some students
    (B) encourage students to improve their family situation
    (C) assume that all students want to know about a variety of family situations
    (D) broaden students' realization of different lifestyles

20. A teacher may use tests for

    (A) diagnosis
    (B) motivation
    (C) grouping students
    (D) all of the above

21. If a teacher introduces a concept, explains and demonstrates it, yet some students still don't understand it, the teacher should

    (A) accept the fact that some students never will comprehend it
    (B) go on to the next concept, because the schedule must be adhered to
    (C) explain the concept in various other ways because students learn in a variety of ways
    (D) continue, because it will become clear to the students later on, when they've had time to think it over

22. Before a teacher plans the lessons for a new unit, he needs to define the

    (A) goal of the unit
    (B) objectives of the unit
    (C) procedures of the unit
    (D) goals and objectives of the unit

23. One disadvantage of essay tests over true–false or multiple-choice tests is that essay tests

    (A) give the students too much freedom in their responses
    (B) offer no choices for the student
    (C) are difficult to standardize
    (D) take too much of the students' time

24. A teacher who usually asks a question to which he expects only one correct answer, is not encouraging

    (A) thinking
    (B) problem-solving
    (C) diverse thinking
    (D) critical thinking

25. Taking diverse information and deriving one solution from it is called

    (A) didactic thinking
    (B) deductive thinking
    (C) inductive thinking
    (D) critical thinking skills

26. The most effective teachers will use

    (A) group discussion for instruction
    (B) individualized programs for instruction
    (C) group teaching for instruction
    (D) each of the above when appropriate

27. A disadvantage of true–false tests is that

    (A) they take so little time that the students don't reflect on the answers
    (B) few statements are completely true or false
    (C) they can readily be standardized
    (D) scoring them is a lengthy procedure

28. If students are not responding to the teacher's questions, a method she could use to encourage responses is to

    (A) wait for a response
    (B) ask a specific student to answer after having asked the question
    (C) ask a specific student to respond, state the question, and wait for a response
    (D) tell the class that it will have detention unless answers are forthcoming

29. The purpose of the introduction to a new unit is

    (A) to arouse the students' interest in the unit
    (B) to inform the students about the objective of the unit
    (C) to show the students how this unit relates to the previous unit
    (D) all of the above

30. Migrant students may have difficulty in classes because they

    (A) are mentally less able to do the work
    (B) have no continuity of curriculum
    (C) may not understand English well
    (D) are not accustomed to the culture

31. A student who scored in the 78th percentile on a grammar test

    (A) answered 78 percent of the questions correctly
    (B) answered 78 percent better than the average score
    (C) scored higher than 78 percent of the students
    (D) scored lower than 78 percent of the students

32. Which of the following indicate the same level of achievement?

    I. High school diploma.
    II. GED Diploma.
    III. Passing the high school equivalency examination

    (A) I and II
    (B) II and III
    (C) I and III
    (D) none of them

33. A teacher would use a standardized test

    (A) as a final examination
    (B) as a unit test
    (C) because they're easy to grade
    (D) to compare her students to national norms

34. The right of parents to review their child's educational records is guaranteed by the

    (A) Buckley Amendment
    (B) Miranda Rule
    (C) Dewey System
    (D) Bennett Amendment

Questions 35 and 36

If a parent is concerned about a grade his child received compared to another student's, and demands to see both students' grades, the teacher should

35. (A) show both records to him
    (B) show only his child's record
    (C) refuse to show either record
    (D) refuse to show any records without express permission from the principal

36. What is the basis for your answer in question 35?

    (A) Parents have the right to see their child's records and the records of classmates for verification of fairness.
    (B) Parents do not have the right to see any student's records.
    (C) Parents do not have the right to see other students' records, but do have the right to see their own child's records.
    (D) Teachers need the principal's permission to divulge confidential information.

37. Lesson objectives should be known and understood by

    (A) the teacher and the students in the class
    (B) the students in the class
    (C) the curriculum coordinator and the teacher
    (D) the teacher

38. Controversy about teaching evolution in schools

    (A) is a recently evolved issue
    (B) does not affect teachers or students
    (C) is an issue of long standing
    (D) is an issue which has been resolved

39. A student would learn fastest by

   (A) hearing material to be learned

   (B) reading material to be learned

   (C) writing material to be learned

   (D) hearing, reading and writing the material to be learned

40. The purpose of administering a pre-test and a post-test to students is to

   (A) measure gains in learning
   (B) keep adequate records
   (C) accustom the students to frequent testing
   (D) measure the value of the material taught

ANSWERS TO SAMPLE TEST 5

1.	**B**	9.	**B**	17.	**B**	25.	**B**	33.	**D**
2.	**A**	10.	**A**	18.	**C**	26.	**D**	34.	**A**
3.	**A**	11.	**B**	19.	**A**	27.	**B**	35.	**B**
4.	**A**	12.	**B**	20.	**D**	28.	**A**	36.	**C**
5.	**D**	13.	**D**	21.	**C**	29.	**D**	37.	**A**
6.	**B**	14.	**D**	22.	**D**	30.	**B**	38.	**C**
7.	**C**	15.	**A**	23.	**C**	31.	**C**	39.	**D**
8.	**C**	16.	**C**	24.	**C**	32.	**D**	40.	**A**

EXPLANATION OF ANSWERS TO SAMPLE TEST 5

1. **B** The primary consideration is the child's maturity.

2. **A** Even though others may be assigned to do copying, the responsibility is that of the teacher, particularly report cards.

3. **A** Direct contact and resolution should be tried before bringing others into the situation.

4. **A** The teacher is responsible for discipline in her class.

5. **D** The student, parents, counselor and principal should all be informed and consulted.

6. **B** Preschool is a transition from home.

7. **C** The activities are expected of teachers.

8. **C** Each culture is different, and in order to get along, the students need to learn the local cultural customs.

9. **B** Computers are best used for reinforcement, not initial learning.

10. **A** The primary consideration is whether the movie is appropriate for the lesson or not.

11. **B** Students have varying educational needs.

12. **B** Defining a word is a good test of whether someone knows the meaning of a word or not.

13. **D** A pre-test is used for diagnosis.

14. **D** Answer choices A, B and C will all enhance the learning experience.

15. **A** The student is guessing.

16. **C** The student should have to spend more time at school.

17. **B** When students progress at widely different rates, group lessons are not as effective as individual lesson plans.

18. **C** To encourage creative thinking, no answers should be discouraged.

19. **A** Teachers need to be sensitive to what may offend or hurt students.

20. **D** Tests can be used for several reasons including diagnosis, motivation and grouping.

21. **C** Students learn in a variety of ways.

22. **D** What is to be learned and how the learning is to be measured needs to be defined.

23. **C** Each essay is different, and grading is more subjective.

24. **C** A teacher who encourages diverse thinking solicits a variety of answers.

25. **B** From a variety of information, a person deduces a solution.

26. **D** Different methods are appropriate for different situations and teachers need to use whichever is best.

27. **B** Most questions have shades of meanings.

28. **A** If given time, ten to fifteen seconds, and no one else answers, students who might not ordinarily volunteer answers will often respond.

29. **D** Introductions to units are transitions. They arouse interest and give a preview of the unit.

30. **B** The students have to get accustomed to new surroundings, teachers, books and curriculum in addition to learning the material.

31. **C** Percentile ranking indicates what percent of students scored lower than that test-taker.

32. **D** All have different standards of achievement.

33. **D** Standardized tests compare students' scores to national norms.

34. **A** The Buckley Amendment guarantees parents the right of access to their children's records.

35. **B** A parent can see his own child's records, but the privacy acts prohibit a teacher from showing records to other students or parents.

36. **C** See question 35, above.

37. **A** Both the teacher and the students should know and understand the objectives.

38. **C** Teaching or not teaching the theory of evo-lution has been and remains a source of contro-versy.

39. **D** The more senses that are involved in learn-ing, the faster the learning.

40. **A** Pre- and post-testing measure gains in learn-ing specific material.

SAMPLE TEST 6

This test is similar to the Florida Teacher Certification Examination. It also provides excellent practice for the teacher certification tests given in Colorado, Illinois, Michigan, and South Carolina. The Professional Knowledge Section can be used to prepare for any state test that includes a professional knowledge component, such as Alabama, Georgia, Kansas, and Texas. In addition, Florida also requires a specialty area test, given on a separate day.

Format of the Florida Teacher Certification Examination

Writing Test	one essay	45 minutes
Basic Skills Test	130 questions	120 minutes
Mathematics	50 questions	
Reading	80 questions	

————————————— *Break* —————————————

Professional Knowledge Test	80 questions	150 minutes

Test-Taking Strategies

You have two hours for the Basic Skills test, which includes both mathematics and reading tests. Distribute your time as you think best. The reading portion does not take very long, so you might consider doing that first, then the mathematics. You will probably find that you can do the reading section in 50 minutes or less, leaving 70 minutes for the math.

No scratch paper is provided, so write on the test booklet.

The number of answer choices varies from question to question.

To be confident of passing the test, you should answer 64 reading questions, 40 mathematics questions and 64 professional knowledge questions correctly.

WRITING
45 Minutes–One Essay

Directions: You have 45 minutes to write an essay on either Topic 1 or Topic 2. The essay topics are intended to measure how well you write, given limitations on time and subject matter. Quality is more important than quantity. Spend some of your time organizing your thoughts. Supporting statements and examples should be specific. Write only on the assigned topic. Write legibly and within the lines provided. Space for notes is provided below.

Topic 1
What is the most important thing you learned from student teaching, and in what way did it change your concept of teaching?

Topic 2
George Whitefield said, "I had rather wear out than rust out." Using your experience and observations, explain why you agree or disagree.

(Write "**Topic 1**" or "**Topic 2.**")

_____

_____

_____

_____

_____

_____

_____

_____

_____

_____

_____

_____

_____

_____

_____

_____

_____

_____

_____

_____

_____

_____

ANSWER SHEETS FOR SAMPLE TEST 6

Basic Skills

Mathematics

	A	B	C	D	E		A	B	C	D	E		A	B	C	D	E		A	B	C	D	E		A	B	C	D	E
1	○	○	○	○	○	11	○	○	○	○	○	21	○	○	○	○	○	31	○	○	○	○	○	41	○	○	○	○	○
2	○	○	○	○	○	12	○	○	○	○	○	22	○	○	○	○	○	32	○	○	○	○	○	42	○	○	○	○	○
3	○	○	○	○	○	13	○	○	○	○	○	23	○	○	○	○	○	33	○	○	○	○	○	43	○	○	○	○	○
4	○	○	○	○	○	14	○	○	○	○	○	24	○	○	○	○	○	34	○	○	○	○	○	44	○	○	○	○	○
5	○	○	○	○	○	15	○	○	○	○	○	25	○	○	○	○	○	35	○	○	○	○	○	45	○	○	○	○	○
6	○	○	○	○	○	16	○	○	○	○	○	26	○	○	○	○	○	36	○	○	○	○	○	46	○	○	○	○	○
7	○	○	○	○	○	17	○	○	○	○	○	27	○	○	○	○	○	37	○	○	○	○	○	47	○	○	○	○	○
8	○	○	○	○	○	18	○	○	○	○	○	28	○	○	○	○	○	38	○	○	○	○	○	48	○	○	○	○	○
9	○	○	○	○	○	19	○	○	○	○	○	29	○	○	○	○	○	39	○	○	○	○	○	49	○	○	○	○	○
10	○	○	○	○	○	20	○	○	○	○	○	30	○	○	○	○	○	40	○	○	○	○	○	50	○	○	○	○	○

Reading

	A	B	C	D	E		A	B	C	D	E		A	B	C	D	E		A	B	C	D	E		A	B	C	D	E
1	○	○	○	○	○	11	○	○	○	○	○	21	○	○	○	○	○	31	○	○	○	○	○	41	○	○	○	○	○
2	○	○	○	○	○	12	○	○	○	○	○	22	○	○	○	○	○	32	○	○	○	○	○	42	○	○	○	○	○
3	○	○	○	○	○	13	○	○	○	○	○	23	○	○	○	○	○	33	○	○	○	○	○	43	○	○	○	○	○
4	○	○	○	○	○	14	○	○	○	○	○	24	○	○	○	○	○	34	○	○	○	○	○	44	○	○	○	○	○
5	○	○	○	○	○	15	○	○	○	○	○	25	○	○	○	○	○	35	○	○	○	○	○	45	○	○	○	○	○
6	○	○	○	○	○	16	○	○	○	○	○	26	○	○	○	○	○	36	○	○	○	○	○	46	○	○	○	○	○
7	○	○	○	○	○	17	○	○	○	○	○	27	○	○	○	○	○	37	○	○	○	○	○	47	○	○	○	○	○
8	○	○	○	○	○	18	○	○	○	○	○	28	○	○	○	○	○	38	○	○	○	○	○	48	○	○	○	○	○
9	○	○	○	○	○	19	○	○	○	○	○	29	○	○	○	○	○	39	○	○	○	○	○	49	○	○	○	○	○
10	○	○	○	○	○	20	○	○	○	○	○	30	○	○	○	○	○	40	○	○	○	○	○	50	○	○	○	○	○

Reading (continued)

	A B C D E		A B C D E		A B C D E		A B C D E		A B C D E
51	○○○○○	57	○○○○○	63	○○○○○	69	○○○○○	75	○○○○○
52	○○○○○	58	○○○○○	64	○○○○○	70	○○○○○	76	○○○○○
53	○○○○○	59	○○○○○	65	○○○○○	71	○○○○○	77	○○○○○
54	○○○○○	60	○○○○○	66	○○○○○	72	○○○○○	78	○○○○○
55	○○○○○	61	○○○○○	67	○○○○○	73	○○○○○	79	○○○○○
56	○○○○○	62	○○○○○	68	○○○○○	74	○○○○○	80	○○○○○

PROFESSIONAL KNOWLEDGE

	A B C D E		A B C D E		A B C D E		A B C D E		A B C D E
1	○○○○○	17	○○○○○	33	○○○○○	49	○○○○○	65	○○○○○
2	○○○○○	18	○○○○○	34	○○○○○	50	○○○○○	66	○○○○○
3	○○○○○	19	○○○○○	35	○○○○○	51	○○○○○	67	○○○○○
4	○○○○○	20	○○○○○	36	○○○○○	52	○○○○○	68	○○○○○
5	○○○○○	21	○○○○○	37	○○○○○	53	○○○○○	69	○○○○○
6	○○○○○	22	○○○○○	38	○○○○○	54	○○○○○	70	○○○○○
7	○○○○○	23	○○○○○	39	○○○○○	55	○○○○○	71	○○○○○
8	○○○○○	24	○○○○○	40	○○○○○	56	○○○○○	72	○○○○○
9	○○○○○	25	○○○○○	41	○○○○○	57	○○○○○	73	○○○○○
10	○○○○○	26	○○○○○	42	○○○○○	58	○○○○○	74	○○○○○
11	○○○○○	27	○○○○○	43	○○○○○	59	○○○○○	75	○○○○○
12	○○○○○	28	○○○○○	44	○○○○○	60	○○○○○	76	○○○○○
13	○○○○○	29	○○○○○	45	○○○○○	61	○○○○○	77	○○○○○
14	○○○○○	30	○○○○○	46	○○○○○	62	○○○○○	78	○○○○○
15	○○○○○	31	○○○○○	47	○○○○○	63	○○○○○	79	○○○○○
16	○○○○○	32	○○○○○	48	○○○○○	64	○○○○○	80	○○○○○

BASIC SKILLS
120 Minutes–130 Questions

Directions: **Choose the best answer for each question and blacken the corresponding space on the Answer Sheets for Sample Test 7. The correct answers and the explanations follow the test.**

MATHEMATICS (50 Questions)

1. Beth and Kay drive separate cars from Stardust to Knightown, a distance of 300 miles. They both start at the same time. Beth drives at 60 miles per hour, while Kay drives at 50 miles per hour. Who will arrive in Knightown first, and by how much?

   (A) Beth by 1 hour
   (B) Kay by 1 hour
   (C) Beth by 5 hours
   (D) They will arrive at the same time.

2. Harry is editing a 180-page book. He edited one quarter of it the first week in May and another quarter of it the second week. He wants to divide the remaining pages evenly over the last two weeks of May. How many pages will he have to edit each of the last two weeks?

   (A) 15 pages
   (B) 45 pages
   (C) 26 pages
   (D) 90 pages

3. $-6 - (+9) =$

   (A) -3
   (B) 3
   (C) 15
   (D) -15

4. Kenny had a balance of $107.52 in his checking account. On Tuesday he wrote checks for $57.61 and $47.16. Wednesday he deposited his paycheck of $452.63. He got his statement from the bank showing service charges of $9.70 on Thursday. In order to balance his checkbook, Kenny should take his beginning balance of $107.52 and

   (A) add $452.63 and $9.70; subtract $57.61 and 47.16
   (B) add $452.63, $57.61, and $47.16; subtract $9.70
   (C) subtract $452.63; add $9.70, $57.61, and $47.16
   (D) add $452.63; subtract $57.61, $47.16, and $9.70

Questions 5 to 7

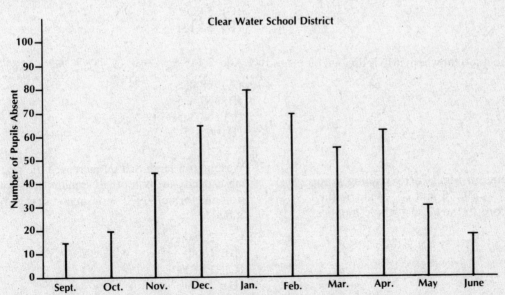

Clear Water School District

5. How many students were absent in December?

   (A) 80
   (B) 60
   (C) 65
   (D) 70

6. Approximately how many absences were there during the school year?

   (A) 450
   (B) 460
   (C) 470
   (D) 480

7. What was the approximate average number of absences each month?

   (A) 35
   (B) 40
   (C) 45
   (D) 50

8. Mr. Jeremy earns $18,408 a year. What is his monthly salary?

   (A) $1,840.80
   (B) $184,080
   (C) $1,534
   (D) $220,896

9. When 173,712 is divided by 231, what is the remainder?

   (A) 117
   (B) 0
   (C) 93
   (D) 233

10. What is the quotient when 5616 is divided by 39?

    (A) 5616
    (B) 144
    (C) 39
    (D) 0

11. The students in Mrs. Carr's reading group score 75, 81, 79, 78 and 73. What is their average score to the closest whole number?

    (A) 75
    (B) 77
    (C) 78
    (D) 79

12. Shona had monthly bank balances of $1,024.57, $1,246.85, $30.47, $117.61, $351.13, $573.37, $1,994.55, $65.76, $1,708.84, $2,007.92, $3,462.01, and $1,280.09. What was her average balance for the year?

    (A) $1,155.27
    (B) $1,155.26
    (C) $1,386.32
    (D) $13,863.17

13. How much more than 7 lb 7 oz is 11 lb 5 oz?

    (A) 3 lb 14 oz
    (B) 4 lb 2 oz
    (C) 3 lb 8 oz
    (D) 18 lb 12 oz

Questions 14 and 15

Thomas is carpeting his den, which measures 17 feet by 27 feet. The carpet he buys cost $9 per square yard.

14. How many square yards of carpet will he have to buy?

    (A) 45
    (B) 51
    (C) 54
    (D) 459

15. How much will the carpeting cost?

    (A) $405
    (B) $459
    (C) $486
    (D) $4,131

16. Add 2,745 + 839 + 62,487 + 987 + 1,247.

    (A) 68,035
    (B) 68,835
    (C) 68,305
    (D) 6,835

17. Washington High School increased the seating capacity at its football stadium to 9,850 from the former 7,970. How many seats were added?

    (A) 2,880
    (B) 1,880
    (C) 17,820
    (D) 1,820

18. A car has a 17-gallon gas tank. If it averages 29 miles per gallon, how far can it travel on a tank of gas?

    (A) 503 miles
    (B) 12 miles
    (C) 46 miles
    (D) 493 miles

19. Widget stock opened for the week at 17 ⅝. The stock gained ⅛ point on Monday, ⅞ on Tuesday, 1½ on Wednesday, ¾ on Thursday and ⅜ on Friday. What was the closing quotation of Widget stock at the end of the week?

    (A) 3⅝
    (B) 20¹¹⁄₈
    (C) 20⅞
    (D) 21¼

20. Jane bought a washing machine for $595. She paid $85 down and will pay the balance in 30 equal monthly installments. How much is each payment?

    (A) $30
    (B) $85
    (C) $17
    (D) $35

21. If a passenger flies 10,000 miles on Horizon Airlines, she will get a free trip. Suzanne flew 4,576 miles in January, 1,379 miles in February and 3,597 miles in March. How many miles will she need to fly in April to qualify for the free trip?

    (A) None, she has flown more than 10,000 miles already.
    (B) 48 miles
    (C) 448 miles
    (D) 488 miles

22. 98 is 35% of what number?

    (A) 133
    (B) 343
    (C) 280
    (D) 350

23. ½ − ⅓ =

    (A) − ⁹⁄₁
    (B) ⅖

    (C) ⅕
    (D) ⅙

24. Kenny has a balance of $107.52 in his checking account. On Tuesday, he wrote checks for $57.61 and $47.16. Wednesday, he deposited his paycheck of $452.63. He got his statement from the bank showing a service charge of $9.70 on Thursday. What is the new balance in Kenny's checking account?

    (A) $465.08
    (B) $655.22
    (C) $444.28
    (D) $445.68

25. To mail a package costs $.20 for the first ounce and $.17 for each additional ounce. How much does a package weigh that costs $2.24 to mail?

    (A) 11.2 oz
    (B) 10.3 oz
    (C) 13 oz
    (D) 13.18 oz

26.

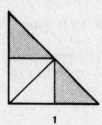 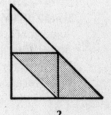

1   2

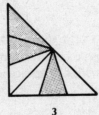 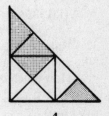

3   4

In which triangles are the shaded portions equivalent?

    (A) none
    (B) 1 and 3
    (C) 1, 2 and 3
    (D) all

27. There was ⅝ of a pie left over from dinner. Howard ate ⅖ of what was left. How much of the pie did Howard eat?

    (A) ¹⁄₄₀
    (B) ⅜
    (C) ¼
    (D) ⅔

28. Using the information from question 27, how much of the pie was left after Howard had his snack?

    (A) ⅜
    (B) ¼
    (C) ⅔
    (D) ⅓

29. Find 0.375 of $28.65 to the nearest cent.

    (A) $10.74
    (B) $107.40
    (C) $1,074.00
    (D) $1,074,000.00

30. Mr. Friesen has worked out the following formula for year-end grades in history class:

    $$\frac{(15\ P + 67\ T + 18\ F)}{100} = \text{final grade}$$

    where P = grade on term paper; T = semester test average; and F = grade on final. What grade will Herman get if he had 74 on his term paper, 87 on his final, and his test average was 69?

    (A) 73
    (B) 76
    (C) 77
    (D) 82

31. Ralph made deposits of $127.50, $1,547.05, and $57.55 to his savings account this month. How much did he add to his savings account?

    (A) $1,740.10
    (B) $1,732.10
    (C) $1,732.05
    (D) $1,740.05

32. The scale on a map is 1 inch = 30 miles. How far apart will two cities be on the map if the actual distance between them is 480 miles?

    (A) 450 inches
    (B) 510 inches

    (C) 16 inches
    (D) 16 miles

33. Harry is editing a 180-page book. He edited ¼ of it the first week in May and ⅓ of the remainder the second week in May. He wants to divide the remaining pages to be edited evenly over the last two weeks of May. How many pages will he have to edit each of the last two weeks?

    (A) 15 pages
    (B) 26 pages
    (C) 45 pages
    (D) 60 pages

34. There are 34 students in each of three first grades. In the other three first grades there are 35, 37, and 31 students, respectively. How many first-grade students are in the school?

    (A) 137
    (B) 205
    (C) 195
    (D) 441

35. The expenses for the AB Company in March were $4,896.31. The gross income was $5,201.13. What was the net income?

    (A) $305.22
    (B) $304.82
    (C) $304.22
    (D) $305.18

36. Horace had a part-time job. Monday he worked 2¾ hours, Tuesday and Wednesday he worked 1⅓ hours each, Thursday he worked 2½ hours, and on Friday he worked 3 hours. How many hours did he work last week?

    (A) 10¹¹⁄₁₂
    (B) 9⁷⁄₁₂
    (C) 9⁵⁄₁₂
    (D) 9⅓

37. Barbara bought the following items: hair-spray, $2.97; cotton swabs, $1.39; cotton puffs, $1.27; shampoo, $2.57; hair rinse, $1.96; comb, $1.34. How much did she spend at the drug store?

    (A) $11.60

(B) $11.45
(C) $11.50
(D) $11.40

38. Carole got 55% on her last test. The passing score is 70%. How much did she need to increase her score to pass?

(A) 125%
(B) 25%
(C) 15%
(D) 10%

39.

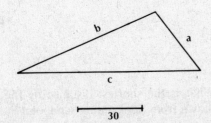

What is the length of side *b* according to the scale?

(A) 60
(B) 75
(C) 40
(D) 90

40. Mike bought a shirt for $12.96 and a tie for $8.77. He gave the clerk $25. How much change should he get?

(A) $3.27
(B) $12.04
(C) $16.23
(D) $21.73

41.

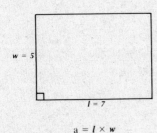
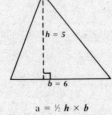

a = l × w   a = ½ h × b

Irene wants to carpet two play areas. The formula for the area is given below each figure. What is the total area to be carpeted?

(A) 15
(B) 23
(C) 35
(D) 50

42. 7.12 [2.3 − (0.6 × 7 − 1.9)] =

(A) −27.056
(B) 0
(C) 10.276
(D) 26.9136

43. What is ½ of ⅟₆₃?

(A) −½
(B) ⅟₆₃
(C) ⅔₃
(D) ½

44. Clark bought a set of tires for $178.15. The tax rate is 6%. How much sales tax did he pay?

(A) $10.69
(B) $29.69
(C) $2.96
(D) $10.78

45. A teacher works seven hours a day for 186 days during the school year. Of that time, ⅔ is nonteaching time, and ⅟₁₅ of the nonteaching time is spent in meetings. How many hours are spent in meetings each year?

(A) 4⅖
(B) 24⅖
(C) 118
(D) 43

46. The Horatio Alger High School cafeteria serves 760 students. One hundred grams of meat is used in each hamburger. If each student gets two hamburgers, how many kilos of beef are used?

(A) 152
(B) 380
(C) 1520
(D) 15,200

47. Carole is making costumes for the school play. Each costume uses ⅝ yard of fabric. How many costumes can she make out of 7 ⅕ yards of fabric?

    (A) ¹/₁₂
    (B) 11
    (C) 25
    (D) 288

48. Mr. Everett's monthly salary is $1,250, of which he saves $137.50. What percentage of his salary does he save?

    (A) 0.11%
    (B) 11%
    (C) 11.25%
    (D) 17.1875%

49. Elaine was born on November 12, 1978. How old was she when she started school on September 9, 1984?

    (A) 6 years, 2 months, 3 days
    (B) 5 years, 9 months, 3 days
    (C) 5 years, 2 months, 27 days
    (D) 5 years, 9 months, 27 days

50.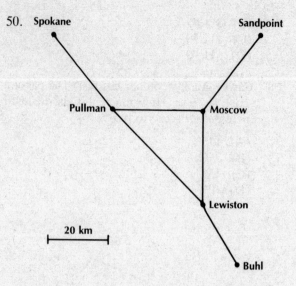

What is the shortest distance by the roads shown from Spokane to Sandpoint?

    (A) 67 km
    (B) 140 km
    (C) 90 km
    (D) 104 km

READING (80 Questions)

Directions: Choose the word that best fits into each blank in the passage.

Questions 1 to 10

One of the things that new teachers or _____ in a new situation fear is losing control of the _____. Letting a class have group discussion or break into _____ for an activity _____ a certain _____ of abdication of control and trust in the group. Without this, however, few teachers can _____ a high level of _____ achievement. How this important facet of _____ is to be _____ is the subject of _____ discussion and debate.

1. (A) teachers
   (B) assistance
   (C) administrators
   (D) students

2. (A) discipline
   (B) reins
   (C) lesson
   (D) class

3. (A) groups
   (B) pieces
   (C) cliques
   (D) friends

4. (A) portends
   (B) involves
   (C) places
   (D) pretends

5. (A) total
   (B) limit
   (C) segment
   (D) amount

6. (A) attest
   (B) set
   (C) attain
   (D) get

7. (A) requirement
   (B) peak
   (C) goal
   (D) aim

8. (A) teaching
   (B) learning
   (C) student
   (D) teacher

9. (A) applied
   (B) approached
   (C) used
   (D) arranged

10. (A) angry
    (B) many
    (C) lengthy
    (D) considerable

Questions 11 to 20

Many teachers who _____ involvement say that it makes a class more _____. It seems to make the time go faster and make a class less boring. It _____ students to concentrate on the _____. They can't "tune out." There _____ many other reasons given for involvement, but the only _____ that it should be _____ is that it is the best method _____ accomplishing the _____ learning goal. This criterion should be used in deciding whether to use any _____ technique.

11. (A) avoid
    (B) advance
    (C) advocate
    (D) avow

12. (A) interesting
    (B) active
    (C) challenging
    (D) action

13. (A) makes
    (B) plods
    (C) coerces
    (D) forces

14. (A) book
    (B) subject
    (C) item
    (D) blackboard

15. (A) are
    (B) seem to be
    (C) were
    (D) will be

16. (A) reason
    (B) purpose
    (C) wary
    (D) method

17. (A) noticed
    (B) used
    (C) discarded
    (D) ignored

18. (A) for
    (B) to
    (C) of
    (D) how

19. (A) specific
    (B) corollary
    (C) momentous
    (D) specious

20. (A) learning
    (B) processed
    (C) training
    (D) teaching

Questions 21 to 30

Adults can learn from listening to _____, but they are more likely to _____ from discussion. Since nearly all _____ learning is self-directed, why do some not _____ in discussion? _____ questioning you will often find that the _____ thinks that she will be _____ and that her ideas are not _____ to the group. This person has been trained not to participate, and until this _____ is overcome, she will not get the full learning _____ that she should from a teaching session.

21. (A) lectures
    (B) tapes
    (C) videos
    (D) discussion

22. (A) achieve
    (B) learn
    (C) advance
    (D) shy

23. (A) valuable
    (B) childhood
    (C) cogent
    (D) adult

24. (A) result
    (B) participate
    (C) recommend
    (D) advise

25. (A) Despite
    (B) Without
    (C) With
    (D) Upon

26. (A) nonparticipant
    (B) participant
    (C) advocate
    (D) instructor

27. (A) ostracized
    (B) deleted
    (C) embarrassed
    (D) challenged

28. (A) tolerated
    (B) viable
    (C) valuable
    (D) received

29. (A) feeling
    (B) idea
    (C) neuroticism
    (D) training

30. (A) benefits
    (B) idea
    (C) joys
    (D) training

Questions 31 to 40

A recent _____ revealed that college stu-
            31
dents don't think that their _____ should be
                            32
humorous. When questioned _____, they
                          33
said that professors who used _____ in the
                             34
classroom were not projecting the correct

_____, and did not seem to take themselves,
   35
the subject, or the _____ seriously enough.
                   36
Interestingly though, students _____ the
                              37
serious material the professor using humor pre-

sented much _____ than the material of
            38
nonhumorous _____. Could it be that these
            39
students think that learning has to be _____?
                                      40

31. (A) book
    (B) survey
    (C) thesis
    (D) theory

32. (A) professors
    (B) friends

(C) parents
(D) counselors

33. (A) further
    (B) again
    (C) later
    (D) persistently

34. (A) charts
    (B) posters
    (C) humor
    (D) experiments

35. (A) image
    (B) position
    (C) posters
    (D) format

36. (A) university
    (B) department
    (C) peers
    (D) students

37. (A) remember
    (B) forget
    (C) like
    (D) enjoy

38. (A) less
    (B) better
    (C) slower
    (D) deeper

39. (A) people
    (B) lectures
    (C) professors
    (D) friends

40. (A) fun
    (B) humorous
    (C) serious
    (D) dull

Questions 41 to 50

Salesmen make a point of _____ your name
                        41
and using it often. Teachers are salesmen of sorts,

too. Think how _____ it feels when someone
              42
remembers your name, and how _____ it
                            43

feels when someone doesn't. It is _____ to
44
learn your students' names as soon as possible.

_____ each student as he comes into the
45
room, _____ on his name and using it will
46
help you remember. If the students keep the same

_____ you will more readily _____ the
47   48
name and the face. Try to think of something

distinctive that will _____ the person's face
49
and name. The more often you use a person's

name, the better you will remember it. What did

you say your _____ is, again?
50

41. (A) saying
    (B) learning
    (C) speaking
    (D) reading

42. (A) happy
    (B) new
    (C) good
    (D) novel

43. (A) good
    (B) poor
    (C) strange
    (D) awful

44. (A) important
    (B) convenient
    (C) pleasant
    (D) customary

45. (A) Meeting
    (B) Greeting
    (C) Seeing
    (D) Watching

46. (A) thinking
    (B) contemplating
    (C) concentrating
    (D) looking

47. (A) names
    (B) friends
    (C) name tags
    (D) places

48. (A) remember
    (B) recall
    (C) associate
    (D) forget

49. (A) link
    (B) combine
    (C) stand out
    (D) erase

50. (A) school
    (B) job
    (C) position
    (D) name

Questions 51 to 60

How you treat your _____ at an early age
51
may affect _____ he becomes a conformist
52
or a (an) _____. Although _____ want
53   54
their children to be well behaved and _____,
55
they want the children to grow up to be indepen-

tent and _____. _____ are influenced
56   57
by their own situation. Parents belonging to lower

economic groups who want their children to

_____ will stress conformity as a way to get
58
ahead. Parents who are secure in _____
59
society encourage their _____ to take risks.
60

51. (A) pet
    (B) wife
    (C) husband
    (D) child

52. (A) whether
    (B) how
    (C) if
    (D) when

53. (A) reprobate
    (B) individualist
    (C) delinquent
    (D) complaint

54. (A) teachers
    (B) parents
    (C) educators
    (D) impediments

55. (A) defenseless
    (B) tidy
    (C) compliant
    (D) complaint

56. (A) creative
    (B) dependent
    (C) quiet
    (D) unobtrusive

57. (A) Children
    (B) Girls
    (C) Boys
    (D) Parents

58. (A) conform
    (B) leave
    (C) succeed
    (D) stay

59. (A) established
    (B) primitive
    (C) edges
    (D) high

60. (A) friends
    (B) children
    (C) spouses
    (D) individuals

Questions 61 to 70

Teacher-education programs have come under much criticism lately. Many _____ advocate
61
doing away with all teacher-education classes, _____ courses on the material to be
62
_____. However, the teacher's knowledge of
63

_____ is of no value to the students
64
_____ the teacher can convey it to those
65
students. To do this, the teacher needs to learn about classroom control, grading, various methods of teaching to ensure maximum _____,
66
how to make a lesson interesting, and where and how to get _____ resources. The teacher also
67
needs to know about child and _____ psy-
68
chology, _____ law, and the educational
69
administrative system. Teacher-education courses are the best way to learn the tools of the _____.
70

61. (A) professors
    (B) teachers
    (C) critics
    (D) students

62. (A) substituting
    (B) using
    (C) having
    (D) without

63. (A) used
    (B) new
    (C) learned
    (D) taught

64. (A) teaching
    (B) subject matter
    (C) facts
    (D) students

65. (A) unless
    (B) when
    (C) if
    (D) whether

66. (A) time
    (B) effort
    (C) lesson
    (D) learning

67. (A) appropriate
    (B) examination
    (C) college
    (D) school

68. (A) children
    (B) adult
    (C) school
    (D) adolescent

69. (A) state
    (B) civil rights
    (C) personal rights
    (D) school

70. (A) teaching
    (B) profession
    (C) learning
    (D) process

Questions 71 to 80

In the _____ for better _____ skills,
     71   72
many companies, followed by several _____
                            73
of the armed _____, have sponsored listen-
          74
ing seminars. The _____ of listening as a
              75
learned skill has _____ filtered down
              76
through the U.S. educational _____. Con-
              77
gress has added speaking and _____ to the
              78
three Rs as _____ skills to be _____ in
     79   80
the public schools.

71. (A) horror
    (B) quest
    (C) wish
    (D) job

72. (A) listening
    (B) speaking
    (C) basic
    (D) upgraded

73. (A) areas
    (B) captains
    (C) generals
    (D) branches

74. (A) guards
    (B) forest
    (C) services
    (D) men

75. (A) good
    (B) promise
    (C) way
    (D) idea

76. (A) slowly
    (B) not
    (C) never
    (D) always

77. (A) branches
    (B) system
    (C) colleges
    (D) methods

78. (A) talking
    (B) hearing
    (C) listening
    (D) mathematics

79. (A) basic
    (B) new
    (C) viable
    (D) popular

80. (A) used
    (B) proved
    (C) held
    (D) taught

PROFESSIONAL KNOWLEDGE
150 Minutes–80 Questions

Directions: Choose the best answer for each question and blacken the corresponding space on the Answer Sheet for Sample Test 3. The correct answers and the explanations follow the test.

1. Which of the following is the most effective way of introducing a topic?

    (A) lecture
    (B) discussion

2. The major benefit of parent-school committees is that

    (A) parents feel part of the school
    (B) teachers don't have to do all the work

3. The school district has proposed a new program. It will be most successful if the people involved in it are

    (A) teachers only, so that it will be run most efficiently
    (B) teachers and parents
    (C) teachers, parents and community

4. The purpose of norm-referenced tests is

    (A) to find out if the students are normal
    (B) to find out what percent of the questions the students got right
    (C) to compare the students with other similar students

5. Jaime scored 60 on a percentile-ranked test. This means that

    (A) 60% of the students taking the test scored higher than Jaime
    (B) 60% of the students taking the test scored lower than Jaime
    (C) Jaime got 60% of the questions right
    (D) Jaime got 60% of the questions wrong

6. When explaining percentile-ranked tests to the public, it is important to state

I. what group took the test
II. that the scores show how students performed in relation to other students
III. that the scores show how students performed according to an absolute measure

    (A) I
    (B) I and II
    (C) I, II and III
    (D) II and III

7. Parent-teacher conferences should be

    (A) scheduled for the convenience of the teacher
    (B) scheduled for the convenience of the parents
    (C) scheduled for the mutual convenience of the teacher and parents

8. Parent-teacher conferences should cover

    (A) problems the student is experiencing
    (B) successes the student has had
    (C) over-all progress

9. Testing is used to

    (A) comply with state requirements
    (B) satisfy parents' concerns
    (C) evaluate students' progress

10. If a teacher wants to let a child know that he has done well, the best way is to

    (A) write a note and place it in his folder
    (B) write a note to be taken home
    (C) tell him he has done well

11. If a child is to be spanked (consistent with state law and school board policy), the teacher should inform the

    (A) principal
    (B) principal and counselor
    (C) principal, counselor and parents
    (D) parent

12. A teacher needs to use good planning and management of time in order to

    (A) leave the school at a reasonable time in the afternoon
    (B) cover all the material she has planned

13. An advantage of weekly or monthly staff meetings is

    (A) learning peers' concerns and news of the school and district
    (B) camaraderie
    (C) learning what is on the weekly bulletin

14. It is beneficial for a teacher who is new to a school to

    (A) keep to herself for a time until she is confident
    (B) get to know a few teachers who have the same type of class
    (C) get to know as many of the teachers and support staff as possible

15. "The students will be able to spell forty words with 95% accuracy." This is a (an)

    (A) goal
    (B) objective
    (C) evaluation
    (D) concept

16. The major advantage of competency-based instruction is that

    (A) both teacher and students will know what the goal is and when the goal has been reached
    (B) goals are stated in concrete terms
    (C) lesson plans don't have to be rewritten continually

17. A lesson plan is a major tool for a teacher in
    I. time management
    II. progress evaluation
    III. contingencies, such as illness

    (A) I, II and III
    (B) III
    (C) II and III
    (D) I and III

18. To involve your class in the democratic process, you would

    (A) let the students plan the next unit to be studied
    (B) let the students present the next unit to be studied
    (C) have a class discussion on what the students would like to learn from the unit

19. Students who are not familiar with standardized tests are likely

    (A) to score lower than what their actual ability is
    (B) accidentally to score better than what their actual ability is

20. A student's score on a test could be skewed by
    I. emotional variations (happiness or grief)
    II. anxiety
    III. physical variations (hunger or lack of sleep)
    IV. surroundings (strange place, noise, heat)

    (A) I, II and III
    (B) I, III and IV
    (C) II, III and IV
    (D) I, II, III and IV

21. Some subjects need to be taught sequentially (one step after another), while others lend themselves to being taught in discrete units. Which of the following subjects is (are) best taught sequentially?

    (A) history
    (B) algebra
    (C) literature
    (D) history and algebra

22. As students get older, differences in their achievement levels

    (A) lessen
    (B) increase

23. In judging students' performance in school, teachers should

    (A) be alert to influences outside school that may affect students' performance
    (B) not allow outside influences to sway their judgment

24. A student who can't remember ever failing a test, even though he has failed many, is coping through

    (A) projection
    (B) regression
    (C) repression
    (D) sublimation

25. When talking in the presence of a child, one should

    (A) talk about him
    (B) talk directly to him
    (C) ignore him

26. If the answer to a question a child asks is beyond his comprehension, it is best to

    (A) tell him that the answer is too difficult
    (B) answer his question even if he won't understand

27. Students' scores on a test were 72, 72, 73, 74, 76, 78, 81, 83, 85. A score of 76 is the

    (A) mean
    (B) median
    (C) mode
    (D) average

28. A multiple-choice question should have from _____ answers.

    (A) 1 to 7
    (B) 2 to 6
    (C) 3 to 5
    (D) 3 to 7

29. In administering a standardized test, great care must be taken to

    (A) follow the proscribed format
    (B) allow for individual student differences
    (C) explain everything in great detail

30. To test students' mastery of mathematics, the most appropriate test is

    (A) multiple-choice format
    (B) true-or-false questions
    (C) completion questions
    (D) essay format

31. A student must write a term paper for both his history class and his literature class. He chooses a topic that is satisfactory to both teachers. Should he be allowed to write only one term paper?

    (A) yes
    (B) no

32. Sources a teacher can use to find appropriate resources for teaching are
    I. school or county media centers
    II. libraries
    III. public agencies
    IV. people in the community

    (A) I, II and III
    (B) II, III and IV
    (C) I, III and IV
    (D) I, II, III and IV

33. After a test on a unit has been given and recorded, the teacher should

    (A) go on to the next unit
    (B) go over the test and explain any questions the students may have
    (C) announce everyone's scores

34. Mainstreaming is the practice of

    (A) teaching the same thing to everyone
    (B) "tracking" students
    (C) grouping students according to ability
    (D) integrating handicapped students into the regular classroom

35. Having a mock presidential election, complete with debates, discussion of issues and voting, teaches students

    (A) the decision-making process
    (B) whether they would like to be politicians or not
    (C) whether to be a Democrat or a Republican

36. The most important fact for a teacher to know about learning methods is

    (A) that she should find the one method that suits her style
    (B) that all of them must be used
    (C) that no one method will work for all students

37. Typing is a subject that lends itself to

    (A) concept teaching
    (B) task teaching
    (C) generalization teaching
    (D) inference and conclusion teaching

38. A person's basic character is generally set by the time she is how many years old?

    (A) 6
    (B) 10
    (C) 18
    (D) 25

39. The teacher who believes that her students should pursue their separate interests on a topic would find the learning results to be

    (A) similar
    (B) successful
    (C) progressive
    (D) inconsistent

40. The best discipline of students is

    (A) benevolently authoritarian
    (B) militaristic
    (C) democratic
    (D) self-motivated

41. Anecdotal records should be used to

    (A) prepare for discipline of a student
    (B) keep a record of a student's grades
    (C) protect the teacher, if necessary
    (D) provide material that may explain a student's behavior

42. Which is less effective in motivating a student?

    (A) ignoring him
    (B) reprimanding him

43. If classes were to be grouped homogeneously, then

    (A) students of widely different abilities would be in the same class
    (B) this would be termed "mainstreaming"
    (C) students of similar ability would be in the same class
    (D) there would be no heterogeneous students in the class

44. Homework in the elementary grades is primarily used

    (A) for punishment
    (B) for reinforcement
    (C) to accustom children to the idea of homework
    (D) to make children feel important

45. Memorization in school is justified when

    (A) it results in a convenience or pleasure for the learner
    (B) it demonstrates the power of the mind
    (C) it demonstrates the discipline of the mind
    (D) it is used as punishment

46. If all of the students in a class passed the pre-test for a unit, the teacher should

    (A) go through the lesson quickly
    (B) administer the post-test
    (C) go through the unit as usual
    (D) go on to the next unit

47. Asking questions in class is best done by

    (A) asking the question, then calling on a particular student
    (B) calling on a particular student, then asking the question

48. At which level of government lies the primary responsibility for schools?

    (A) federal
    (B) state
    (C) county
    (D) local

49. It is hard to tell whether a student is guessing or not on a _____ test.

    (A) multiple-choice
    (B) completion
    (C) matching
    (D) true-or-false
    (E) essay

50. If a teacher wants to know whether the students completely understand a concept in high school social science, the test he would use would be

    (A) multiple-choice

(B) completion
(C) matching
(D) true-or-false
(E) essay

51. You want students to identify presidents of the United States with their administrations, so the test you use is

  (A) multiple-choice
  (B) completion
  (C) matching
  (D) true-or-false
  (E) essay

52. Programmed learning material would be most likely to be found in

  (A) a class divided in three groups
  (B) independent study
  (C) a class in which the teacher tries to individualize the instruction

53. It is possible that some children who are good readers in the early grades are merely

  (A) quiet
  (B) trying to please teacher and parents
  (C) interested in the reading material
  (D) myopic

54. A student will usually remember what he has learned if it is

  (A) important for a test
  (B) repeated
  (C) interesting to him

55. Jonathan doesn't learn anything he hears; he must see it to remember it. In order to facilitate learning, he could

  (A) use a computer
  (B) read supplementary textbooks
  (C) take notes and study them
  (D) all of the above

56. One time that Sharon takes an IQ test, her score is 103. The next time it is 99. You conclude that

  (A) Sharon's intelligence is decreasing
  (B) Sharon didn't try as hard on the second test
  (C) the scores are not significantly different

57. Lesson plans

  (A) are a formality and a waste of time
  (B) should be strictly adhered to
  (C) should be flexible

58. Movies shown in the classroom

  (A) fill up time
  (B) are a waste of time
  (C) are most effective if followed by discussion

59. Team teaching

  (A) is a waste of taxpayers' money
  (B) makes the best use of both teachers' talents
  (C) is going out of style
  (D) is a new concept in teaching

60. Jeff is a second grader who continually pushes and shoves other children. His teacher says, "He cannot keep his hands to himself." What can the teacher suspect as the cause of Jeff's behavior?

  (A) Jeff has been mistreated at home.
  (B) Jeff needs the companionship of other children.
  (C) Jeff is a bully.

61. Boys in elementary school need a great deal of physical action. To fulfill this need in the classroom, a teacher could

  (A) have the class make models of what is being studied
  (B) have the children act out stories
  (C) have spelling and arithmetic relay races
  (D) have two-minute stretching and running-in-place breaks every hour
  (E) all of the above

62. A student is having behavior problems in class. The teacher should discuss the problem and possible solutions with the following people in which order?

  (A) principal, counselor, parents, student
  (B) parents, counselor, student, principal
  (C) counselor, student, principal, student
  (D) student, parents, counselor, principal
  (E) student, counselor, principal, parents

63. The greatest influence on a child is

    (A) the school environment
    (B) his or her peers
    (C) the home environment

64. Forty-year-olds have slightly less ability to learn than do twenty-year-olds. However, as many college-age students have learned to their dismay, older students do learn as well if not better than their younger counterparts. The difference between innate ability and performance can be attributed to

    (A) motivation
    (B) interest
    (C) attention
    (D) better use of available time
    (E) all of the above

65. Recently increased community involvement in schools was a result of

    (A) interest in schools
    (B) encouragement by school districts
    (C) dissatisfaction with the schools

66. The most prominent educational issue of the mid 1980s is

    (A) accountability
    (B) busing
    (C) mainstreaming
    (D) Headstart
    (E) bilingual education

67. The most publicized educational report in the early 1980s was

    (A) *Johnny Still Can't Read*
    (B) *José Can't Read*
    (C) *Educational Excellence*
    (D) *A Nation at Risk*
    (E) *Bilingualism in America*

68. One measure of accountability implemented by many states is

    (A) entrance tests for high school
    (B) exit tests from high school
    (C) entrance tests for colleges
    (D) exit tests from colleges

69. Some class activities require quiet behavior on the part of the students, while at other times more liveliness is warranted. What would be your criterion of inappropriate student behavior in a classroom?

    (A) how often the student had done this before
    (B) whether the student was at his or her desk
    (C) the level of loudness of the student
    (D) whether the behavior was disruptive to other students

70. As a result of reports showing American students lagging behind students in other countries in education, American educators are now stressing

    (A) the study of foreign languages
    (B) educational excellence
    (C) exchange programs
    (D) double homework
    (E) fewer extracurricular activities

71. Which is more important for learning to occur?

    (A) readiness
    (B) training

72. When corporal punishment is to be administered, it is best to

    (A) spank in the privacy of an empty classroom to save the child embarrassment
    (B) spank in the principal's office
    (C) let the principal do the spanking
    (D) have a witness and inform the parents and the principal

73. What can a teacher do for students in his class who are not on grade level?

    (A) give them materials on their level and let them work at a pace that is reasonable for them, trying to bring them up to grade level
    (B) give them the same work as the other students, only not so much, so that they won't feel embarrassed
    (C) give them the same work as the other students, because they will absorb as much as they are capable of

74. The best way to get students interested in a new topic, such as camping, is to

    (A) tell them about your camping experiences
    (B) ask a forest ranger to talk about camping
    (C) show the class a film about camping
    (D) ask them to relate their camping experiences

75. Showing one student's grades to another student

    (A) is not professional
    (B) creates the incentive for the student to improve
    (C) should be done only in certain circumstances

Questions 76 to 78

You have recently given a test to your sophomore biology class. The grades were low, and the students claim that the test was unfair.

76. What should you do?

    (A) Check the test to see whether their claim is valid.
    (B) Increase everyone's score by one grade.
    (C) Dismiss this as sour grapes.
    (D) Report the students who complained to the vice-principal.

77. What could cause your test to be unfair?

    (A) The test included items not in the readings or lectures.
    (B) The test items were primarily on peripheral matter.
    (C) The test was too long.
    (D) all of the above

78. What can you do to assure that your tests are fair?

    (A) Ask each student to submit one question.
    (B) Write twenty questions for the test, and let each student answer any ten of the questions.
    (C) Make all of the questions true or false.
    (D) Use the objectives for the unit as the guide for the test.

79. An integrated curriculum

    (A) emphasizes to the students the interrelationship of the courses they are studying
    (B) bases the curriculum on the various ethnic cultures of the students
    (C) has students of various ethnic backgrounds on the curriculum development committee

80. An error frequently made about children is

    (A) overestimating their intellect
    (B) overestimating their need for rest
    (C) underestimating their need for rest
    (D) underestimating their intellect

ANSWERS TO SAMPLE TEST 6

BASIC SKILLS

Mathematics

1. A	11. B	21. C	31. B	41. D
2. B	12. B	22. C	32. C	42. B
3. D	13. A	23. D	33. C	43. B
4. D	14. B	24. D	34. B	44. A
5. C	15. B	25. C	35. B	45. B
6. B	16. C	26. D	36. A	46. A
7. C	17. B	27. B	37. C	47. B
8. C	18. D	28. B	38. C	48. B
9. B	19. D	29. A	39. B	49. D
10. B	20. C	30. A	40. A	50. C

Reading

1. A	17. B	33. A	49. A	65. A
2. D	18. C	34. C	50. D	66. D
3. A	19. A	35. A	51. D	67. A
4. B	20. D	36. D	52. A	68. D
5. D	21. A	37. A	53. B	69. D
6. C	22. B	38. B	54. B	70. B
7. C	23. D	39. C	55. C	71. B
8. A	24. B	40. D	56. A	72. A
9. B	25. D	41. B	57. D	73. D
10. D	26. A	42. C	58. C	74. C
11. C	27. C	43. D	59. A	75. D
12. A	28. C	44. A	60. B	76. A
13. D	29. D	45. B	61. C	77. B
14. B	30. A	46. C	62. A	78. C
15. A	31. B	47. D	63. D	79. A
16. A	32. A	48. C	64. B	80. D

PROFESSIONAL KNOWLEDGE

1.	B	17.	A	33.	B	49.	D	65. C
2.	A	18.	C	34.	D	50.	E	66. A
3.	C	19.	A	35.	A	51.	C	67. D
4.	C	20.	D	36.	C	52.	B	68. B
5.	B	21.	D	37.	B	53.	D	69. D
6.	B	22.	B	38.	B	54.	C	70. B
7.	C	23.	A	39.	D	55.	D	71. A
8.	C	24.	C	40.	D	56.	C	72. D
9.	C	25.	B	41.	D	57.	C	73. A
10.	C	26.	B	42.	A	58.	C	74. D
11.	C	27.	B	43.	C	59.	B	75. A
12.	B	28.	C	44.	C	60.	B	76. A
13.	A	29.	A	45.	A	61.	E	77. D
14.	C	30.	C	46.	D	62.	E	78. D
15.	B	31.	A	47.	A	63.	C	79. A
16.	A	32.	D	48.	B	64.	E	80. D

EXPLANATION OF ANSWERS TO SAMPLE TEST 6

BASIC SKILLS

MATHEMATICS

1. **A** rate × time = distance. *Or* distance ÷ rate = time
   Beth: 300 miles ÷ 60 mph = 5 hours
   Kay: 300 miles ÷ 50 mph = 6 hours
   Beth will arrive 6 − 5 = 1 hour sooner than Kay

2. **B** Harry edits ¼ + ¼ = ½ of the book the first two weeks in May. Harry has 1 − ½ = ½ of the book left to edit. He will have to edit ½ of 180 = 90 pages in the next two weeks.
   $$90 \div 2 = 45 \text{ pages each week}$$

3. **D** −6 − (+9) =
   −6 − 9 = −15

4. **D** You add deposits; subtract checks and service charges.

5. **C** Use your answer sheet to line up the figures.

6. **B** 15 + 20 + 45 + 65 + 80 + 70 + 55 + 62(+ or −) + 30 + 18(+ or −) = 460

7. **C** $\dfrac{460}{10 \text{ months}} = 46$ 45 is closest

8. **C** It will be less than ¹⁄₁₀ of his annual salary. Eliminate A, B, and D.
   $$\frac{\$18,408.00}{12} = \$1,534.00$$

9. **B** Since 231 divides evenly into 173,712, there is no remainder.

10. **B** In division, *quotient* means answer. Estimate.
    $$\frac{5,600}{40} = \text{about } 140$$

11. **B** The score will be near the middle. Eliminate A.
    $$73 + 75 + 78 + 79 + 81 = 386$$
    $$386 \div 5 = 77\tfrac{1}{5}$$

12. **B** Eliminate D immediately. Align your columns and decimals carefully when you add the monthly balances.

    $1,024.57
    1,246.85
    30.47
    117.61
    351.13
    573.37
    1,994.55
    65.76
    1,708.84
    2,007.92
    3,462.01
    + 1,280.09
    —————
    $13,863.17   Eliminate C.

    $\dfrac{\$13,863.17}{12} = \$1,155.26\tfrac{5}{12}$

13. **A** Subtract.   11 lb 5 oz
                        − 7 lb 7 oz
    Borrow. (1 lb = 16 oz)
    11 lb 5 oz = 10 lb 21 oz
                  − 7 lb 7 oz
                  —————
                     3 lb 14 oz

14. **B** Area = 17 × 27 = 459 sq ft
    9 sq ft = 1 sq yd
    $$\frac{459}{9} = 51 \text{ sq yd}$$

15. **B** 51 × $9 = $459

16. **C** First, estimate: 3,000
                              1,000
                             62,000
                              1,000
                              1,000
                             ————
                             68,000 Eliminate D.

Align the numbers.

$$\begin{array}{r} 2{,}745 \\ 839 \\ 62{,}487 \\ 987 \\ +\ 1{,}247 \\ \hline \ldots 05 \end{array}$$

This is as far as you need to add in order to decide on the correct answer.

17. **B**

$$\begin{array}{r} 9{,}850 \\ -\ 7{,}970 \\ \hline 1{,}880 \end{array}$$

18. **D** Estimate. $30 \times 17 = 510$

19. **D**

$17\frac{5}{8}$, $\frac{1}{8}$, $\frac{7}{8}$, $1\frac{1}{2}$, $\frac{3}{4}$, $+\ \frac{3}{8}$ Change to eighths: $17\frac{5}{8}$, $\frac{1}{8}$, $\frac{7}{8}$, $1\frac{4}{8}$, $\frac{6}{8}$, $+\ \frac{3}{8}$

$18\ \frac{26}{8} = 21\frac{1}{4}$

20. **C**

$ 595 price
− 85 down payment

$ 510 amount to be financed $\frac{\$510}{30} = \$17$

21. **C**

$$\begin{array}{r} 4{,}576 \\ 1{,}379 \\ 3{,}597 \\ \hline 9{,}552 \end{array}$$

Suzanne flew 9,552 miles

$$\begin{array}{r} 10{,}000 \\ -\ 9{,}552 \\ \hline 448 \end{array}$$

448 miles left

22. **C** $\frac{\text{is}}{\text{of}}$ $\frac{98 \times 100}{35} = 280$

23. **D** $\frac{1}{2} - \frac{1}{3} = \frac{1 \times 3}{2 \times 3} - \frac{1 \times 2}{3 \times 2} = \frac{3 - 2}{6} = \frac{1}{6}$

24. **D**

Plus: balance $ 107.52
deposit 452.63
$ 560.15

Minus: check $57.61
check 47.16
service charge 9.70
$ 114.47

$ 560.15
− 114.68

$ 445.68 balance

25. **C**

$$\begin{array}{r} \$2.24 \\ .20 = 1 \text{ oz} \\ \hline \$2.04 \end{array}$$

$\frac{\$2.04}{.17} = 12$ oz

$1 + 12 = 13$ oz

26. **D** In each case the shaded part is ½ of the whole triangle.
1. $\frac{2}{4} = \frac{1}{2}$ 2. $\frac{2}{4} = \frac{1}{2}$ 3. $\frac{3}{6} = \frac{1}{2}$
4. $\frac{4}{8} = \frac{1}{2}$

27. **B** $\frac{5}{8} \times \frac{3}{5} = \frac{3}{8}$

28. **B** $\frac{5}{8} - \frac{3}{8} = \frac{2}{8} = \frac{1}{4}$

29. **A** You want about $\frac{1}{3}$ of $28.65. That is close to $10.
Only A fits.

30. **A** Substitute in the formula. Multiply before adding.

$$\frac{(15 \times 74 + 67 \times 69 + 18 \times 87)}{100} =$$

$$\frac{1{,}110 + 4{,}623 + 1{,}566}{100} =$$

$$\frac{7299}{100} = 72.99$$

31. **B**

$$\begin{array}{r} \$\ \ 127.50 \\ 1{,}547.05 \\ 57.55 \\ \hline \$1{,}732.10 \end{array}$$

You will need to add only as far as the 2 to choose the correct answer.

32. **C** $\frac{480}{30} = 16$ inches

33. **C** $180 \times \frac{1}{4} = 45$ pages week 1. $180 - 45 = 135$ pages left
$135 \times \frac{1}{3} = 45$ pages week 2. $135 - 45 = 90$ pages left

$\frac{90}{2} = 45$ pages each week

34. **B** $34 + 34 + 34 + 35 + 37 + 31 = 205$

35. **B**

$ 5,201.13	**income**
- 4,896.31	**expenses**
$ 304.82	**net income**

36. **A**

		change to twelfths:
Mon.	$2\frac{3}{4}$	$2\frac{9}{12}$
Tues.	$1\frac{1}{3}$	$1\frac{4}{12}$
Wed.	$1\frac{1}{3}$	$1\frac{4}{12}$
Thurs.	$2\frac{1}{2}$	$2\frac{6}{12}$
Fri.	3	3
		$9\frac{23}{12}$

$9\frac{23}{12} = 9 + 1\frac{11}{12} = 10\frac{11}{12}$ hours

37. **C**

$$\begin{array}{r} \$2.97 \\ 1.39 \\ 1.27 \\ 2.57 \\ 1.96 \\ 1.34 \\ \hline \$11.50 \end{array}$$

38. **C**

$$\begin{array}{r} 70\% \\ -55\% \\ \hline 15\% \end{array}$$

39. **B** Mark off the length of the scale on the edge of your answer sheet. Lay the edge of your answer sheet along side b and mark on line b where the answer sheet mark is. Repeat as necessary to estimate the length.

40. **A** purchases $\begin{array}{r} \$\,12.96 \\ 8.77 \\ \hline \$\,21.73 \end{array}$ money tendered $\begin{array}{r} \$\,25.00 \\ -21.73 \\ \hline \$\,3.27 \end{array}$

41. **D**

rectangle $a = l \times w$, $a = 7 \times 5$, $a = 35$ triangle $a = \frac{1}{2}\,h \times b$, $a = \frac{1}{2} \times 5 \times 6$, $a = 15$

Add the areas: $35 + 15 = 50$

42. **B** Do the operation inside the bracket before removing the bracket. Remove brackets from the inside out. This is the opposite of peeling an onion. Do multiplication and division from left to right, then addition and subtraction from left to right.

$7.12 \times [2.3 - (.6 \times 7 - 1.9)] =$
$7.12 \times [2.3 - (4.2 - 1.9)] =$
$7.12 \times [2.3 - 2.3] =$
$7.12 \times [0] = 0$

Anything multiplied by 0 equals 0.

43. **B** $\frac{1}{7} \times \frac{1}{9} = \frac{1}{63}$

44. **A** $178.15 × 0.06 = $10.689.

45. **B** You can do this in steps:

7 hours × 186 days = 1302 hours

$1302 \times \frac{2}{7} = \frac{2604}{7} = 372$ hours nonteaching time

$372 \times \frac{1}{15} = 24\frac{4}{5}$ hours spent in meetings

Or you can do it all at once:

7 hours × 186 days × $\frac{2}{7} \times \frac{1}{15} = \frac{124}{5} = 24\frac{4}{5}$ hours

46. **A** 1000 grams = 1 kilo

$$\frac{760 \text{ students} \times 100 \text{ grams} \times 2 \text{ hamburgers}}{1{,}000 \text{ grams}} = 152 \text{ kilos.}$$

47. **B** $7\frac{1}{5} \div \frac{5}{8} = \frac{36}{5} \div \frac{5}{8} = \frac{36}{5} \times \frac{8}{5} = \frac{288}{25} = 11\frac{13}{25}$

48. **B** $\frac{\$\ 137.50}{\$1{,}250.00} \times 100 = 11\%$

49. **D**

	Year	Month	Day
	1984	9	9
Borrow (1 mo = 30 days)	1984	8	39
	−1978	11	12
			27 days
Borrow (1 yr = 12 months)	1983	20	
	−1978	11	
	5 yr	9 mo	27 days

50. **C** The shortest route is Spokane–Pullman–Moscow–Sandpoint. Follow the procedure in question 39.

READING

Questions 1 to 10

One of the things that new teachers or teachers (1) in a new situation fear is losing control of the class (2). Letting a class have group discussion or break into groups (3) for an activity involves (4) a certain amount (5) of abdication of control and trust in the group. Without this, however, few teachers can attain (6) a high level of goal (7) achievement. How this important facet of teaching (8) is to be approached (9) is the subject of considerable (10) discussion and debate.

Questions 11 to 20

Many teachers who <u>advocate</u> involvement say that it
11
makes a class more <u>interesting</u>. It seems to make the
12
time go faster and make a class less boring. It <u>forces</u>
13
students to concentrate on the <u>subject</u>. They can't
14
"tune out." There <u>are</u> many other reasons given for
15
involvement, but the only <u>reason</u> that <u>it should be used</u>
16   17
is that it is the best method <u>of</u> accomplishing the
18
specific learning goal. This <u>criterion</u> should be used in
19
deciding whether to use any <u>teaching</u> technique.
20

Questions 21 to 30

Adults can learn from listening to <u>lectures</u>, but they are
21
more likely to <u>learn</u> from discussion. Since nearly all
22
<u>adult</u> learning is self-directed, why do some not
23
<u>participate</u> in discussion? <u>Upon</u> questioning you will
24   25
often find that the <u>nonparticipant</u> thinks that she will be
26
<u>embarrassed</u> and that her ideas are not <u>valuable</u> to the
27   28
group. This person has been trained not to participate,

and until this <u>training</u> is overcome, she will not get the
29
full learning <u>benefits</u> that she should from a teaching
30
session.

Questions 31 to 40

A recent <u>survey</u> revealed that college students don't
31
think that their <u>professors</u> should be humorous. When
32
questioned <u>further</u>, they said that professors who used
33
humor in the classroom were not projecting the correct
34
image and did not seem to take themselves, the subject,
35
or the <u>students</u> seriously enough. Interestingly, though,
36
students <u>remember</u> the serious material the professor
37
using humor presented much <u>better</u> than the material
38
of nonhumorous <u>professors</u>. Could it be that these
39
students think that learning has to be <u>dull</u>?
40

Questions 41 to 50

Salesmen make a point of <u>learning</u> your name and
41
using it often. Teachers are salesmen of sorts, too.

Think how <u>good</u> it feels when someone remembers
42
your name, and how <u>awful</u> it feels when someone
43
doesn't. It is <u>important</u> to learn your students' names as
44
soon as possible. <u>Greeting</u> each student as he comes
45
into the room, <u>concentrating</u> on his name and using it
46
will help you remember. If the students keep the same

<u>places</u> you will more readily <u>associate</u> the name and the
47   48
face. Try to think of something distinctive that will <u>link</u>
49
the person's face and name. The more often you use a

person's name, the better you will remember it. What

did you say your <u>name</u> is, again?
50

Questions 51 to 60

How you treat your <u>child</u> at an early age may affect
51
<u>whether</u> he becomes a conformist or an <u>individualist</u>.
52   53
Although <u>parents</u> want their children to be well
54
behaved and <u>compliant</u>, they want the children to grow
55
up to be independent and <u>creative</u>. <u>Parents</u> are influ-
56   57
enced by their own situation. Parents belonging to

lower economic groups who want their children to

<u>succeed</u> will stress conformity as a way to get ahead.
58
Parents who are secure in <u>established</u> society encourage
59
their <u>children</u> to take risks.
60

Questions 61 to 70

Teacher-education programs have come under much

criticism lately. Many <u>critics</u> advocate doing away with
<u> 61</u>

all teacher-education classes, <u>substituting</u> courses on
<u>   62</u>

the material to be <u>taught</u>. However, the teacher's
<u>   63</u>

knowledge of <u>subject matter</u> is of no value to the
<u>   64</u>

students <u>unless</u> the teacher can convey it to those
<u>   65</u>

students. To do this, the teacher needs to learn about

classroom control, grading, various methods of teach-

ing to ensure maximum <u>learning</u>, how to make a lesson
<u>   66</u>

interesting, and where and how to get <u>appropriate</u>
<u>   67</u>

resources. The teacher also needs to know about child

and <u>adolescent</u> psychology, <u>school</u> law and the educa-
<u>   68</u>   <u> 69</u>

tional administrative system. Teacher-education

courses are the best way to learn the tools of the

<u>profession</u>.
<u> 70</u>

Questions 71 to 80

In the <u>quest</u> for better <u>listening</u> skills, many companies,
<u>   71</u>   <u>   72</u>

followed by several <u>branches</u> of the armed <u>services</u>,
<u>   73</u>   <u> 74</u>

have sponsored listening seminars. The <u>idea</u> of listening
<u>   75</u>

as a learned skill has <u>slowly</u> filtered down through the
<u>   76</u>

U.S. educational <u>system</u>. Congress has added speaking
<u>   77</u>

and <u>listening</u> to the three Rs as <u>basic</u> skills to be <u>taught</u>
<u>   78</u>   <u> 79</u>   <u> 80</u>

in the public schools.

PROFESSIONAL KNOWLEDGE

1. **B** Discussion involves students immediately.

2. **A** Parent-school committees develop the involvement of parents.

3. **C** The more people involved, the more successful a project will be.

4. **C** Norm-referenced tests compare students with other students.

5. **B** A student who scored 60% on a percentile-ranked test scored better than 60% of the students taking the test.

6. **B** Identify the norm group and explain the meaning of the score.

7. **C** Scheduling for mutual convenience is best.

8. **C** Parent-teacher conferences are the time to discuss general progress.

9. **C** Testing should evaluate students' progress.

10. **C** Oral praise is most meaningful.

11. **C** Inform all who will be affected.

12. **B** Effective planning helps a teacher accomplish her goals.

13. **A** Faculty meetings provide an opportunity to keep abreast of what is happening.

14. **C** The sooner you know all the people who make a school run, the better.

15. **B** An objective states a desired result in concrete terms.

16. **A** Competency-based instruction clarifies goals and objectives.

17. **A** A lesson plan helps with time management, progress evaluation and substitute teaching.

18. **C** Democracy in the classroom is not turning control of the class over to the students but involving them in the educational process.

19. **A** Students who are unfamiliar with standardized tests are at a disadvantage compared with students who are used to them.

20. **D** Students' scores can be affected by any number of variables.

21. **D** History and algebra are suitable for sequential teaching.

22. **B** As students mature, their achievement levels vary more.

23. **A** Teachers should be alert to outside problems students may have that can impair progress.

24. **C** Repression is forgetting something painful.

25. **B** Children, like adults, should be treated politely, like human beings. Talking about them as though they were statues is rude.

26. **B** Answer children's questions. It is amazing how much they understand.

27. **B** The median is the middle score when the scores are arranged in progressive numerical order.

28. **C** Three to five answer choices provide adequate variety.

29. **A** The validity of standardized tests depends on the tests being administered identically.

30. **C** Completion questions (find the answer) best test mathematical skills.

31. **A** If one term paper will suffice, it is pointless to write two. The second one would become mere busy work.

32. **D** A teacher should draw on the widest possible range of resources available. It improves the program and fosters community involvement.

33. **B** If the teacher doesn't go over the test and explain the answers, the students don't learn from the test.

34. **D** Mainstreaming is an effort to provide as normal surroundings as possible for handicapped students.

35. **A** Participation in mock elections teaches students about a facet of the decision-making process.

36. **C** A teacher's job has been described as teaching the same thing seven different ways. Children learn in a variety of ways.

37. **B** Typing is a task that students learn primarily by doing.

38. **B** It is generally considered that a child's character is formed before the age of 10.

39. **D** Students need direction in their learning in order for a base amount of similar learning to take place.

40. **D** Self-motivated discipline is what society strives for.

41. **D** Anecdotal records, detailed records of a student's behavior over a period of time, should be used to shed light on that behavior.

42. **A** Ignoring a student does not motivate him.

43. **C** Homogeneous grouping is the grouping of students of like achievement levels.

44. **C** Teachers try to prepare their students for what is ahead by giving them small amounts of homework.

45. **A** Learning poems can be a pleasure and learning the multiplication tables is a convenience.

46. **D** If the students pass the pre-test, they obviously know the material, and the unit need not be taught.

47. **A** If the students don't know who will be called on to answer, then all the students will pay attention to the question.

48. **B** The individual states have the primary responsibility for education.

49. **D** A student has a 50% chance of guessing correctly on a true-false test. This type of test lends itself most to guessing.

50. **E** A student can explain why he thinks as he does on an essay test.

51. **C** Matching tests are useful in history, geography, and science, where categories exist that can be matched.

52. **B** Programmed learning materials were designed for individual study.

53. **D** Myopic children tend to be good readers because they focus well at close range, as for reading, and not at long range.

54. **C** We learn most readily those things in which we are interested.

55. **D** All the choices would reinforce his visual learning.

56. **C** The four-point difference is not significant.

57. **C** Lesson plans are guides, and should be used as such.

58. **C** Discussion solidifies students' thinking after seeing a movie or performance.

59. **B** Team teaching can use the best abilities of both teachers. One may be a musician, the other an artist. The children receive the benefits of both their talents.

60. **B** Jeff may need the closeness of companionship. He is trying to get it but doesn't know how to do it in an acceptable manner.

61. **E** All of the suggestions use physical energy in the learning process.

62. **E** The teacher should try to solve the problem at the lowest level. If the problem is resolved at any stage, he should not proceed to the next stage.

63. **C** The home has the most influence on a child.

64. **E** Older adults may have more motivation to learn and interest in the subject, pay more attention, and make better use of their time. This more than makes up for any lessening in their ability to learn.

65. **C** Dissatisfaction with schools has increased community involvement and caused new laws to be passed and stricter standards to be enforced.

66. **A** Accountability is the most prominent recent educational issue. The other choices were current earlier than accountability.

67. **D** *A Nation at Risk* was the report of the Andrew Carnegie Foundation on the decline in American education.

68. **B** Exit tests from high school have been implemented by many school districts and states.

69. **D** If behavior is disruptive to other students it is inappropriate.

70. **B** Excellence in education is being emphasized in a variety of ways.

71. **A** Readiness and training are both important, but without readiness, training is useless.

72. **D** A witness is necessary to protect the teacher, and the sooner the teacher informs both the principal and the parents, the better.

73. **A** Students learn best when they can succeed at their own level.

74. **D** Students are interested when they participate and when what they contribute is considered important.

75. **A** A student's grades are confidential.

76. **A** Perhaps the students' claim is valid.

77. **D** Tests should reflect both the material that was to be studied and the time allotted for completing the tests.

78. **D** Using the unit objectives as a guide for the test ensures that you will test what you have taught and that the test will reflect the objectives of the unit.

79. **A** An integrated curriculum is designed to connect all the subjects so that the students will understand their relationship. No subject is an island unto itself.

80. **D** People often underestimate children's intelligence.

ARCO

BOOKS FOR GRADUATE SCHOOL AND BEYOND

ARCO'S SUPERCOURSES

SuperCourse for the GMAT
SuperCourse for the GRE
SuperCourse for the LSAT
SuperCourse for the MCAT
SuperCourse for the TOEFL

TOEFL

TOEFL: Test of English as a Foreign Language
TOEFL Grammar Workbook
TOEFL Reading and Vocabulary Workbook
TOEFL Skills for Top Scores

ARCO'S CRAM COURSES

GMAT Cram Course
GRE Cram Course
LSAT Cram Course

TEACHER CERTIFICATION

CBEST: California Educational Basic Skills Test
NTE: National Teacher Examinations
PPST: Pre-Professional Skills Tests

HEALTH PROFESSIONS

Nursing School Entrance Examinations
PCAT: Pharmacy College Admission Test

GRADUATE SCHOOL GUIDES

Getting into Law School: Strategies for the 90's
Getting into Medical School: Strategies for the 90's
The Grad Student's Guide to Getting Published

GRADUATE & PROFESSIONAL SCHOOL ENTRANCE

GMAT: Graduate Management Admission Test
GRE: Graduate Record Examination
GRE • GMAT Math Review
Graduate Record Examination in Biology
Graduate Record Examination in Computer Science
Graduate Record Examination in Engineering
Graduate Record Examination in Psychology
GRE • LSAT Logic Workbook
LSAT: Law School Admission Test
MAT: Miller Analogies Test
MCAT Sample Exams

AVAILABLE AT BOOKSTORES EVERYWHERE

PRENTICE HALL